MW00786195

Creating GUI Applications wxPython

Michael Driscoll

Published by Michael Driscoll
Ankeny, IA

Cover art by Varya Kolesnikova

ISBN 9780996062893

90000 >

9 780996 062893

Contents

Acknowledgments 1

Introduction 2
   Who is this book for? 2
   About the Author 2
   Conventions 3
   Requirements 3
   Integrated Development Environments (IDEs) 4
   Book Source Code 5
   Reader Feedback 5
   Errata 5

Chapter 1 - An Intro to wxPython 6
   What is a GUI? 6
   Hello World 7
   Hello with Classes 8
   Events 11
   Absolute Positioning vs Sizers 14
   Wrapping Up 20

Chapter 2 - Creating an Image Viewer 21
   Finding the Right Widget 22
   Displaying an Image 23
   Making Working Buttons 26
   Loading an Image 29
   Wrapping Up 32

Chapter 3 - Enhancing the Image Viewer 33
   Opening a Folder 34
   Adding New Buttons 38
   Hooking up Previous / Next 41
   Playing a Folder 44
   Switching to PubSub 45
   Other Notes on PubSub 48
   Wrapping Up 48

Chapter 4 - Creating a Database Viewer **49**

Installing SQLAlchemy 49

Installing ObjectListView 50

Creating the Database Model 50

Populating the Database 53

Creating a Database Viewer 54

Wrapping Up 59

Chapter 5 - Creating a Database Editor **61**

Prerequisites 61

Model - View - Controller 62

The Model 62

The View 64

The Controller 70

Editing the Database with a UI 74

Connecting the View and Controller 82

Wrapping Up 84

Chapter 6 - The Humble Calculator **86**

Figuring Out the Logic 86

Is eval() Evil? 87

Designing the Calculator 87

Creating the Initial Calculator 88

Using a Validator 96

Creating a Better eval() 100

Wrapping Up 103

Chapter 7 - Creating a Tarball Archiver **104**

Creating a Command Line Interface 104

Archiving Multiple Items 110

Adding a GUI 111

Wrapping Up 127

Chapter 8 - Creating an MP3 Tag Editor **128**

Finding an MP3 Package 128

Designing the MP3 Tagger 129

Creating the Main Application 130

Editing MP3s 136

Adding New Features 139

Wrapping Up 144

Chapter 9 - Creating an Application for NASA's API **145**

Using NASA's API 146

Designing the User Interface 149

Creating the NASA Search Application 150
The Download Dialog 157
Adding Advanced Search 161
Wrapping Up 172

Chapter 10 - Creating a PDF Merger / Splitter Utility **173**
Installing PyPDF2 173
Designing the Interface 173
Creating the Application 175
Using Threads in wxPython 194
Enhancing PDF Merging with Threads 194
Wrapping Up 197

Chapter 11 - Creating a File Search Utility **199**
Designing Your File Search Utility 199
Creating the File Search Utility 200
The Text Search Utility 210
Installing the Dependencies 211
Designing a Text Search Utility 211
Creating a Text Search Utility 212
Wrapping Up 226

Chapter 12 - Creating an FTP Application **228**
Designing the FTP Client 228
Creating Your First Prototype 229
Refactoring the Code 240
Wrapping Up 249

Chapter 13 - Creating an XML Editor **251**
The lxml Package 251
Designing the Main App 252
Introducing the wx.TreeCtrl 253
Creating the Basic User Interface 258
Creating an XML Editor 275
Boomslang XML 305
Wrapping Up 307

Chapter 14 - Distributing Your Application **308**
Installing PyInstaller 308
Generating an Executable 309
The spec file 311
Creating Executables for Mac 312
Creating Executables for Linux 312
Learning More About PyInstaller 313

What About Installers? 313
Creating an Installer with Inno Setup 313
Code Signing 324
Wrapping Up 325

Appendix A - The wxPython Demo **326**
Learning to Use the Demo 327
Modifying Demo Code 334
Extracting Demo Code 337
Wrapping Up 342

Appendix B - The Widget Inspection Tool **343**
Using the Widget Inspection Tool 343
Wrapping Up 350

Acknowledgments

Writing a book takes a lot of work. Finding people who are willing to review rough versions of the book is difficult and sometimes not even possible. I was fortunate while writing this book to have several amazing people who helped me out by reading early versions of the book. I want to thank Charles McKnight for his many insights into my chapters. Tony Cappellini and Steve Nicholson were quite helpful in finding text issues and asking pertinent questions. Sundeep Agarwal also had many good ideas for improvements.

I also had help from Ignace, Geert Dobbels and Oliver Schoenborn as well as several others. I can't name everyone who helped me because some of them just used handles or their emails were lost. But I am grateful for all the help I received. Every bug report, no matter how small, has helped make this book better for the next person who reads it.

Special thanks goes out to all the core developers of the wxPython GUI Toolkit. Without them, this book wouldn't even exist!

Thank you!

Mike

Introduction

Welcome to **Creating GUI Applications with wxPython**. In this book, we will learn how to create several different desktop applications using the wxPython GUI toolkit. Each of the applications that we create will run on Windows, Mac and Linux. All of the code is open source and free for you to use and change at will. We will start off the book with a quick introduction to the wxPython framework itself and then we will jump into learning how to create fun little applications.

At the end of the book, I will discuss how you can distribute your applications to users.

This book will be using **Python 3.7** and **wxPython 4**.

Who is this book for?

This book is for anyone who would like to learn how to create cross-platform graphical user interfaces with Python. You should already know the Python programming language and it would help if you already know something about event-driven programming and object oriented programming. This book isn't really an intro to wxPython either. Instead, we will spend most of the chapters creating simple and functional applications and improving them. This will help you understand how all the pieces fit together when you are creating your own applications or enhancing the ones in this book.

If you would like an introduction to wxPython, you can see the following resources:

- wxPython documentation - https://wxpython.org/Phoenix/docs/html/index.html
- zetcode's wxPython tutorial - http://zetcode.com/wxpython/

About the Author

Mike Driscoll has been programming with the Python language for more than a decade. He has also been an active user and documenter of the wxPython GUI toolkit for almost as long as he's been using Python. When Mike isn't programming for work, he writes about Python on his blog: https://www.blog.pythonlibrary.org/. He has worked with Packt Publishing and No Starch Press as a technical reviewer for their books. He has also written several books.

You can see a full listing here:

- https://www.blog.pythonlibrary.org/books/

Conventions

As with most technical books, this one includes a few conventions that you need to be aware of. New topics and terminology will be in **bold**.

Code examples will look like the following:

```
import wx

app = wx.App(False)
frame = wx.Frame(None, title='Test')
frame.Show()
app.MainLoop()
```

Most code examples should work if you were to copy and paste them into your code editor, unless we are looking at a smaller portion of code explicitly.

Requirements

You will need a working version of the Python programming language to use this book. This book's examples were written using Python 3.6 and 3.7. If you do not have Python 3, you can get it here:

- https://python.org/download/

The wxPython package supports Python 3.4 - 3.7. The wxPython toolkit does **not** come included with Python. However you can install it with pip:

```
pip install wxPython
```

Some people recommend installing 3rd party packages such as wxPython using the following syntax:

```
python3 -m pip install wxPython --user
```

This will cause whichever version of Python 3 is mapped to your **python3** shortcut to install wxPython to itself. When you just run pip by itself, it is not always clear where the package will be installed.

> Note: Linux users may need to install some dependencies before pip can install wxPython. See the README file on the wxPython Github page for additional details. There is also an Extras directory on the wxPython website that has pre-built wheels for certain flavors of Linux here: https://extras.wxpython.org/wxPython4/extras/linux/. If you go that route, then you can install wxPython by using the following command: `pip install -U -f URL/to/wheel`

If you prefer to install packages into a Python virtual environment, you can use Python 3's venv package or the 3rd party package to do so. For more information on Python virtual environments, see the following URL:

- https://docs.python-guide.org/dev/virtualenvs/

Another method for installing into a Python virtual environment is the use of **pipenv**. The pipenv package is basically pip+virtualenv as an all-in-one tool.

You can use it like this:

```
pipenv install wxPython
pipenv shell
```

Any additional requirements will be explained later on in the book.

> Note: If you are using **Anaconda**, you may see a message like this when attempting to run wxPython: *This program needs access to the screen. Please run with a Framework build of python, and only when you are logged in on the main display of your Mac.* This occurs because you need to use **pythonw** when running wxPython, so you may need to adjust your settings in Anaconda to make it work correctly.

Integrated Development Environments (IDEs)

Python comes with an Integrated Development Environment called IDLE. However it can be a bit buggy to use when working with wxPython or PyQt. I usually use WingIDE Pro as my Python IDE of choice. However there are a couple of other popular options:

- PyCharm
- VS Code

Some developers like to use Vim or Sublime Text as well. There are benefits to using a Python-specific IDE though:

- Better syntax highlighting
- Built-in linters
- Better auto-complete
- Debugging

Both PyCharm and WingIDE have community editions that are free to use. VS Code is also free to use and has plugins for most popular programming languages. All three of these programs work on all major platforms as well.

You can also check out the following link for additional options:

- https://wiki.python.org/moin/IntegratedDevelopmentEnvironments

Now you should be all set up and ready to start programming.

Book Source Code

The book's source code can be found on Github:

- https://github.com/driscollis/applications_with_wxpython

Reader Feedback

I welcome feedback about my writings. If you'd like to let me know what you thought of the book, you can send comments to the following address:

- comments@pythonlibrary.org

Errata

I try my best not to publish errors in my writings, but it happens from time to time. If you happen to see an error in this book, feel free to let me know by emailing me at the following:

- errata@pythonlibrary.org

Now let's get started!

Chapter 1 - An Intro to wxPython

The wxPython toolkit is a cross-platform Graphical User Interface (GUI) Framework that is currently maintained primarily by Robin Dunn. It provides Python bindings to the underlying wxWidgets toolkit, which is written in C++. The wxPython toolkit was first released in 1998 and is very stable. The community surrounding wxPython is quite nice and very welcoming and helpful to newcomers. You will probably see the term **Phoenix** in reference to **wxPython 4**. Phoenix was the code name for the Python 3 port of wxPython. The previous versions of wxPython are not completely compatible with wxPython 4.

If you have legacy wxPython applications or you find an old example that you want to convert to wxPython 4, then you will want to consult the following two URLs:

- Classic vs Phoenix:
    - https://wxpython.org/Phoenix/docs/html/classic_vs_phoenix.html
- wxPython Project Phoenix Migration Guide:
    - https://wxpython.org/Phoenix/docs/html/MigrationGuide.html

The focus of this chapter is on giving you a quick introduction to **wxPython 4**.

What is a GUI?

Before you dig in to wxPython, I thought it would be good to explain what a GUI is. A graphical user interface is an interface that is drawn on screen that the user can then interact with. A user interface is made up of several common components such as:

- The main window
- Menu / toolbar
- Buttons
- Text entry
- Labels

Collectively, these are known as **widgets**. The wxPython toolkit provides dozens and dozens of widgets, including many complex custom widgets that are written in pure Python. As a developer, you will take these widgets and arrange them in a pleasing way for the user to interact with.

Let's get started by creating a "hello world" type application.

Hello World

When you create a user interface with wxPython, you will almost always need to create a wx.Frame and a `wx.Panel`. The `wx.Frame` is the window object that contains all the other widgets. It is literally a frame. The `Panel` is a bit different. It is a container as well, but it also enables the ability to tab between widgets. Without the `Panel`, tabbing will not work the way you expect. You can use Panels to group widgets as well.

Let's create an example `Frame` to start out:

```python
# hello_world.py

import wx


app = wx.App(False)
frame = wx.Frame(None, title='Hello World')
frame.Show()
app.MainLoop()
```

The first thing you will notice is that you import the wx module. This is a key import as you will need it for any of wxPython's core widgets. Next you instantiate the Application object: `wx.App`. You must have a `wx.App` instance to run anything in wxPython. However you may only have one of them at a time. You will note that I have passed in `False` as its first argument. What this does is it prevents wxPython from catching stdout and redirecting it to a new frame that is automatically generated by wxPython. You can play around with this as it's useful for debugging, but not something that you want to have enabled in production most of the time.

For the next step, you will create the `wx.Frame` instance. The frame has one required argument.

It is pretty standard to see the above though, but to be even more explicit you could rewrite that line to the following:

```python
frame = wx.Frame(parent=None, title='Hello World')
```

As you can see, the frame requires you to pass in a parent. In this case, since this is the primary entry point to your application, you set the parent to None. We also set the title argument to a string because if you didn't, then it defaults to an empty string which is kind of boring. Next you call the frame's `Show()` method to make it visible on-screen.

Finally to get the application itself to run, you must call the app object's `MainLoop()` method. This starts the event loop so that your wxPython application can respond to the keyboard and widget events. When you run this code, you should see a window that looks like this:

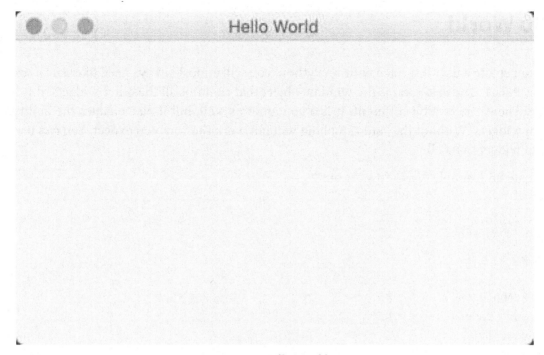

Fig. 1-1: Hello World

While this code works, you will rarely write code that looks like the example above. Instead, most wxPython code that you will read and write is put into classes.

Hello with Classes

The reason that most code in wxPython is put into classes is because you will want to make your code more modular. To do that, you put the widgets related to the frame in the frame class and the widgets that are grouped into a panel in the panel class. You will find that this is true in all of Python's GUI frameworks, such as **Tkinter** or **PyQt**.

Let's take a moment and update the example above so that it uses classes:

```python
# hello_with_classes.py

import wx


class MyFrame(wx.Frame):

    def __init__(self):
        wx.Frame.__init__(self, None, title='Hello World')
        self.Show()
```

```python
if __name__ == '__main__':
    app = wx.App(redirect=False)
    frame = MyFrame()
    app.MainLoop()
```

In this example you will subclass wx.Frame and name your subclass MyFrame. Then you set up the frame in much the way as you did before except that the code for the frame goes into your __init__() method. You also need to call self.Show() to make the frame visible. The application creation is still at the end of the code as before. You also instantiate your new frame class here.

You aren't done with your modification yet. Python 3 recommends using super() when working with classes. The built-in super() function's primary purpose in wxPython is used for referring to the parent class without actually naming it. If you have some free time, I highly recommend you Google Raymond Hettinger's article on super() as it is quite helpful in understanding why it is so useful.

Anyway, let's update your code so that it uses super() too:

```python
# hello_with_classes_super.py

import wx


class MyFrame(wx.Frame):

    def __init__(self):
        super().__init__(None, title='Hello World')
        self.Show()


if __name__ == '__main__':
    app = wx.App(redirect=False)
    frame = MyFrame()
    app.MainLoop()
```

You will see a lot of legacy code that does not use super(). However since this is a Python 3 book, you will use good practices and use super() for your examples.

Note that in Python 2, you were required to call super like this:

```python
super(MyFrame, self).__init__(None, title='Hello World')
```

Let's move on and add a Panel class with a button to your example:

```python
# hello_with_panel.py

import wx


class MyPanel(wx.Panel):

    def __init__(self, parent):
        super().__init__(parent)

        button = wx.Button(self, label='Press Me')


class MyFrame(wx.Frame):

    def __init__(self):
        super().__init__(None, title='Hello World')
        panel = MyPanel(self)
        self.Show()


if __name__ == '__main__':
    app = wx.App(redirect=False)
    frame = MyFrame()
    app.MainLoop()
```

Here you add a panel that contains one widget: a button. You will notice that a panel should have a parent, which in this case is a Frame. You can make other widgets be the parent of a panel though. For example, you can nest panels inside of each other, or make a wx.Notebook into their parent. Regardless, you only want **one** panel as the sole widget for a frame. The panel will automatically expand to fill the frame as well if it is the only child widget of the frame. If you add a panel and a button to the frame without giving them a position or putting them in a sizer, then they will end up stacking up on top of each other. We will talk more about this later on in this chapter.

> Note: wx.Panel widgets enable tabbing between widgets on Windows. So if you want to be able to tab through the widgets in a form you have created, you are required to have a panel as their parent.

Anyway, when I ran this code, it ended up looking like this:

Fig. 1-2: Hello World with a Panel & Button

Now let's talk a little bit about event handling in wxPython.

Events

Events are what happens when the user uses your application. For example, when the user presses a button on their keyboard while your application is in focus, this will fire a KeyEvent. If the user clicks on a widget on your application, it will fire some kind of widget event. You can capture these events by creating an event binding. What this means is that you are creating a listener for a particular event that you want your application to react to. For example, if you have a button in your application, you probably want that button to do something when the user presses it. To actually get the button to do something, you will need to bind the button to the button press event.

Let's update the previous example so that the button actually does something:

```python
# button_event.py

import wx


class MyPanel(wx.Panel):

    def __init__(self, parent):
        super().__init__(parent)
```

```python
        button = wx.Button(self, label='Press Me')
        button.Bind(wx.EVT_BUTTON, self.on_button_press)

    def on_button_press(self, event):
        print('You pressed the button')

class MyFrame(wx.Frame):

    def __init__(self):
        super().__init__(None, title='Hello World')
        panel = MyPanel(self)
        self.Show()


if __name__ == '__main__':
    app = wx.App(redirect=False)
    frame = MyFrame()
    app.MainLoop()
```

Here you call the button's `Bind()` method and tell it to bind to an event: `wx.EVT_BUTTON`. This is the button press event. The second argument is the function that you want to call when the button is pressed. Finally you create the event handler function, `on_button_press()`. You will notice that it takes an event argument. When you catch an event in wxPython, it will pass an event object to the function that you have bound to the event. This event object usually has information in it that identifies which widget called the function and a bunch of other information.

If you run this code, you should see it print out **"You pressed the button"** to stdout each time the button is pressed. Give it a try!

Before you continue, I want to mention that you can also bind the event like this:

```python
self.Bind(wx.EVT_BUTTON, self.on_button_press, button)
```

If you do the binding this way, you are telling wxPython that you are binding the function to the `wx.Panel` instead of the `wx.Button`. This allows us to bind multiple widgets to the same event but different event handlers and then use `event.Skip()` to control which events get bubbled up the layers. In this example, the button in on the bottom layer, the panel is in the next layer up and the frame is at the top layer.

Let's update the code one more time:

```python
# event_hierarchy.py

import wx


class MyPanel(wx.Panel):

    def __init__(self, parent):
        super().__init__(parent)

        button = wx.Button(self, label='Press Me')
        self.Bind(wx.EVT_BUTTON, self.panel_button_handler, button)
        button.Bind(wx.EVT_BUTTON, self.on_button_press)

    def panel_button_handler(self, event):
        print('panel_button_handler called')

    def on_button_press(self, event):
        print('on_button_press called')
        event.Skip()

class MyFrame(wx.Frame):

    def __init__(self):
        super().__init__(None, title='Hello World')
        panel = MyPanel(self)
        self.Show()


if __name__ == '__main__':
    app = wx.App(redirect=False)
    frame = MyFrame()
    app.MainLoop()
```

Here you bind EVT_BUTTON to both the panel and the button object, but you have them call different event handlers. When you press the button, its event handler gets called immediately and it will print out the appropriate string. Then you call event.Skip() so that the EVT_BUTTON event goes up to the next event handler, if one exists. In this case, you have one for the panel and it fires as well. If you wanted to, you could also bind the frame to EVT_BUTTON and catch it there as well. At any of these points, you could remove the call to event.Skip() and the event would stop propagating at that event handler.

Absolute Positioning vs Sizers

wxPython supports both absolute positioning of widgets and relative positioning of widgets. Relative positioning of widgets requires the use of special container objects called Sizers or Layouts. A sizer allows you to resize your application and have the widgets resize along with it. If you are using absolute positioning, the widgets cannot expand or change position at all so when you resize your application, you will find that some of your widgets may get cut off. This can also happen if you load your application on a computer that is using a low resolution display. It is always recommended that you use sizers as they will make your application much nicer to use on multiple displays and screen sizes.

If you would like to play around with absolute positioning, all you need to do is update the call to the instantiation of the wx.Button you created earlier.

Here is an example:

```python
button = wx.Button(self, label='Press Me', pos=(100, 10))
```

The new argument here is called pos for Position. It takes a tuple of **x** and **y** coordinates in pixels. The start location, or origin, is the top left or (0, 0). In the example above, you tell wxPython to place the button 100 pixels from the left-hand side of the panel and 10 pixels from the top.

This is what it looks like when you do that:

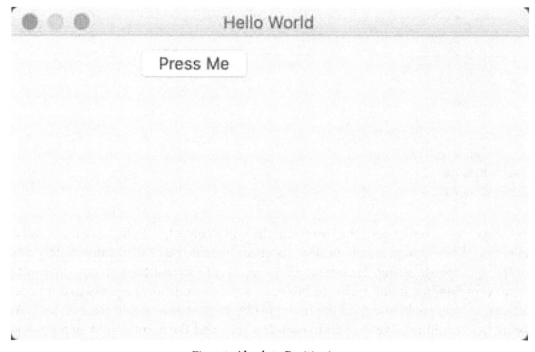

Fig. 1-3: Absolute Positioning

Now let's try using a sizer.

The wxPython toolkit has several sizers you can use:

- `wx.BoxSizer`
- `wx.StaticBoxSizer`
- `wx.GridSizer`
- `wx.FlexGridSizer`
- `wx.WrapSizer`

You can also nest sizers in each other. For demonstration purposes, you will focus on `wx.BoxSizer`. Let's try to center the button in our application both horizontally and vertically.

Here is an example using a slightly modified version of our previous code:

```python
# simple_sizer.py

import wx

class MyPanel(wx.Panel):

    def __init__(self, parent):
        super().__init__(parent)

        button = wx.Button(self, label='Press Me')

        main_sizer = wx.BoxSizer(wx.HORIZONTAL)
        main_sizer.Add(button, proportion=0,
                       flag=wx.ALL | wx.CENTER,
                       border=5)
        self.SetSizer(main_sizer)


class MyFrame(wx.Frame):

    def __init__(self):
        super().__init__(None, title='Hello World')
        panel = MyPanel(self)
        self.Show()


if __name__ == '__main__':
    app = wx.App(redirect=False)
    frame = MyFrame()
    app.MainLoop()
```

The main portion of code that we care about are these three lines:

```
main_sizer = wx.BoxSizer(wx.HORIZONTAL)
main_sizer.Add(button, proportion=0, flag=wx.ALL | wx.CENTER, border=5)
self.SetSizer(main_sizer)
```

This creates a `BoxSizer` that is Horizontally oriented, which is actually the default. Next you add the button object to our sizer and tell the sizer that the proportion of the widget should be 0, which means that the widget should be minimally sized. Then you pass in two flags: `wx.ALL` and `wx.CENTER` The first tells wxPython that you want to apply a border on all four sides of the widget while the second argument tells wxPython to center the widget. Finally you set the border to 5 pixels and since you passed in the wx.ALL flag earlier, that means you want a 5-pixel border on the top, bottom, left and right of the widget.

When I ran this, I got the following:

Fig. 1-4: Using a sizer

Interesting. The widget appears to be centered vertically in a horizontal sizer. If you look at the documentation you will find that horizontal sizers center between the bottom and the top of the parent while vertically oriented sizers align left and right.

 Note: Sizers are invisible to the user, so they can be hard to visualize. You can make them appear if you use the **Widget Inspection Tool** which is helpful for debugging layouts that aren't working well. Go to https://wxpython.org/Phoenix/docs/html/wx.lib.mixins. inspection.html for an example or check out Appendix B for more information.

Let's try changing the proportion flag:

```
main_sizer.Add(button, proportion=1, flag=wx.ALL | wx.CENTER, border=5)
```

Now the proportion is 1 which tells wxPython to make that widget fill 100% of the space:

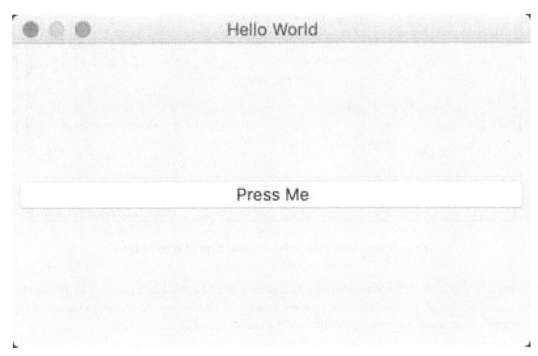

Fig. 1-5: Sizer with a proportion of 1

As you can see, the button is now stretched out horizontally across the entire application.

If you would like to make the button stretch in both directions, you can append the wx.EXPAND flag:

```
main_sizer.Add(button, proportion=1, flag=wx.ALL | wx.CENTER | wx.EXPAND, border=5)
```

Which will now make your application look like this on Windows and Linux:

Fig. 1-6: Sizer with proportion of 1 and Expand on Windows

 Note: On Mac OSX, the button retains its standard height and cannot be made higher in this manner. Instead, you would need to use a custom button or add an image to the standard button that would increase its height beyond the standard size.

If you happened to have multiple widgets in your sizer, then the proportion flag would work differently. Let's say you have two buttons and you add the first button with a proportion of 1 and the second button with a proportion of 0. This will cause the first button to take up as much space as it can while leaving the second button at its minimal size.

Here is the updated code:

```python
# sizer_with_two_widgets.py

import wx


class MyPanel(wx.Panel):

    def __init__(self, parent):
        super().__init__(parent)

        button = wx.Button(self, label='Press Me')
        button2 = wx.Button(self, label='Second button')
```

```python
        main_sizer = wx.BoxSizer(wx.HORIZONTAL)
        main_sizer.Add(button, proportion=1,
                       flag=wx.ALL | wx.CENTER | wx.EXPAND,
                       border=5)
        main_sizer.Add(button2, 0, wx.ALL, 5)
        self.SetSizer(main_sizer)


class MyFrame(wx.Frame):

    def __init__(self):
        super().__init__(None, title='Hello World')
        panel = MyPanel(self)
        self.Show()


if __name__ == '__main__':
    app = wx.App(redirect=False)
    frame = MyFrame()
    app.MainLoop()
```

And here is the result on Mac OSX:

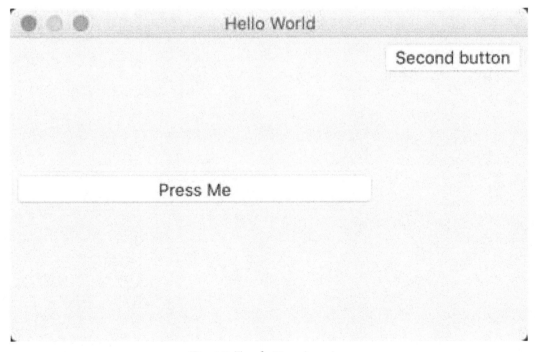

Fig. 1-7: Two buttons in a sizer

Note: The first button will be stretched out in both direction on Windows and Linux, like the screenshot in 1-6. However on Mac OSX, the height cannot be changed for `wx.Button`*. If you want the same behavior across all three platforms, you will need to use a generic button instead.*

I highly recommend playing around with the different flags and proportions using a variety of widgets. You should also check out the documentation which has lots of interesting examples in the Sizer Overview:

- https://wxpython.org/Phoenix/docs/html/sizers_overview.html

Wrapping Up

There is much, much more about wxPython that could be covered here. There are dozens upon dozens of widgets and neat features that you could talk about. However if you did that, then this chapter would end up becoming a book unto itself. This chapter is more for people to get a taste of how wxPython works so that you will be better prepared for creating actual cross-platform applications in the following chapters.

So without further ado, let's start creating!

Chapter 2 - Creating an Image Viewer

You can create pretty much anything if you put your mind to it. The biggest challenge is figuring out how to get started. Several years ago, I wanted to see how hard it would be to create a user interface that I could use to view photographs that I had taken.

Here are the two features that I required for my first version:

- Can load and display at least jpgs
- Resizes the photo so it fits on-screen

That seems really simple. In fact, I would highly recommend that when creating a proof of concept, you should always keep the number of features small. Otherwise you may spend too much time cramming unnecessary features into something that you may end up throwing out. The next step is to think about how you want your user interface to look. I find that sketching it out by hand or in software is a good way to go as it helps me see visually how the application could end up.

You can use pen and paper or you can use something like **Qt Creator** or **Visual Studio** to create really basic UIs that you would then have to code up in wxPython. I usually go for the pen and paper route, but I also have a utility called **Balsamiq Mockups** that is good for creating simple mock ups without any code or bulky applications.

I will be using that for my mock up here:

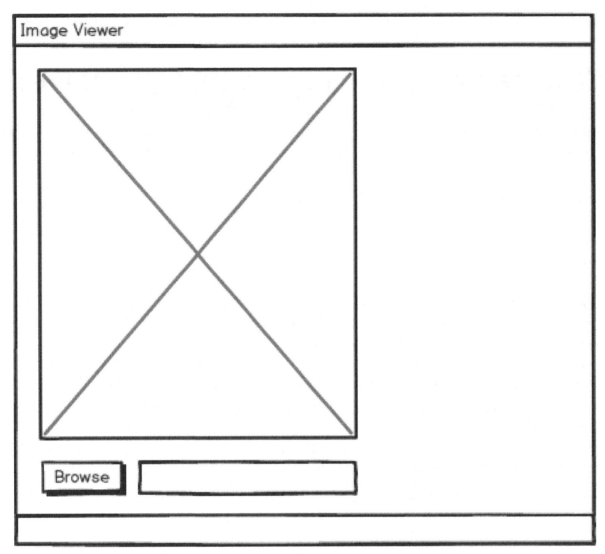

Fig. 2-1: Mockup Image Viewer

Now let's learn how to actually display a photo using wxPython. Feel free to download the code from Github if you'd like to follow along or just type the code out yourself.

Finding the Right Widget

Sometimes finding the right widget can be a challenge. Whenever I am starting out doing something completely new, I will do some research to see what is available to me. I use the following websites the most for research when it comes to wxPython:

- Google
- The wxPython documentation - > https://wxpython.org/Phoenix/docs/html/index.html
- The wxPython demo

In this case, since I know I want to display an image, I would probably look on Google and check the demo. The wxPython demo actually has a couple of candidates that I could use:

- `wx.Image`
- `wx.StaticBitmap`
- `wx.lib.agw.thumbnailctrl.ThumbnailCtrl`

The quickest method of choosing which one to actually use is to analyze what the demo itself is using. In most of the examples that I saw, it was using `wx.StaticBitmap` to display the image to the user. So we will use that as well. You will find that `wx.Image` is actually used as well for converting image files into a format that StaticBitmap can display to the user.

The `wx.Image` widget supports the following formats:

- BMP
- PNG
- JPEG
- GIF (not animated)
- PCX
- TIFF
- TGA
- IFF
- XPM
- ICO
- CUR
- ANI

For full details, see https://wxpython.org/Phoenix/docs/html/wx.Image.html

Anyway, you can use wx.Image to load your image into `wx.StaticBitmap` for display to the user. Let's get started actually coding something up.

Displaying an Image

The first task to tackle is the creation of the widget that will display an image to the user. Let's create a simple interface that has a `StaticBitmap` widget and a button.

I will focus on the `Panel` portion first as it has most of the code that you care about:

```python
# image_viewer.py

import wx

class ImagePanel(wx.Panel):

    def __init__(self, parent, image_size):
        super().__init__(parent)

        img = wx.Image(*image_size)
        self.image_ctrl = wx.StaticBitmap(self,
                                          bitmap=wx.Bitmap(img))
        browse_btn = wx.Button(self, label='Browse')

        main_sizer = wx.BoxSizer(wx.VERTICAL)
        main_sizer.Add(self.image_ctrl, 0, wx.ALL, 5)
        main_sizer.Add(browse_btn)
        self.SetSizer(main_sizer)
        main_sizer.Fit(parent)
        self.Layout()
```

Here you create a subclass of wx.Panel that you call ImagePanel. Next you create an instance of wx.Image. This is used as an initial placeholder image for when you first load up your user interface. The wx.Image widget accepts a width and height as its arguments. To keep things simple, you can just pass in a tuple and unpack the width and height using Python's * operator.

The wx.StaticBitmap requires a bitmap of some sort and the wx.Image works well for this use case. Speaking of the StaticBitmap, that is exactly what you create next. Note that you use wxPython's wx.Bitmap to turn your wx.Image instance into something that your StaticBitmap can use. Then you create a **Browse** button and finally you add the two widgets to your sizer. The button is not bound to any events, so it won't do anything yet if you click it.

The second to last line tells wxPython to Fit() the sizer to the size of the parent. This causes wxPython to attempt to match the sizer's minimal size and reduces whitespace around the widgets.

The last ling calls the panel's Layout() method, which will force a layout of all the children widgets. It is especially useful when adding and removing widgets to a sizer or parent widget. In this case, it can be useful when working with Fit() and when working with image related widgets that can have their contents change.

Now let's add the following code to your Python file so that you can run your new application:

```python
class MainFrame(wx.Frame):

    def __init__(self):
        super().__init__(None, title='Image Viewer')
        panel = ImagePanel(self, image_size=(240,240))
        self.Show()


if __name__ == '__main__':
    app = wx.App(redirect=False)
    frame = MainFrame()
    app.MainLoop()
```

This code creates a simple subclass of wx.Frame, instantiates your panel and shows the frame to the user. If you don't instantiate the panel class here, no widgets will be shown on-screen.

When you run this code, you should see something like the following:

Fig. 2-2: Image Viewer Skeleton

That is pretty close to your sketch except that it doesn't have the text box that should contain the path to the currently open image. Let's add that and make the button do something too!

Making Working Buttons

This next step in building your application is to make your **Browse** button do something. So let's add the text control and make the **Browse** button do something useful!

Copy the code from the previous example into a new file called **image_viewer_button_event.py** and update the ImagePanel class to the following:

```python
# image_viewer_button_event.py

import wx

class ImagePanel(wx.Panel):

    def __init__(self, parent, image_size):
        super().__init__(parent)

        img = wx.Image(*image_size)
        self.image_ctrl = wx.StaticBitmap(self,
                                          bitmap=wx.Bitmap(img))

        browse_btn = wx.Button(self, label='Browse')
        browse_btn.Bind(wx.EVT_BUTTON, self.on_browse)

        self.photo_txt = wx.TextCtrl(self, size=(200, -1))

        main_sizer = wx.BoxSizer(wx.VERTICAL)
        hsizer = wx.BoxSizer(wx.HORIZONTAL)

        main_sizer.Add(self.image_ctrl, 0, wx.ALL, 5)
        hsizer.Add(browse_btn, 0, wx.ALL, 5)
        hsizer.Add(self.photo_txt, 0, wx.ALL, 5)
        main_sizer.Add(hsizer, 0, wx.ALL, 5)

        self.SetSizer(main_sizer)
        main_sizer.Fit(parent)
        self.Layout()
```

The piece that you should focus on here is adding an event binding to your button object.

Here is the relevant code:

```
browse_btn.Bind(wx.EVT_BUTTON, self.on_browse)
```

All this does is tell wxPython that you will now do something when the user presses the Browse button. The something that you will do is call the on_browse() method.

Let's write that next:

```python
def on_browse(self, event):
    """
    Browse for an image file
    @param event: The event object
    """
    wildcard = "JPEG files (*.jpg)|*.jpg"
    with wx.FileDialog(None, "Choose a file",
                       wildcard=wildcard,
                       style=wx.ID_OPEN) as dialog:
        if dialog.ShowModal() == wx.ID_OK:
            self.photo_txt.SetValue(dialog.GetPath())
```

The first item to discuss is your wildcard variable. This variable holds the file types that the user is able to select when using your application. In this case, you are limiting the user to only be able to view JPEG images. The next step is to create an instance of wxPython's wx.FileDialog. We set its parent to None and give it a title, the wildcard and what style to use.

In this case, we want it to be an open file dialog, so we set the style to wx.ID_OPEN. Then you show the dialog to the user modally. Modal means that the dialog will appear on top of your application and prevent the user from interacting with it until they either choose a file or dismiss the dialog.

The file dialog will use the native operating system's file dialog.

On my Mac, I got this when I clicked the Browse button:

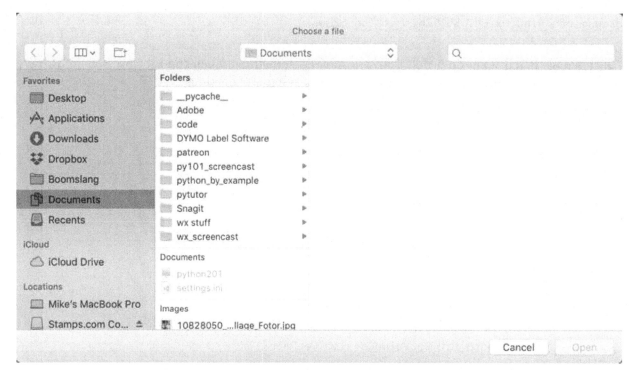

Fig. 2-3: File Browser Dialog

If you happen to run this code on Windows or Linux, the file dialog will look like that operating system's default file dialog. When the user presses OK, then the dialog will set the text control's value to the path of the file that the user selected. Python's with statement will automatically call the dialog's Destroy() method for you and prevent the dialog from hanging in your computer's memory.

Try running this code and selecting a JPEG file on your local system.

You should end up with something like this:

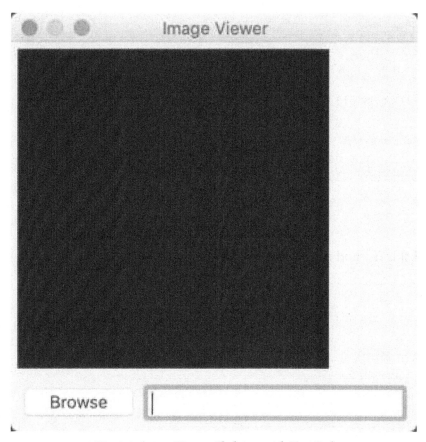

Fig. 2-4: Image Viewer Skeleton with TextCtrl

You will notice that the image still isn't being loaded in your application. Let's learn how to do that!

Loading an Image

Loading and displaying the image is actually quite easy to do with wxPython. But first you need to add an instance attribute that determines the maximum size allowed for the image. This will prevent our application from loading an image into the control that is too large to be displayed. We will add this attribute at the beginning of your `wx.Panel` subclass. Take the code from the previous section and copy and paste it into a new file named **image_viewer_working.py**.

Then update it to include a new instance attribute called `self.max_size`:

```
# image_viewer_working.py

import wx

class ImagePanel(wx.Panel):

    def __init__(self, parent, image_size):
        super().__init__(parent)
        self.max_size = 240


        # Rest of code snipped for brevity
```

Leave the rest of this method alone. The next step is to update your on_browse() method to call a new method:

```
def on_browse(self, event):
    """

    Browse for an image file
    @param event: The event object
    """

    wildcard = "JPEG files (*.jpg)|*.jpg"
    with wx.FileDialog(None, "Choose a file",
                       wildcard=wildcard,
                       style=wx.ID_OPEN) as dialog:
        if dialog.ShowModal() == wx.ID_OK:
            self.photo_txt.SetValue(dialog.GetPath())
            self.load_image()
```

Here you call a new method when the user presses the **OK** button in the open file dialog called load_image().

This is the method you need to write next:

```
def load_image(self):
    """

    Load the image and display it to the user
    """

    filepath = self.photo_txt.GetValue()
    img = wx.Image(filepath, wx.BITMAP_TYPE_ANY)

    # scale the image, preserving the aspect ratio
    W = img.GetWidth()
    H = img.GetHeight()
```

```
if W > H:
    NewW = self.max_size
    NewH = self.max_size * H / W
else:
    NewH = self.max_size
    NewW = self.max_size * W / H
img = img.Scale(NewW,NewH)

self.image_ctrl.SetBitmap(wx.Bitmap(img))
self.Refresh()
```

Here you grab the file path that is in your text control. Then you attempt to load that image using wxPython's wx.Image class and tell it to accept pretty much any of the supported file types by using the wx.BITMAP_TYPE_ANY flag. Of course, you currently have the file dialog itself set to only allow you to pick JPG files. But if you loosened up that restriction, you could accept other image types.

The next thing you do is some scaling to make sure that the image gets scaled to fit your max size, which is 240 pixels. You can use your image object's Scale() method here and pass it your calculated width and height.

Finally you use your StaticBitmap control's SetBitmap() method to actually display the image to the user. It requires you to pass it an instance of wx.Bitmap, so you use wx.Bitmap to create one of those on the fly and put it into your StaticBitmap control. Lastly you call the panel's Refresh() method to force a refresh.

I ran this code and used it to open up the cover image for one of my other books:

Fig. 2-5: Displaying an image

Try opening a few of your own photos to verify it works for you too!

Wrapping Up

We learned a lot about how wxPython works and how easy it is to write an application that can load and display images. The full code for this chapter ended up being only 79 lines including docstrings. I think that is quite good for a simple cross-platform application. However this photo viewer is pretty limited. It would be nice if you could load up a folder of images and then have a "previous" and "next" button to cycle through the photos in said folder. We will look into how to add that feature and another one in the next chapter!

Chapter 3 - Enhancing the Image Viewer

When you first write a piece of software, you might think that when it is released, you are finished with the project. In reality, you are now committed to support that project for its life or until it has been replaced with something new. What this means is that all too often when writing software, you won't be able to ship with all the features that you wanted to and so the features that were dropped will end up being added in some future version. Plus you will need to fix any bugs that arise and possibly add other new features that your users request.

As was noted in the previous chapter, your image viewer is a bit too simplistic. So in this chapter you will look into how you might add the following features:

- Open a folder of images (jpgs)
- Add a previous button
- Add a next button
- Add a play button

The previous and next buttons should allow the user to cycle through the photos in the opened folder. The play button should "play" the folder. In other words, when you press play, it should cycle through all the photos with a delay between cycling.

Here is a sketch of what I was thinking of:

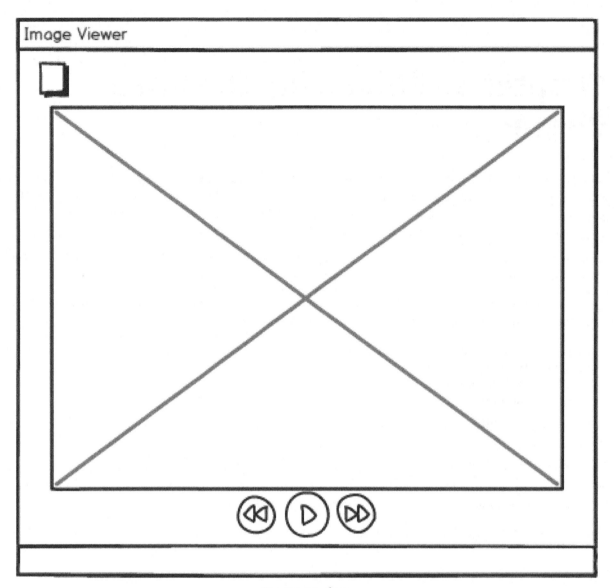

Fig. 3-1: Mockup

Let's start out by learning how to open a folder.

Opening a Folder

The first step that you want to do is create a new file with the following name:

- **image_viewer_folder.py**.

Inside of it, you can write the following code:

```python
# image_viewer_folder.py

import glob
import os
import wx


class ImagePanel(wx.Panel):

    def __init__(self, parent, image_size):
        super().__init__(parent)
        self.max_size = 240
        self.photos = []

        img = wx.Image(*image_size)
        self.image_ctrl = wx.StaticBitmap(
            self, bitmap=wx.Bitmap(img))

    def update_photo(self, image):
        """
        Update the currently shown photo
        """
        img = wx.Image(image, wx.BITMAP_TYPE_ANY)
        # scale the image, preserving the aspect ratio
        W = img.GetWidth()
        H = img.GetHeight()
        if W > H:
            NewW = self.max_size
            NewH = self.max_size * H / W
        else:
            NewH = self.max_size
            NewW = self.max_size * W / H
        img = img.Scale(NewW, NewH)

        self.image_ctrl.SetBitmap(wx.Bitmap(img))
        self.Refresh()
```

Here you create the same subclass that you had created in the previous chapter, but you removed all the widgets except for the StaticBitmap. We also have added a new instance attribute called photos and you added a method called update_photo() which you will use to update the photo widget. Note that this is exactly the same as the example from the previous chapter when it comes to updating the StaticBitmap widget.

The next step is to create a way to show a wx.DirDialog, which will let the user choose a folder of photos. Now you could use another wx.Button to open said dialog, but this is actually the sort of thing that menus and toolbars are made for. So for this example, you will add a toolbar with an open folder button.

Let's add the following class to the same file you just created:

```python
class MainFrame(wx.Frame):

    def __init__(self):
        super().__init__(None, title='Image Viewer', size=(400, 400))
        self.panel = ImagePanel(self, image_size=(240,240))
        self.create_toolbar()
        self.Show()

    def create_toolbar(self):
        """
        Create a toolbar
        """
        self.toolbar = self.CreateToolBar()
        self.toolbar.SetToolBitmapSize((16,16))

        open_ico = wx.ArtProvider.GetBitmap(
            wx.ART_FILE_OPEN, wx.ART_TOOLBAR, (16,16))
        openTool = self.toolbar.AddTool(
            wx.ID_ANY, "Open", open_ico, "Open an Image Directory")
        self.Bind(wx.EVT_MENU, self.on_open_directory, openTool)

        self.toolbar.Realize()
```

Here you create your subclass of wx.Frame and instantiate your wx.Panel subclass, ImagePanel. Please note that you are saving the panel instance as an instance attribute, which will give us easy access to the panel's attributes from within the Frame's class. We will look at a better way of communicating between classes later on in this chapter, but this will work fine for a non-complex application.

The next step is where you call the create_toolbar() method. This method calls the Frame's CreateToolBar() method, which basically instantiates a toolbar object. We then tell that toolbar object what size its toolbar buttons are via SetToolBitmapSize().

Then you add a button using the toolbar object's AddTool() method. This takes an id, a label, the bitmap object and a shortHelp parameter. The shortHelp parameter is a string that is used for the toolbar button's tooltip. Finally you bind the toolbar button object to wx.EVT_MENU and tell it to call a method named on_open_directory() when it is clicked.

Let's write that method next:

```python
def on_open_directory(self, event):
    """

    Open a directory dialog
    """
    with wx.DirDialog(self, "Choose a directory",
                        style=wx.DD_DEFAULT_STYLE) as dlg:
        if dlg.ShowModal() == wx.ID_OK:
            self.folder_path = dlg.GetPath()

            photos = glob.glob(os.path.join(self.folder_path, '*.jpg'))
            self.panel.photos = photos
            if photos:
                self.panel.update_photo(photos[0])
```

In this example, you create your wx.DirDialog instance using Python's with statement. This will automatically destroy the dialog at the end so you don't have to. Then you show the dialog modally via the ShowModal() method in the same way that you did with the File dialog from the previous chapter. If the user presses the OK button, then you get the path of the chosen folder and save it off.

Then you use Python's glob module to search that folder for JPG files. The glob module will return a list of paths to any JPG files it finds or an empty list if it finds nothing at all. Finally you set the panel instance's photos attribute to that list and tell it to update the photo that is shown to the user if the list has any items in it. In this case, the photo shown is the first item in the list.

Let's add these final four lines of code so you can run this example:

```python
if __name__ == '__main__':
    app = wx.App(redirect=False)
    frame = MainFrame()
    app.MainLoop()
```

When I ran this example, this is what my application looked like:

Fig. 3-2: Initial new version of Image Viewer

Now let's add the **Previous**, **Play** and **Next** buttons to your application!

Adding New Buttons

Adding three new buttons isn't very hard, but one thing I have discovered over my many years of programming is that it is usually a good idea to write some "helper" functions here and there for repetitive code. In this case, you have three buttons that you want in a horizontal row. If you coded it all out, you would need to do the following steps several times:

- Instantiate the button
- Bind the button event
- Add the button to a sizer

You can put these steps into a function or method like this:

```python
def btn_builder(self, label, sizer, handler):
    """
    Builds a button, binds it to an event handler and adds it to a sizer
    """
    btn = wx.Button(self, label=label)
    btn.Bind(wx.EVT_BUTTON, handler)
    sizer.Add(btn, 0, wx.ALL|wx.CENTER, 5)
```

This can reduce some of the visual clutter in your code and if you make it generic enough, you can reuse this code in other projects. Let's try applying this code to your example. Take the code from the previous example and save it as **image_viewer_nav_buttons.py**.

Then modify it as follows:

```python
# image_viewer_nav_buttons.py

import glob
import os
import wx

class ImagePanel(wx.Panel):

    def __init__(self, parent):
        super().__init__(parent)
        self.max_size = 240
        self.photos = []
        self.layout()

    def layout(self):
        """
        Layout the widgets on the panel
        """

        self.main_sizer = wx.BoxSizer(wx.VERTICAL)
        btn_sizer = wx.BoxSizer(wx.HORIZONTAL)

        img = wx.Image(self.max_size, self.max_size)
        self.image_ctrl = wx.StaticBitmap(self, wx.ID_ANY,
                                          wx.Bitmap(img))
        self.main_sizer.Add(self.image_ctrl, 0, wx.ALL|wx.CENTER, 5)
        self.image_label = wx.StaticText(self, label="")
        self.main_sizer.Add(self.image_label, 0, wx.ALL|wx.CENTER, 5)
```

```
        btn_data = [("Previous", btn_sizer, self.on_previous),
                    ("Slide Show", btn_sizer, self.on_slideshow),
                    ("Next", btn_sizer, self.on_next)]
        for data in btn_data:
            label, sizer, handler = data
            self.btn_builder(label, sizer, handler)

        self.main_sizer.Add(btn_sizer, 0, wx.CENTER)
        self.SetSizer(self.main_sizer)
```

Note that you have removed the image_size parameter here. You will also need to remove it from the MainFrame class.

Next you have a new method named layout() that you put all of your widget instantiation and bindings into. We also create two wx.BoxSizers here. To create three buttons, you create a list of tuples. Each tuple has a label string, the sizer to use and the event handler that should be called for that button.

Now let's look more closely at that btn_builder() method:

```
def btn_builder(self, label, sizer, handler):
    """
    Builds a button, binds it to an event handler and adds it to a sizer
    """
    btn = wx.Button(self, label=label)
    btn.Bind(wx.EVT_BUTTON, handler)
    sizer.Add(btn, 0, wx.ALL|wx.CENTER, 5)
```

Here you create an instance of wx.Button using the label that is passed in. Then you bind its EVT_BUTTON to the specified handler. Finally you Add() the button to the specified sizer object. No muss, no fuss.

If you want your code to run, then you also need to stub out those event handlers / methods:

```
def on_next(self, event):
    pass


def on_previous(self, event):
    pass


def on_slideshow(self, event):
    pass
```

Obviously these methods don't do anything. They are there to make the code runnable. You should now be able to run this code and see your new buttons:

Fig. 3-3: Image Viewer buttons

Now you need to make those buttons do something useful!

Hooking up Previous / Next

You hooked up the buttons to event handlers in the previous section within the btn_builder() method when you called each button's Bind() method. What you need to do now is actually add the necessary logic to the event handlers so that something useful occurs when the user presses the "Previous" or "Next" button.

To make this work correctly, you need to add a couple more attributes to your class:

```
# image_viewer_prev_next.py

import glob
import os
import wx

class ImagePanel(wx.Panel):

    def __init__(self, parent):
        super().__init__(parent)
        self.max_size = 240
        self.photos = []
        self.current_photo = 0
        self.total_photos = 0
        self.layout()
```

Here you added two new attributes:

- current_photo
- total_photos

We set both of these to zero. The current_photo attribute refers to the index that you are currently on in the list that is held in the photos attribute. The total_photos attribute is the total number of paths that are in the photos list.

Now that you have that out of the way, let's update the Previous and Next button event handlers:

```
def on_next(self, event):
    """
    Loads the next picture in the directory
    """
    if not self.photos:
        return

    if self.current_photo == self.total_photos - 1:
        self.current_photo = 0
    else:
        self.current_photo += 1
    self.update_photo(self.photos[self.current_photo])

def on_previous(self, event):
    """
    Displays the previous picture in the directory
```

```
    """

    if not self.photos:
        return

    if self.current_photo == 0:
        self.current_photo = self.total_photos - 1
    else:
        self.current_photo -= 1
    self.update_photo(self.photos[self.current_photo])
```

In both of these event handlers, you do a check to verify that your photos list is not empty. If it is, then you return because there aren't any images to show right now. Otherwise you use basic math to determine what the next index should be.

If you press "Next" and the current photo is the total minus one, then you know you have reached the end of the folder and need to reset the current photo to zero. Otherwise you increase the number. Then you update the photo control. We do the same basic operations in the "Previous" button's event handler except in reverse.

We also need to update the on_open_directory() method in your Frame class in such a way that it updates the panel's total_photos amount.

Let's find out how to do that:

```
def on_open_directory(self, event):
    """
    Open a directory dialog
    """
    with wx.DirDialog(self, "Choose a directory",
                    style=wx.DD_DEFAULT_STYLE) as dlg:
        if dlg.ShowModal() == wx.ID_OK:
            self.folder_path = dlg.GetPath()

            photos = glob.glob(os.path.join(self.folder_path, '*.jpg'))
            self.panel.photos = photos
            if photos:
                self.panel.update_photo(photos[0])
                self.panel.total_photos = len(photos)
            else:
                self.panel.reset()
```

Once you have made all those changes, you should now be able to use the "Previous" and "Next" buttons in your image viewer application unless you choose a directory that doesn't have any photos. In that case, you need to have the reset() method written in your panel class:

```python
def reset(self):
    img = wx.Image(self.max_size,
                   self.max_size)
    bmp = wx.Bitmap(img)
    self.image_ctrl.SetBitmap(bmp)
    self.current_photo = 0
    self.photos = []
```

This code will reset the image control widget back to its original state. It will also reset the current_photo and photos instance attributes to their initial values.

Playing a Folder

We are still missing the functionality of being able to "play" the folder. In this section, you will learn what you need to do to make this feature possible. Our first task is to learn about timers. The wxPython toolkit has a handy class called **wx.Timer** that allows you to execute code at specified intervals.

Let's modify your ImagePanel class so that it has one:

```python
# image_viewer_slideshow.py


import glob
import os
import wx


class ImagePanel(wx.Panel):

    def __init__(self, parent):
        super().__init__(parent)
        self.max_size = 240
        self.photos = []
        self.current_photo = 0
        self.total_photos = 0
        self.layout()

        self.slideshow_timer = wx.Timer(self)
        self.Bind(wx.EVT_TIMER, self.on_next, self.slideshow_timer)
```

Here you create your timer object and set its **owner** to the panel (i.e. self). Then you bind the wx.EVT_TIMER to the panel and the timer object. It will call your on_next() method each time the timer event fires. Of course, the timer is currently not running, so you need to start it.

A good place to put the timer start code is in your on_slideshow() event handler:

```
def on_slideshow(self, event):
    """
    Starts and stops the slideshow
    """
    btn = event.GetEventObject()
    label = btn.GetLabel()
    if label == "Slide Show":
        self.slideshow_timer.Start(3000)
        btn.SetLabel("Stop")
    else:
        self.slideshow_timer.Stop()
        btn.SetLabel("Slide Show")
```

Just for fun, you extract the button object by using the event's GetEventObject() method. Then you pull out the label and check to see what it is. If it is "Slide Show", then you start the timer and change the label. This allows us to press the button again to stop the timer. Note that when you start the timer, you pass in a value of 3000 milliseconds, which translates to 3 seconds. If everything works correctly, you should see the photos auto-advance every three seconds.

Switching to PubSub

I wanted to take a step back here and talk a bit about why I usually don't recommend interacting with classes by using the class instance as you have done so far in this example. The reason is that this can get very complex when your application has many views or frames. Keeping track of which panel or widget belongs to which can lead to errors and difficult bugs.

Instead of using this method, I usually recommend using the **Publish / Subscribe** pattern. This pattern basically says that you want to create a publisher that sends out messages to subscribers or listeners. Each listener can take that message and use it accordingly.

You see this all the time with client/server applications and more advanced versions of it in distributed application programming. The wxPython toolkit includes a module for this pattern called pubsub which you will find in wx.lib.pubsub. However this is now deprecated within wxPython, so you will want to switch to a package called PyPubSub by Oliver Schoenborn and available on the Python Package Index. This package is what wx.lib.pubsub was originally based on.

To install PyPubSub, you may use pip:

```
pip install pypubsub
```

Once that is installed, you will also need to copy the previous example into a new file and save it as **image_viewer_pubsub.py**.

Now let's modify the ImagePanel class within it to add the following:

```python
# image_viewer_pubsub.py

import glob
import os
import wx
from pubsub import pub


class ImagePanel(wx.Panel):

    def __init__(self, parent):
        super().__init__(parent)
        self.max_size = 240
        self.photos = []
        self.current_photo = 0
        self.total_photos = 0
        self.layout()

        pub.subscribe(self.update_photos_via_pubsub, "update")

        self.slideshow_timer = wx.Timer(self)
        self.Bind(wx.EVT_TIMER, self.on_next, self.slideshow_timer)
```

Here you import `pub` from `pubsub`. Then you create a subscriber by calling `pub.subscribe`. The subscriber takes two arguments:

- The function to call
- The named topic.

Now let's add the `update_photos_via_pubsub()` method to finish your changes to your panel subclass:

```python
def update_photos_via_pubsub(self, photos):
    """
    Update the photo attributes via pubsub
    """
    self.photos = photos
    self.total_photos = len(self.photos)
    self.update_photo(self.photos[0])
```

Here you create a method that accepts a Python list of paths to the photos. So instead of updating your panel in your Frame subclass, you can now update it within your `ImagePanel`. The last change you need to apply is to remove the portion of the code that was setting the above items from your Frame's subclass. To do that, you need to modify the on_open_directory() method in the MainFrame class.

Here is the original:

```python
def on_open_directory(self, event):
    """
    Open a directory dialog
    """
    with wx.DirDialog(self, "Choose a directory",
                      style=wx.DD_DEFAULT_STYLE) as dlg:
        if dlg.ShowModal() == wx.ID_OK:
            self.folder_path = dlg.GetPath()

            photos = glob.glob(os.path.join(self.folder_path, '*.jpg'))
            self.panel.photos = photos
            if photos:
                self.panel.update_photo(photos[0])
                self.panel.total_photos = len(photos)
            else:
                self.panel.reset()
```

and here is the changed version:

```python
def on_open_directory(self, event):
    """
    Open a directory dialog
    """
    with wx.DirDialog(self, "Choose a directory",
                      style=wx.DD_DEFAULT_STYLE) as dlg:
        if dlg.ShowModal() == wx.ID_OK:
            self.folder_path = dlg.GetPath()

            photos = glob.glob(os.path.join(self.folder_path, '*.jpg'))
            if photos:
                pub.sendMessage("update", photos=photos)
            else:
                self.panel.reset()
```

As you can see, you no longer need to set any attributes or call any methods on self.panel if there are photos. Now you pass the paths to the photos indirectly to the ImagePanel class using PubSub. If you had other parts of your application that needed this information, they could also be subscribed to this message and get it too.

Applications can grow quickly, so if you think you will be needing to communicate across multiple classes in your application, then using PubSub early will save you a lot of headaches.

Other Notes on PubSub

PyPubSub has a message data specification (MDS) that you can use for catching messaging errors. You can set the message data specification yourself or let PyPubSub infer it automatically. When someone sends data that does not match the specification, you will see an exception gets thrown.

PyPubSub also supports event notification. This will allow you to hook into PyPubSub to call a callback / method whenever listeners are added, removed, messaged, new topics are defined, etc. This is useful for debugging.

Note that PyPubSub is not inherently thread-safe in wxPython. You will need to use one of wxPython's thread-safe methods with PyPubSub for it to work correctly. wxPython's thread-safe methods are `wx.CallAfter`, `wx.CallLater`, and `wx.PostEvent`.

For the most up-to-date information on PyPubSub, you should always check its documentation on ReadTheDocs:

- https://pypubsub.readthedocs.io/en/v4.0.3/

Wrapping Up

We learned about a lot of fun new topics in this chapter. For example, you learned how to use `wx.Timer` objects effectively. We also learned how to use PyPubSub, which can come in handy for more complex programs.

Here are a few enhancements you can try on your own:

- Try switching out the Previous, Play and Next buttons for other types of buttons
- Use images instead of text labels on the buttons
- Add a menubar
- Add a status bar
- Create a "play list" of your favorite photos
- Display thumbnails that allow you to click and enlarge

There is so much more that you could do with this application. You have to put the time and effort into it to make your program work the way you want! For example, you might want to be able to open other image file types. To allow for that, you could use a config file that you can read and write to using Python's configparser module. If you are looking for a challenge, that is a good starting point!

Chapter 4 - Creating a Database Viewer

As a programmer, application developer or whatever hat you end up wearing when you're coding, you will find yourself interacting with databases at some point. Databases are a part of life for programmers and they are something that most users end up interacting with in some form or another whether they realize it or not. The Python programming language comes with a module called sqlite3 that is built-in to the standard library:

- https://docs.python.org/3/library/sqlite3.html

You will find that a lot of programs use SQLite because it is a nice, lightweight, disk-based database that doesn't require you to set up a separate server. Programs like Mozilla's Firefox use SQLite for storing Bookmarks, web history, etc. In this chapter, you will be using wxPython to create a database viewer that will give us the ability to view what is in a SQLite database. The concepts in this chapter can be used to load other databases too. You will need to find the right Python module to connect to that database. Fortunately, all the popular databases have some kind of Python bindings.

The other tool you will be using in this chapter is **SQLAlchemy**, which is an Object Relational Mapper or ORM. It basically translates SQL into Python so you don't need to know SQL to work with a database. The real beauty of SQLAlchemy in my mind is that it also abstracts the connection to the database in such a way that you can use the same code in SQLAlchemy to connect to multiple database back-ends and work with them. This is not the case if you are using the Python bindings directly since they all work a little differently.

Installing SQLAlchemy

You can install **SQLAlchemy** quite easily using pip:

```
pip install sqlalchemy
```

This should install everything you need to use SQLAlchemy successfully. At the time of writing, the current version was 1.2.14, so make sure you have that version or newer.

You can learn more about SQLAlchemy here:

- https://www.sqlalchemy.org/

Installing ObjectListView

You will also be using a custom wxPython widget that is provided as a 3rd party download. The package is called **ObjectListView** and provides a really nice tabular widget that I personally find very useful when working with databases and other data formats that require a grid-like interface.

You can get `ObjectListView` from the Python Packaging Index here:

- https://pypi.org/project/ObjectListView/

Or you can install it using pip:

```
pip install ObjectListView
```

Now that you have all your dependencies installed, let's learn how to make a database!

Creating the Database Model

For this chapter, you will use SQLite for your database and SQLAlchemy for your interface to that database. SQLAlchemy has a couple of different ways that you can use it. You can use the ORM side or you can use the SQL Expression Language side, which allows you to use SQL code directly in Python. Both ways of using SQLAlchemy are complex, but I personally prefer to use the ORM method, so that is what you will do here. Now you need to decide what kind of database you want to do.

I read a lot of books myself, so I thought it would be fun to create a really simple database that contains two tables. The first table will be a `Book` table with two columns: the title of the book and its author. The second table will be used for storing the `Book`'s characters, so you will call this table `Character`. It will have the first and last name of the character as well as a foreign key from the Book table, which is the `Book`'s id.

Let's see how this all plays out in code though. Open up your favorite Python editor and create a new file called **model.py**.

Then enter the following code into it:

```python
# model.py

from sqlalchemy import create_engine
from sqlalchemy.orm import relationship, backref, sessionmaker
from sqlalchemy.ext.declarative import declarative_base
from sqlalchemy import Column, ForeignKey, Integer, String

engine = create_engine('sqlite:///books.db', echo=True)
Base = declarative_base()
```

Here you import the various pieces that you need from the `sqlalchemy` package. Then you create an engine object. This is used for database connections and allows us to create the database. The `echo` parameter tells SQLAlchemy to echo out the SQL commands that SQLAlchemy does to stdout. The `declarative_base()` call at the end will return a base class that you use to create `Table` objects and also allows us to map Python to SQL.

Let's go ahead and define our table classes:

```python
class Book(Base):
    """
    The Book model - defines the Book table
    """
    __tablename__ = "books"

    id = Column(Integer, primary_key=True)
    title = Column(String)
    author = Column(String)

    def __init__(self, title, author):
        self.title = title
        self.author = author


class Character(Base):
    """"""
    __tablename__ = "characters"

    id = Column(Integer, primary_key = True)
    first_name = Column(String)
    last_name = Column(String)
    book_id = Column(ForeignKey("books.id"))
    book = relationship("Book", backref=backref("characters",
                                                order_by=id))
```

```python
    def __init__(self, first_name, last_name):
        self.first_name = first_name
        self.last_name = last_name

    @property
    def fullname(self):
        """
        Returns the full name
        """
        return "%s %s" % (self.first_name, self.last_name)

    def __repr__(self):
        """
        Override the official string representation of Character
        """
        return "<Character('%s')>" % self.fullname
```

The first class subclasses your Base class. The name of the table is defined via the __tablename__ class attribute. The other class attributes define the columns in the table. You will note that you can tell the Columns what type they are as well as setting the primary key of the table. The only truly required class method that you need is the __init__ method. However for the Character class, I added some helper methods to generate the fullname of the character and to modify the string representation of the class.

So now you have the Table definitions (i.e. the classes). How do you actually create the database?

By adding the following lines of code! Make sure these are not indented at all:

```python
# Create the tables
Base.metadata.create_all(engine)
```

Now if you stopped here and ran the code, you would end up with some output that includes the following:

```
CREATE TABLE characters (
    id INTEGER NOT NULL,
    first_name VARCHAR,
    last_name VARCHAR,
    book_id INTEGER,
    PRIMARY KEY (id),
    FOREIGN KEY(book_id) REFERENCES books (id)
)
```

Note that this is a snippet of the output generated from running this script.

This output tells us what SQLAlchemy is doing, which in this case is creating an empty table. Let's find out how to actually add some data to your databases!

Populating the Database

When you are using SQLAlchemy to interact with the database and you are using its ORM methodology, you will need to create a session object.

Add the following code to the end of your **model.py** script and make sure it is not indented at all:

```
# Create a session object so you can populate the database
Session = sessionmaker(bind=engine)
session = Session()


# Add data to the tables
new_char = Character("Hermione", "Granger")
new_char.book = Book("Harry Potter", "JK Rowling")
session.add(new_char)
new_char = Character("Sherlock", "Holmes")
new_char.book = Book("The Adventure of the Creeping Man",
                     "Arthur Conan Doyle")
session.add(new_char)
session.commit()
```

Here you create your Session object. You can think of it as a database cursor. Then you create some instances of your database classes. To add an instance to the database, you call your session object's add() method. This will basically stage the data to be committed. To actually save your data to the database, you must call the commit() method on your session object, which is what you do at the end of this code. At this point, each of the tables should have two entries a piece.

Note that you can run this script multiple times without it overwriting the database. However each time you run this script, you will add the entries multiple times, so it's not really recommended.

Now let's learn how you can create a viewer that you can use to view your tables!

Creating a Database Viewer

Now you must decide how you want your user interface to look. There are many options. You could use a toolbar button to open the database file in much the same way that you did for your Image Viewer application. Or you could create a menubar with a menu item that opens a **File Browser** dialog. But to keep it even simpler, I think you should use a wx.Button to open the file and a wx.ComboBox for the tables.

Here is the mockup of my idea:

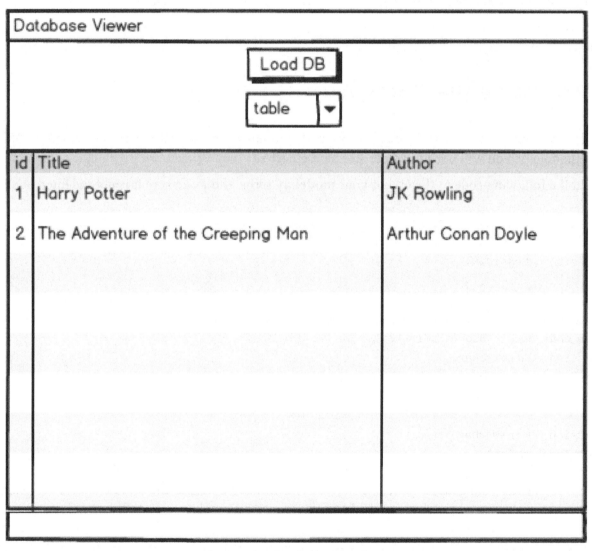

Fig. 4-1: Database viewer mockup

In this example you have your two widgets for loading the database and changing tables. Your mockup also shows a table widget. That table widget will be your ObjectListView widget.

Let's see how you can get this interface coded up:

```python
# db_viewer.py

import os
import wx

from ObjectListView import ObjectListView, ColumnDefn
from sqlalchemy import create_engine, MetaData, Table
from sqlalchemy.orm import mapper, sessionmaker, clear_mappers


class GenericDBClass(object):
    """
    Stub of a database class for ObjectListView
    """
    pass
```

Here are the various imports that you need. As you can see, you don't need to import all the various classes and functions from SQLAlchemy as you did when you created the model since this code isn't going to be used to create a database. You also import a couple of items from ObjectListView. Finally you create a stub class, which you will use with ObjectListView. The reason for this is that ObjectListView uses objects for loading its data and since you are making your database viewer generic, you don't want it to be constrained to loading only one database.

Now let's look at the first method in your wx.Panel subclass:

```python
class MainPanel(wx.Panel):

    def __init__(self, parent):
        super().__init__(parent)

        self.db_data = []
        self.current_directory = os.getcwd()

        self.dataOlv = ObjectListView(self,
                                      style=wx.LC_REPORT|wx.SUNKEN_BORDER)

        # load DB
        loadDBBtn = wx.Button(self, label="Load DB")
        loadDBBtn.Bind(wx.EVT_BUTTON, self.loadDatabase)
        self.table_names = []
        self.tableCbo = wx.ComboBox(self, value="", choices=self.table_names)
        self.tableCbo.Bind(wx.EVT_COMBOBOX, self.loadTable)
```

```
# Create some sizers
main_sizer = wx.BoxSizer(wx.VERTICAL)

main_sizer.Add(loadDBBtn, 0, wx.ALL|wx.CENTER, 5)
main_sizer.Add(self.tableCbo, 0, wx.ALL|wx.CENTER, 5)
main_sizer.Add(self.dataOlv, 1, wx.ALL|wx.EXPAND, 5)

self.SetSizer(main_sizer)
```

This code is your widget setup and layout code.

Here you create your three widgets:

- wx.Button for loading the database
- wx.ComboBox for changing which table is shown
- ObjectListView for displaying the currently selected table's data

You also bind a couple of events. The first is the button event which you will use to load your database via a method called loadDatabase(). The second is a combo box event (wx.EVT_COMBOBOX) that will fire when the user makes a choice from the combo box. This event will trigger the loadTable() method.

Let's look at that method next:

```
def loadTable(self, event):
    """
    Load the table into the ObjectListView widget
    """
    current_table = self.tableCbo.GetValue()
    metadata = MetaData(self.engine)
    table = Table(current_table, metadata, autoload=True, autoload_with=self.engine)
    self.columns = table.columns.keys()

    clear_mappers()
    mapper(GenericDBClass, table)

    Session = sessionmaker(bind=self.engine)
    session = Session()
    self.db_data = session.query(GenericDBClass).all()

    self.setData()
    self.Layout()
```

This is where a lot of the magic is located in this code. Here you use SQLAlchemy's special ability: **reflection**. Reflection is a neat process that SQLAlchemy can use to get information about a table from a database without us needing to create a model class for it. When the user selects a table from the combo box, you grab the table name. Then you load up the database's metadata using SQLAlchemy's `MetaData` class. Next you create a `Table` object on the fly and pass it the table name, the metadata object and tell it to `autoload`.

Next you grab the column's keys from the table and then clear the SQLAlchemy mappers. The reason for doing this is that in normal use cases, a `Table` class is only ever mapped once. However since you want the ability to load up different tables within a database as well as open multiple databases, you need to clear the mappers before remapping one temporarily.

You can read more about this subject here:

- https://docs.sqlalchemy.org/en/latest/orm/mapping_api.html#sqlalchemy.orm.configure_mappers

Anyway, once that is done you can go ahead and create your mapping. Then you instantiate a session object and pull out all the data using a query that is equivalent to this:

```
SELECT * FROM table_name
```

Normally this is probably NOT something that you would do as the database could have millions of records. If it did, then you risk the chance of crashing your application and possibly your database. However since you are interacting with a SQLite database of your own, this won't happen. In fact, most SQLite databases should be fine with this, but feel free to change this line to query for the first ten records or so if you want to.

Finally you need to call the `setData()` method and tell the panel to `Layout()`, which basically tells it to refresh itself.

Now let's find out what the `setData()` method does:

```python
def setData(self, data=None):
    """
    Update the ObjectListView widget's contents
    """
    olv_columns = []
    for column in self.columns:
        olv_columns.append(ColumnDefn(
            column.title(), "left", 120, column.lower()))
    self.dataOlv.SetColumns(olv_columns)

    self.dataOlv.SetObjects(self.db_data)
```

Here you can take the list of columns that you created in the previous function and create them in your `ObjectListView` widget. You can guess how wide the columns should be by setting it to 120 pixels wide and see if it looks okay. Then you call `SetColumns()` which actually adds them to the widget. To add the actual data to the widget, you need to call `SetObjects()`, to which you pass the data from your SQLAlchemy call. This works because you set the column names to be the same as the SQLALchemy record object names.

Normally when you use `ObjectListView`, you will have a class as a model of what each column should look like. Then when you create the widget, you can set the `ColumnDefn`'s last argument to match whichever class attribute you want it to be. In this case, you set it to a lowercase version of the column name. Anyway, just trust me: it works great!

The next step is to add the `loadDatabase()` method:

```python
def loadDatabase(self, event):
    """
    Create a file dialog to open a database file

    Load the database file into the application

    Populate the table combobox
    """
    wildcard = "All files (*.*)|*.*"
    with wx.FileDialog(
        self, message="Choose a file",
        defaultDir=self.current_directory,
        defaultFile="",
        wildcard=wildcard,
        style=wx.FD_OPEN | wx.FD_CHANGE_DIR
    ) as dlg:
        if dlg.ShowModal() == wx.ID_OK:
            db_path = dlg.GetPath()
        else:
            return

    self.engine = create_engine('sqlite:///%s' % db_path, echo=True)

    self.table_names = self.engine.table_names()
    self.tableCbo.SetItems(self.table_names)
    self.tableCbo.SetValue(self.table_names[0])
    self.loadTable("")
```

This piece of code does the actual loading of the database itself. This will cause a modal **File Dialog** to appear which allows the user to go find a database file. If the user finds one AND presses the OK button, then you will load it up and extract a few details from the database. For example, you pull the table names out of the database, which you use in your combo box. You also set the combo box to the first table name in the list and then tell your `ObjectListView` widget to go ahead and load that table's data automatically.

Now let's add the subclass for the `wx.Frame`:

```python
class MainFrame(wx.Frame):

    def __init__(self):
        super().__init__(
            parent=None, title="Database Viewer",
            size=(800,600))
        panel = MainPanel(self)
        self.Show()


if __name__ == '__main__':
    app = wx.App(redirect=False)
    frame = MainFrame()
    app.MainLoop()
```

This final bit of code creates your `wx.Frame` and loads the panel.

When I ran this code against my copy of the database, I got the following:

Fig. 4-1: Database viewer

Wrapping Up

At this point you should be able to use the database viewer to load up other SQLite databases too. For example, the latest version of Mozilla Firefox still uses SQLite for storing cookies, history and lots of other metadata. This application works great for viewing that data.

Of course, viewing data usually isn't the only thing that you want to do, so in the next chapter you will create a simple database editing application.

Chapter 5 - Creating a Database Editor

Databases are wonderful ways to store and manage data. They make finding your data easier, especially if you write a nice interface for searching the database. In this chapter, you will look at how to create a straight forward database that you can interact with using wxPython. One of my hobbies is reading books. In light of this, I thought it would be fun to create a database that stores the following information about a book and its author:

- title
- author
- ISBN
- publisher
- last name
- first name

The last two items on this list are there for when you want to store additional information about other people who are a part of the creation of the book, such as an illustrator or a co-author.

You will be using **SQLAlchemy** and **SQLite** in this chapter as you did in the previous one for interacting with your database.

Here are the features that you will want to support in your application:

- Create a database
- Add records
- Display records
- Modify records
- Delete records
- Search

Let's get ready to create something great!

Prerequisites

As with the previous chapter, you will need the following packages in addition to wxPython to create this application:

- SQLAlchemy
- ObjectListView

You can use pip to install both of these.

Model - View - Controller

There is a programming design pattern that is commonly used when developing user interfaces called **Model-View-Controller** or MVC. The idea is that you can divide your application into three interconnected parts. What this allows is better code reuse and parallel development.

Let's take a look at the three components of MVC:

- Model - This component is the code you use to house and manage the data of your application. A database is a good example of a model.
- View - The view is what is shown to the user. In other words, this is what your wxPython widgets are.
- Controller - The controller takes the inputs and turns them into commands for either the model or the view or both.

You will try to follow this architecture in your database editor application.

The Model

As you might expect, the **Model** is where you will have your SQLAlchemy code. You will also have a model class for your `ObjectListView` widget that amounts to a UI model. The SQLAlchemy models define your database's tables and how they reference each other. This code will also create your database if it does not already exist. To get started, let's create a Python file named **model.py**. Or name it what you will as long as you know what it is.

Once you have your file created, add the following code:

```python
# model.py

from sqlalchemy import Table, Column, create_engine
from sqlalchemy import Integer, ForeignKey, String, Unicode
from sqlalchemy.ext.declarative import declarative_base
from sqlalchemy.orm import backref, relation

engine = create_engine("sqlite:///books.db", echo=True)
Base = declarative_base()
metadata = Base.metadata
```

Here you have the imports you need to create your database. Then you actually create your SQLAlchemy engine like you did in the previous chapter. This will create your SQLite database file and set the SQL output `echo` to `True`. This causes SQLAlchemy to send all the SQL commands that it runs to stdout so you can see what it is doing. In a released product, you would probably want to disable this functionality or put it into a configuration file.

Next you create a declarative base class and you grab its metadata for use later on in this module.

Now let's create your first class:

```python
class OlvBook(object):
    """
    Book model for ObjectListView
    """

    def __init__(self, id, title, author, isbn, publisher,
                 last_name, first_name):
        self.id = id  # unique row id from database
        self.title = title
        self.author = author
        self.isbn = isbn
        self.publisher = publisher
        self.last_name = last_name
        self.first_name = first_name
```

This class is what you will use as your book model for the ObjectListView widget. It contains all the attributes you want to display to the user as well as a couple of attributes that you won't show to the user, such as the id.

Note: While using id as a parameter is nice, id is also a keyword in Python. If you plan to use Python's id, then you shouldn't be creating your own version of it.

Now let's go ahead and create your first SQLAlchemy table class:

```python
class Person(Base):
    """"""

    __tablename__ = "people"

    id = Column(Integer, primary_key=True)
    first_name = Column("first_name", String(50))
    last_name = Column("last_name", String(50))

    def __repr__(self):
        """"""
        return "<Person: %s %s>" % (self.first_name, self.last_name)
```

When I originally created the Person class, I thought it would be useful for adding additional authors to a book or perhaps an illustrator's or editor's name. You could conceivably create a class for holding publisher information instead, if you wanted to.

Regardless, this class defines the people table which has three columns: id, first_name and last_name.

The next class you will create is the Book class:

```
class Book(Base):
    """ """

    __tablename__ = "books"

    id = Column(Integer, primary_key=True)
    author_id = Column(Integer, ForeignKey("people.id"))
    title = Column("title", Unicode)
    isbn = Column("isbn", Unicode)
    publisher = Column("publisher", Unicode)
    person = relation("Person", backref="books", cascade_backrefs=False)


metadata.create_all(engine)
```

This class defines your books table and six columns:

- id - Your primary key
- author_id - The Foreign Key that you use to hook this table to the people table
- title - The title of the book
- isbn - The ISBN of the book
- publisher - The publisher's name
- person - The other piece of the puzzle for hooking the people table to the book table

This final piece of code also creates your database if it does not already exist. Go ahead and run this script when you have all the classes set up so that the SQLite database gets created.

Now you are ready to move on to the view!

The View

The **View**, or the GUI, is what the user will see and interact with on-screen. Let's take a moment and try to sketch out what you want your View / GUI to look like.

Here are the features I want it to do:

- Be able to search
- Display the book table's content in a tabular way
- Add a book
- Edit a book

- Delete a book
- Show everything in my library

With those features in mind, here is a sketch of what I think it should look like:

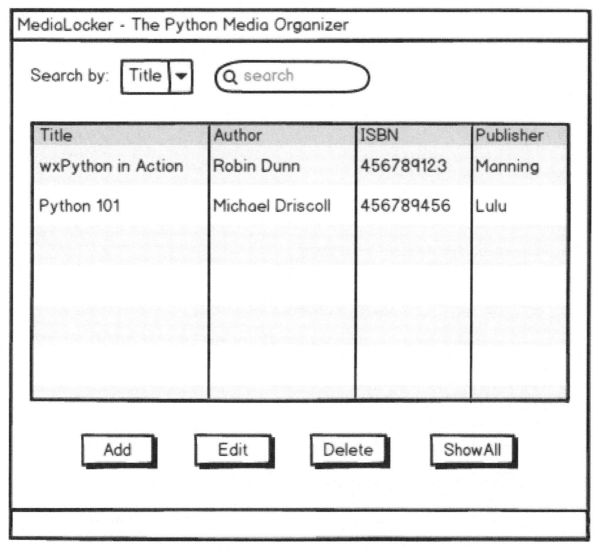

Fig. 5-1: Mockup

Let's get to work and see if you can come up with some code that can turn this vision into a reality! To start, you should create a Python file. Since this is the file that you are likely to run your application from, calling it **view.py** probably doesn't make sense. You could call it **main.py** if you like. Or if you have a name for your application, then that is probably a good name to give to your main script.

For the purposes of this example, you will stick with naming the file **main.py**.

You can start this example with the following code:

```python
# main.py

import wx
from ObjectListView import ObjectListView, ColumnDefn


class BookPanel(wx.Panel):
    """
    The book panel widget - holds majority of the widgets
    in the UI
    """

    def __init__(self, parent):
        super().__init__(parent)

        self.book_results = []

        main_sizer = wx.BoxSizer(wx.VERTICAL)
        search_sizer = wx.BoxSizer(wx.HORIZONTAL)
        btn_sizer = wx.BoxSizer(wx.HORIZONTAL)
        font = wx.Font(10, wx.SWISS, wx.NORMAL, wx.BOLD)

        # create the search related widgets
        categories = ["Author", "Title", "ISBN", "Publisher"]
        search_label = wx.StaticText(self, label="Search By:")
        search_label.SetFont(font)
        search_sizer.Add(search_label, 0, wx.ALL, 5)

        self.categories = wx.ComboBox(self, value="Author", choices=categories)
        search_sizer.Add(self.categories, 0, wx.ALL, 5)

        self.search_ctrl = wx.SearchCtrl(self, style=wx.TE_PROCESS_ENTER)
        self.search_ctrl.Bind(wx.EVT_TEXT_ENTER, self.search)
        search_sizer.Add(self.search_ctrl, 0, wx.ALL, 5)

        self.book_results_olv = ObjectListView(self, style=wx.LC_REPORT
                                               |wx.SUNKEN_BORDER)
        self.book_results_olv.SetEmptyListMsg("No Records Found")
        self.update_book_results()
```

This is the beginning of your wx.Panel subclass. Here you set up an attribute, self.book_results, and a couple of widgets. You also instantiate three sizers. You need a main sizer, a sizer for your search widgets (the ones along the top) and a button's sizer for the buttons along the bottom of your user interface. You also create your search widgets here and the tabular widget, `ObjectListView`.

Now let's add the rest of the widgets to the __init__ as well:

```python
# create the button row
add_record_btn = wx.Button(self, label="Add")
add_record_btn.Bind(wx.EVT_BUTTON, self.add_record)
btn_sizer.Add(add_record_btn, 0, wx.ALL, 5)

edit_record_btn = wx.Button(self, label="Edit")
edit_record_btn.Bind(wx.EVT_BUTTON, self.edit_record)
btn_sizer.Add(edit_record_btn, 0, wx.ALL, 5)

delete_record_btn = wx.Button(self, label="Delete")
delete_record_btn.Bind(wx.EVT_BUTTON, self.delete_record)
btn_sizer.Add(delete_record_btn, 0, wx.ALL, 5)

show_all_btn = wx.Button(self, label="Show All")
show_all_btn.Bind(wx.EVT_BUTTON, self.on_show_all)
btn_sizer.Add(show_all_btn, 0, wx.ALL, 5)

main_sizer.Add(search_sizer)
main_sizer.Add(self.book_results_olv, 1, wx.ALL|wx.EXPAND, 5)
main_sizer.Add(btn_sizer, 0, wx.CENTER)
self.SetSizer(main_sizer)
```

Here you create the button row that runs along the bottom of your user interface. You bind each of these buttons to event handlers and then you finish by adding the search and button sizers to the main sizer. You also add the `ObjectListView` widget in at this point too.

Note: You could use the `btn_builder()` method from chapter 3 here to make this code a bit nicer.

Here is the order that you can add them to the main sizer:

- Search widgets
- ObjectListView (table)
- Button widgets

Now you need to stub out the event handlers for the buttons and search function:

```
def add_record(self, event):
    """

    Add a record to the database
    """

    pass


def edit_record(self, event):
    """

    Edit a record
    """

    pass


def delete_record(self, event):
    """

    Delete a record
    """

    pass


def show_all_records(self, event):
    """

    Updates the record list to show all of them
    """

    pass


def search(self, event):
    """

    Searches database based on the user's filter
    choice and keyword
    """

    pass
```

These methods don't really do much. They are placeholders to remind you that you still need to write this functionality so that the application will work. You do need to write one more method for the panel subclass to be complete though and that method is for updating the ObjectListView's contents.

The update method is as follows:

```python
def update_book_results(self):
    """
    Updates the ObjectListView's contents
    """
    self.book_results_olv.SetColumns([
            ColumnDefn("Title", "left", 350, "title"),
            ColumnDefn("Author", "left", 150, "author"),
            ColumnDefn("ISBN", "right", 150, "isbn"),
            ColumnDefn("Publisher", "left", 150, "publisher")
        ])
    self.book_results_olv.SetObjects(self.book_results)
```

This code defines the column labels in your table-like widget. It also sets the text alignment, width of the column and which attribute of the OlvBook class you created in the model to use for populating its data. Currently the value of self.book_results is an empty list, so the widget will not show any data.

The last bit of code you need to write is for creating the wx.Frame instance:

```python
class BookFrame(wx.Frame):
    """
    The top level frame widget
    """

    def __init__(self):
        """Constructor"""
        super().__init__(
            None, title="Media Organizer",
            size=(800, 600))
        panel = BookPanel(self)

        self.Show()


if __name__ == "__main__":
    app = wx.App(False)
    frame = BookFrame()
    app.MainLoop()
```

This is pretty similar to what you have written in previous chapters, so I don't think it really needs any explanation.

When you run your code, you should now have a user interface that looks something like this:

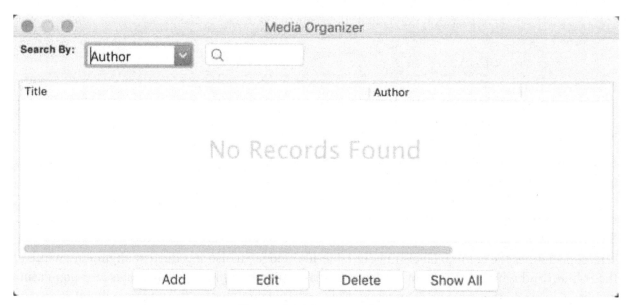

Fig. 5-2: Initial user interface

None of the buttons work yet. However you can't fix those until you have written the controller.

The Controller

The **Controller** is kind of the "glue" of your application. The View will be calling the controller to communicate with the Model. The controller will get what it needs from the Model and then update the View. It's actually kind of elegant how it all ends up working together. This is especially nice when you are working on a team as you can have one of your coworkers work on the view while your data engineer does the model and you get to do the controller.

In this example, you need seven functions in the Controller:

- An add record function
- A database connector
- A function to convert database results to something the View can display
- A delete record function
- An edit record function
- A function that returns all records from the book table
- A search function

Let's create each of these in turn in a script that I am going to call **controller.py**.

The first function will be for adding records to the database:

```python
# controller.py

from model import Book, Person, OlvBook
from sqlalchemy import create_engine
from sqlalchemy.orm import sessionmaker


def add_record(session, data):
    """
    Data should be a dictionary of two dictionaries in the following format:

    {"author":{"first_name":"John", "last_name":"Doe"},
     "book":{"title":"Some book", "isbn":"1234567890",
             "publisher":"Packt"}
    }
    """
    book = Book()
    book.title = data["book"]["title"]
    book.isbn = data["book"]["isbn"]
    book.publisher = data["book"]["publisher"]
    author = Person()
    author.first_name = data["author"]["first_name"]
    author.last_name = data["author"]["last_name"]
    book.person = author

    session.add(book)
    session.commit()
```

This function is actually a really good way to demonstrate how you can use wxPython as an interface to a SQL database. Here you create an instance of your Book class, which is a SQLAlchemy Base class that you use to model the data in the database. Then you set its attributes according to the data you passed in. Now this data that you pass in is in the format mentioned in this function's docstring, which is a dictionary of dictionaries.

Once you have the book instance all set up, you create a Person instance and set its attributes too. Finally you create a SQLAlchemy session object by calling the connect_to_database() function, which you get to next. But first let's mention that the last two lines of this code will add the book to the database and commit the data to the database.

Here you will learn how to connect to the database:

```
def connect_to_database():
    """

    Connect to the SQLite database and return a Session object
    """
    engine = create_engine("sqlite:///books.db", echo=True)
    Session = sessionmaker(bind=engine)
    session = Session()
    return session
```

This function is all about connecting to the database and then returning the session object. This function should only be called once by the application and the session object should be re-used.

Now let's create a conversion function:

```
def convert_results(results):
    """

    Convert results to OlvBook objects
    """
    books = []
    for record in results:
        author = "%s %s" % (record.person.first_name,
                            record.person.last_name)
        book = OlvBook(record.id, record.title, author,
                    record.isbn, record.publisher,
                    record.person.last_name,
                    record.person.first_name
                    )
        books.append(book)
    return books
```

The convert_results() function is used in conjunction with the search function, which you will get to in a minute. This function will convert a SQLAlchemy result set into a list of OlvBook instances that you will then use in the ObjectListView widget. Basically, this is the glue function between a database query and displaying the result on-screen.

Now let's add a delete function:

```python
def delete_record(session, id_num):
    """
    Delete a record from the database
    """
    record = session.query(Book).filter_by(id=id_num).one()
    session.delete(record)
    session.commit()
```

The delete_record() function will use the unique id number of the row in the database to look it up and then delete it from the database. you do this by running a SQL query using SQLAlchemy. Once the record is deleted, you will need to update the user interface, but that is the work of another function.

Now let's create a function for editing a database entry:

```python
def edit_record(session, id_num, row):
    """
    Edit a record
    """
    record = session.query(Book).filter_by(id=id_num).one()
    record.title = row["title"]
    record.person.first_name = row["first_name"]
    record.person.last_name = row["last_name"]
    record.isbn = row["isbn"]
    record.publisher = row["publisher"]
    session.add(record)
    session.commit()
```

The edit_record() function will connect to the database and use the id number to look up the correct record in the database. Then it will take the settings from the passed in row dictionary and modify the record accordingly. When you are done modifying the record, you can add it to the session object and commit it to disk.

This is the get_all_records() function:

```python
def get_all_records(session):
    """
    Get all records and return them
    """
    result = session.query(Book).all()
    books = convertResults(result)
    return books
```

This function will run a query that extracts all the records from the Book table. Then it converts those results to a format that the ObjectListView can consume and returns it.

The final function is the search_records() function:

```python
def search_records(session, filter_choice, keyword):
    """
    Searches the database based on the filter chosen and the keyword
    given by the user
    """
    if filter_choice == "Author":
        qry = session.query(Person)
        result = qry.filter(Person.first_name.contains('%s' % keyword)).all()
        records = []
        for record in result:
            for book in record.books:
                records.append(book)
        result = records
    elif filter_choice == "Title":
        qry = session.query(Book)
        result = qry.filter(Book.title.contains('%s' % keyword)).all()
    elif filter_choice == "ISBN":
        qry = session.query(Book)
        result = qry.filter(Book.isbn.contains('%s' % keyword)).all()
    else:
        qry = session.query(Book)
        result = qry.filter(Book.publisher.contains('%s' % keyword)).all()
    books = convertResults(result)

    return books
```

This function will use a string to determine what kind of query you should run against the database. You can query for the author, the title of the book, the ISBN or the publisher. The query is pretty much the same in all cases, although for the author you have to query against the Person table instead of the Book table. Then you extract the book or books that the author wrote and make that the result.

Editing the Database with a UI

The last item on your feature list is creating a couple of dialogs for adding records to the database and editing existing entries. There are several popular organizational methods that developers like to use. You can put all of your user interface into a single file, such as the **view.py**. Or you can separate things out and group items into new files. For this example, I thought it made more sense to create a **dialogs.py** file that you would use for any dialogs that you need to show the user.

If you plan ahead a bit, you can also craft the dialog class in such a way that you can use it for both adding and editing records in the database. You will try to keep that in mind when you write your class.

Let's learn how to create our RecordDialog class:

```python
# dialogs.py

import controller
import wx


class RecordDialog(wx.Dialog):
    """
    Add / Modify Record dialog
    """

    def __init__(self, session, row=None, title="Add", addRecord=True):
        """Constructor"""
        super().__init__(None, title="%s Record" % title)
        self.addRecord = addRecord
        self.selected_row = row
        self.session = session
        if row:
            book_title = self.selected_row.title
            first_name = self.selected_row.first_name
            last_name = self.selected_row.last_name
            isbn = self.selected_row.isbn
            publisher = self.selected_row.publisher
        else:
            book_title = first_name = last_name = isbn = publisher = ""
```

Here you need to import the controller module and the wx module. Then you subclass wx.Dialog class. Since you want this class to act as both the record adding and editing class, you pass in a title so that the title of the dialog is correct depending on the context. You also default the title "Add" and the addRecord parameter to True. You could make these required parameters if you want to, but for convenience, I decided to give them defaults.

The next step is to set some instance variables that hold which record was passed in (if any) as well as the database session object. You also extract the book's metadata from the row object if it exists. Now you need to create the actual user interface. You have a choice before you. You can put all the

UI code into the __init__() method or you can create a separate class method. Since this UI will be fairly small, I am going to include it in the __init__(). However if you were to add new features to this dialog, you might want to move this code into a separate method.

Let's get the UI started by creating a few sizers:

```
# create the sizers
main_sizer = wx.BoxSizer(wx.VERTICAL)
author_sizer = wx.BoxSizer(wx.HORIZONTAL)
btn_sizer = wx.BoxSizer(wx.HORIZONTAL)
```

You create a top-level sizer and two horizontally oriented sizers which will basically hold rows of widgets.

Speaking of which, let's add a couple of widgets now:

```
# create some widgets
size = (80, -1)
font = wx.Font(10, wx.SWISS, wx.NORMAL, wx.BOLD)
title_lbl = wx.StaticText(self, label="Title:", size=size)
title_lbl.SetFont(font)
self.title_txt = wx.TextCtrl(self, value=book_title)
main_sizer.Add(self.row_builder([title_lbl, self.title_txt]),
               0, wx.ALL)
```

In this example, you create a centered label that will run along the top of the dialog. Then you add a second label next to a text control for inputting or editing the book's title.

Now let's add the author related widgets:

```
author_lbl = wx.StaticText(self, label="Author:", size=size)
author_lbl.SetFont(font)
author_sizer.Add(author_lbl, 0, wx.ALL, 5)
self.author_first_txt = wx.TextCtrl(self, value=first_name)
author_sizer.Add(self.author_first_txt, 1, wx.ALL, 5)
self.author_last_txt = wx.TextCtrl(self, value=last_name)
author_sizer.Add(self.author_last_txt, 1, wx.ALL, 5)
main_sizer.Add(author_sizer, 0, wx.ALL)
```

These three widgets relate to the author's first and last name. You need one label (wx.StaticText) and two text controls (wx.TextCtrl). You add each of these controls to the author related sizer and you set the font on the label.

Now let's add the ISBN and Publisher widgets:

```
isbn_lbl = wx.StaticText(self, label="ISBN:", size=size)
isbn_lbl.SetFont(font)
self.isbn_txt = wx.TextCtrl(self, value=isbn)
main_sizer.Add(self.row_builder([isbn_lbl, self.isbn_txt]),
               0, wx.ALL)


publisher_lbl = wx.StaticText(self, label="Publisher:", size=size)
publisher_lbl.SetFont(font)
self.publisher_txt = wx.TextCtrl(self, value=publisher)
main_sizer.Add(self.row_builder([publisher_lbl, self.publisher_txt]),
               0, wx.ALL)
```

This code is pretty much the same as the previous snippet except that you have two labels this time around.

The last widgets you need to add are the buttons:

```
ok_btn = wx.Button(self, label="%s Book" % title)
ok_btn.Bind(wx.EVT_BUTTON, self.on_record)
btn_sizer.Add(ok_btn, 0, wx.ALL, 5)
cancel_btn = wx.Button(self, label="Close")
cancel_btn.Bind(wx.EVT_BUTTON, self.on_close)
btn_sizer.Add(cancel_btn, 0, wx.ALL, 5)


main_sizer.Add(btn_sizer, 0, wx.CENTER)
self.SetSizerAndFit(main_sizer)
```

Here you have an OK button to accept the changes and an Cancel button to exit the dialog without saving any changes.

If you were to run the application with a couple of stubbed out event handlers it would look like this:

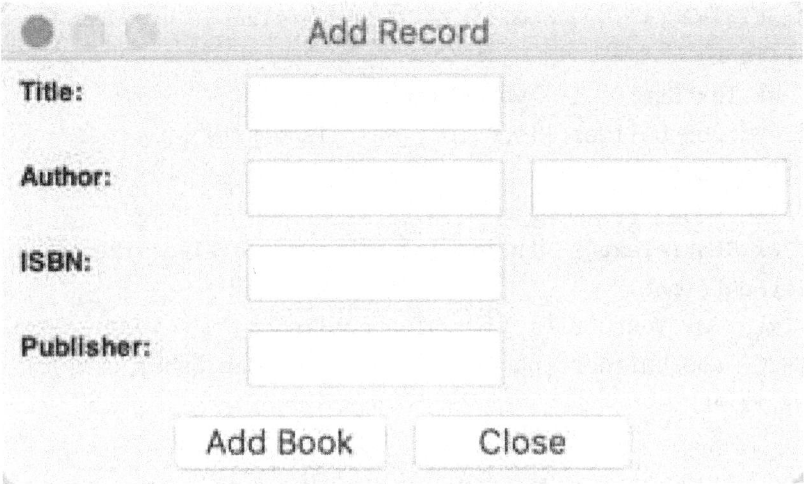

Fig. 5-3: Add / Modify Dialog

Now you need to create a method that you will use to get whatever the user enters into the form. You will call this method get_data():

```python
def get_data(self):
    """
    Gets the data from the widgets in the dialog

    Also display an error message if required fields
    are empty
    """
    author_dict = {}
    book_dict = {}

    fName = self.author_first_txt.GetValue()
    lName = self.author_last_txt.GetValue()
    title = self.title_txt.GetValue()
    isbn = self.isbn_txt.GetValue()
    publisher = self.publisher_txt.GetValue()

    if fName == "" or title == "":
        show_message("Author and Title are Required!",
                     "Error")
        return None, None

    if "-" in isbn:
        isbn = isbn.replace("-", "")
    author_dict["first_name"] = fName
    author_dict["last_name"] = lName
```

```
        book_dict["title"] = title
        book_dict["isbn"] = isbn
        book_dict["publisher"] = publisher

        return author_dict, book_dict
```

This is the method that you would use for validating your input data. In this case, you check to see if the user has entered a first name and a title. If they have not, you will call the show_message() function and tell the user that they missed a required field. There is a widget level validation you can add via a wx.Validator. This would probably be a better method for validating the inputs, but I want to keep this brief if I can. Feel free to check that out on your own as a fun enhancement you could add yourself.

Anyway, the rest of this code is for creating two dictionaries that represent the author and the book and then returns both of those newly created dictionaries.

Let's move on and learn how to add a record to the database using the user interface:

```
def on_add(self):
    """
    Add the record to the database
    """
    author_dict, book_dict = self.get_data()
    if author_dict is None or book_dict is None:
        return

    data = ({"author":author_dict, "book":book_dict})
    controller.add_record(self.session, data)

    # show dialog upon completion
    show_message("Book Added",
                 "Success!", wx.ICON_INFORMATION)

    # clear dialog so we can add another book
    for child in self.GetChildren():
        if isinstance(child, wx.TextCtrl):
            child.SetValue("")
```

Here you call the get_data() method to get the two dictionaries. Then you create a tuple and send that along to the controller's add_record() function. Next you should display a MessageDialog to the user that confirms that the record was added successfully. One immediate improvement here would be to have the add_record() function return True or False in regards to whether or not it actually was added successfully. Feel free to add that yourself if you'd like to. The last piece of code loops over the widgets in the dialog and clears the text controls so that the user can add another record if they want to.

The next method to look at is how to close the dialog:

```python
def on_close(self, event):
    """
    Close the dialog
    """
    self.Close()
```

This code is pretty straight-forward. All you need to do is call the dialog's `Close()` method. The `Close()` method makes the dialog close and you have to make sure that you destroy it yourself so it doesn't hang out in memory. Since you will be opening this dialog using Python's `with` statement (shown in the next section), wxPython will automatically call the dialog's `Destroy()` method for you implicitly.

Now let's find out how you can edit a record using the user interface:

```python
def on_edit(self):
    """
    Edit a record in the database
    """
    author_dict, book_dict = self.get_data()
    combo_dict = {**author_dict, **book_dict}
    controller.edit_record(self.session, self.selected_row.id, combo_dict)
    show_message("Book Edited Successfully!", "Success",
                 wx.ICON_INFORMATION)
    self.Close()
```

Once again, you call the `get_data()` method to get the data that the user entered. Then you flatten the two dictionaries into one. Next you call the controller's `edit_record()` function and pass it the session, the unique ID for the row you are editing and the data to be changed. Finally you show a `MessageDialog` to the user to inform them of the success of their change. Since the editing is done at this point, you call the Destroy method here to close the dialog.

Let's take a look at what happens when the user presses the OK button:

```python
def on_record(self, event):
    """
    Add or edit a record
    """
    if self.addRecord:
        self.on_add()
        self.title_txt.SetFocus()
    else:
        self.on_edit()
```

The event handler, on_record(), is called when the user presses OK. Here you check if the user is adding or editing a record and call the appropriate method. If the user is adding a record, you will reset the focus back to the first field after the record is added.

For convenience's sake, you can create a helper function like this to make building rows of widgets simpler:

```python
def row_builder(self, widgets):
    """
    Helper function for building a row of widgets
    """
    sizer = wx.BoxSizer(wx.HORIZONTAL)
    lbl, txt = widgets
    sizer.Add(lbl, 0, wx.ALL, 5)
    sizer.Add(txt, 1, wx.ALL, 5)
    return sizer
```

All this method does is create a sizer and then extracts the StaticText and TextCtrl widgets from the passed in parameter. Then it adds those widgets to the sizer and returns the sizer itself.

The final function you want to look at is the show_message() function. Please note that this is a function and is not a part of the dialog class so be sure to dedent it appropriately:

```python
def show_message(message, caption, flag=wx.ICON_ERROR):
    """
    Show a message dialog
    """
    msg = wx.MessageDialog(None, message=message,
                           caption=caption, style=flag)
    msg.ShowModal()
    msg.Destroy()
```

All this code does is create a MessageDialog using the passed in message, caption and flag and shows it to the user. The user then dismisses the dialog which causes it to destroy itself.

Connecting the View and Controller

Now that you have the controller and the dialogs fleshed out, you need to actually use those functions in the main application. So in this section, you will learn how to hook up the Application's View to the Controller. You will be updating the methods in the BookPanel class that is in your **main.py** file here. You will need to add the following imports to the top of the file:

- os
- controller
- dialogs

Now let's get started by updating the add_record() method:

```python
def add_record(self, event):
    """
    Add a record to the database
    """
    with dialogs.RecordDialog(self.session) as dlg:
        dlg.ShowModal()

    self.show_all_records()
```

Adding a record should be simple for the user. So here you create an instance of the RecordDialog class from the **dialogs.py** module you created and show it to the user. Note that this is also where you pass in your database session object. Regardless of whether the user adds a record or not, you always Destroy() the dialog and refresh the contents of the main application so that it always shows the latest data by calling the show_all_records() method.

Now let's update the edit_record() method:

```python
def edit_record(self, event):
    """
    Edit a record
    """
    selected_row = self.book_results_olv.GetSelectedObject()
    if selected_row is None:
        dialogs.show_message('No row selected!', 'Error')
        return

    with dialogs.RecordDialog(self.session,
                              selected_row,
                              title='Modify',
```

```
                        addRecord=False) as dlg:
    dlg.ShowModal()

self.show_all_records()
```

In this code, you grab the currently selected item in the `ObjectListView` widget. This allows us to edit the item. Of course, the user may not have chosen anything yet, so you check to see if there is anything selected and if there is not, then you display a `MessageDialog` letting them know.

If the user has selected an item, then you create an instance of `RecordDialog` as you did before, but this time you pass in the database session object, the selected row, a different title and change the `addRecord` flag to `False`. This tells your dialog class to load the data into the dialog's fields so that the user can edit them.

Next up, you will need to modify the `delete_record()` method:

```
def delete_record(self, event):
    """
    Delete a record
    """
    selected_row = self.book_results_olv.GetSelectedObject()
    if selected_row is None:
        dialogs.show_message('No row selected!', 'Error')
        return
    controller.delete_record(self.session, selected_row.id)
    self.show_all_records()
```

Once again, you attempt to extract the selected row from the user interface. If there is nothing selected, you let the user know. Otherwise you call the controller's `delete_record()` function and give it your database `session` object and the record's unique identifier. Finally you refresh the user interface.

Speaking of refreshing the UI, let's learn how that works:

```
def show_all_records(self):
    """
    Updates the record list to show all of them
    """
    self.book_results = controller.get_all_records(self.session)
    self.update_book_results()
```

This method calls other controller's `get_all_records()` method, which will execute a SQL query for all the current records in the database and return them. Then you call `update_book_results()` to update the application.

Now let's learn how you can hook up the search capability:

```python
def search(self, event):
    """
    Searches database based on the user's filter
    choice and keyword
    """
    filter_choice = self.categories.GetValue()
    keyword = self.search_ctrl.GetValue()
    self.book_results = controller.search_records(
        self.session, filter_choice, keyword)
    self.update_book_results()
```

The search() method will get the user's category choice. Then it will get the user's string that they entered into the search control. The next step is to pass that information on to the controller's search_records() function. This function executes a SQL query using that information and returns the results, it any. Then you update the user interface accordingly.

The last method that you need to update is the on_show_all() method, which is an event handler that you have bound to the **Show All** button:

```python
def on_show_all(self, event):
    """
    Updates the record list to show all the records
    """
    self.show_all_records()
```

All this code does is call the show_all_records() method. Technically you could call show_all_-records() directly if you modified it slightly to accept the event object, but in this case I thought it was better to create a separate event handler method. This helps to keep the two methods short and makes changing them easier as well.

Wrapping Up

Creating a simple database editor in wxPython is a bit complicated. However if you open up the code for the main application, you will notice that it is only 164 lines of code, which isn't all that bad for a user interface. At this point, you now have a working editor. The next step would be to figure out what kinds of improvements you would like to meet. You could add more validation via wx.Validator. There is also a neat set of widgets in wx.lib.masked that you could use to make inputting data like the ISBN more uniform while also preventing the user from entering alphanumeric characters.

If this application was to be deployed in a business, you would want to swap out SQLite for a robust database, such as Microsoft SQL Server or PostgreSQL. Changing out the backend would make a really good learning opportunity for you.

Finally I would like to mention that a friend of mine took a version of this code and refactored it a bit into a project we ended up calling **MediaLocker** which you can find on Bitbucket here: https://bitbucket.org/driscollis/medialocker/src/default/ . It hasn't been updated in a long time, but it does make a good case study of how to refactor and enhance code.

Chapter 6 - The Humble Calculator

A lot of beginner tutorials start with "Hello World" examples. There are plenty of websites that use a calculator application as a kind of "Hello World" for GUI beginners. Calculators are a good way to learn because they have a set of widgets that you need to lay out in an orderly fashion. They also require a certain amount of logic to make them work correctly.

For this calculator, let's focus on being able to do the following:

- Addition
- Subtraction
- Multiplication
- Division

I think that supporting these four functions is a great starting place and also give you plenty of room for enhancing the application on your own.

Figuring Out the Logic

One of the first items that you will need to figure out is how to actually execute the equations that you build.

For example, let's say that you have the following equation:

```
1 + 2 * 5
```

What is the solution? If you read it left-to-right, the solution would seem to be 3 * 5 or 15. But multiplication has a higher precedence than addition, so it would actually be 10 + 1 or 11. How do you figure out precedence in code? You could spend a lot of time creating a string parser that groups numbers by the operand or you could use Python's built-in eval function. The eval() function is short for evaluate and will evaluate a string as if it was Python code.

A lot of Python programmers actually discourage the user of eval().

Let's find out why.

Is eval() Evil?

The eval() function has been called "evil" in the past because it allows you to run strings as code, which can open up your application's to nefarious evil-doers. You have probably read about SQL injection where some websites don't properly escape strings and accidentally allowed dishonest people to edit their database tables by running SQL commands via strings. The same concept can happen in Python when using the eval() function.

A common example of how eval() could be used for evil is as follows:

```
eval("__import__('os').remove('file')")
```

This code will import Python's os module and call its remove() function, which would allow your users to delete files that you might not want them to delete.

There are a couple of approaches for avoiding this issue:

- Don't use eval()
- Control what characters are allowed to go to eval()

Since you will be creating the user interface for this application, you will also have complete control over how the user enters characters. This actually can protect you from eval's insidiousness in a straight-forward manner. You will learn two methods of using wxPython to control what gets passed to eval(), and then you will learn how to create a custom eval() function at the end of the chapter.

Designing the Calculator

Let's take a moment and try to design a calculator using the constraints mentioned at the beginning of the chapter.

Here is the sketch I came up with for the calculator:

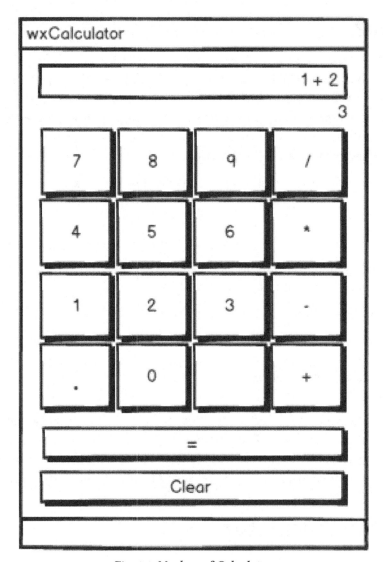

Fig. 6-1: Mockup of Calculator

Note that you only care about basic arithmetic here. You won't have to create a scientific calculator, although that might be a fun enhancement to challenge yourself with. Instead, you will create a nice, basic calculator.

Let's get started!

Creating the Initial Calculator

Whenever you create a new application, you have to consider where the code will go. Does it go in the wx.Frame class, the wx.Panel class, some other class or what? It is almost always a mix of different classes when it comes to wxPython. As is the case with most wxPython applications, you will want to start by coming up with a name for your application. For simplicity's sake, let's call it **wxcalculator.py** for now.

The first step is to add some imports and subclass the `Frame` widget.

Let's take a look:

```python
# wxcalculator.py

import wx


class CalcFrame(wx.Frame):

    def __init__(self):
        super().__init__(
            None, title="wxCalculator",
            size=(350, 375))
        panel = CalcPanel(self)
        self.SetSizeHints(350, 375, 350, 375)
        self.Show()



if __name__ == '__main__':
    app = wx.App(False)
    frame = CalcFrame()
    app.MainLoop()
```

This code is very similar to what you have seen in the past. You subclass `wx.Frame` and give it a title and initial size. Then you instantiate the panel class, `CalcPanel` (not shown) and you call the `SetSizeHints()` method. This method takes the smallest (width, height) and the largest (width, height) that the frame is allowed to be. You may use this to control how much your frame can be resized or in this case, prevent any resizing. You can also modify the frame's style flags in such a way that it cannot be resized too.

Here's how:

```python
class CalcFrame(wx.Frame):

    def __init__(self):
        no_resize = wx.DEFAULT_FRAME_STYLE & ~ (wx.RESIZE_BORDER |
                                                wx.MAXIMIZE_BOX)
        super().__init__(
            None, title="wxCalculator",
            size=(350, 375), style=no_resize)
        panel = CalcPanel(self)
        self.Show()
```

Take a look at the `no_resize` variable. It is creating a `wx.DEFAULT_FRAME_STYLE` and then using bitwise operators to remove the resizable border and the maximize button from the frame.

Let's move on and create the `CalcPanel`:

```python
class CalcPanel(wx.Panel):

    def __init__(self, parent):
        super().__init__(parent)
        self.last_button_pressed = None
        self.create_ui()
```

I mentioned this in an earlier chapter, but I think it bears repeating here. You don't need to put all your interfacer creation code in the init method. This is an example of that concept. Here you instantiate the class, set the `last_button_pressed` attribute to None and then call `create_ui()`. That is all you need to do here.

Of course, that begs the question. What goes in the `create_ui()` method?

Well, let's find out:

```python
def create_ui(self):
    main_sizer = wx.BoxSizer(wx.VERTICAL)
    font = wx.Font(12, wx.MODERN, wx.NORMAL, wx.NORMAL)

    self.solution = wx.TextCtrl(self, style=wx.TE_RIGHT)
    self.solution.SetFont(font)
    self.solution.Disable()
    main_sizer.Add(self.solution, 0, wx.EXPAND|wx.ALL, 5)
    self.running_total = wx.StaticText(self)
    main_sizer.Add(self.running_total, 0, wx.ALIGN_RIGHT)

    buttons = [['7', '8', '9', '/'],
               ['4', '5', '6', '*'],
               ['1', '2', '3', '-'],
               ['.', '0', '', '+']]
    for label_list in buttons:
        btn_sizer = wx.BoxSizer()
        for label in label_list:
            button = wx.Button(self, label=label)
            btn_sizer.Add(button, 1, wx.ALIGN_CENTER|wx.EXPAND, 0)
            button.Bind(wx.EVT_BUTTON, self.update_equation)
        main_sizer.Add(btn_sizer, 1, wx.ALIGN_CENTER|wx.EXPAND)
```

```
equals_btn = wx.Button(self, label='=')
equals_btn.Bind(wx.EVT_BUTTON, self.on_total)
main_sizer.Add(equals_btn, 0, wx.EXPAND|wx.ALL, 3)

clear_btn = wx.Button(self, label='Clear')
clear_btn.Bind(wx.EVT_BUTTON, self.on_clear)
main_sizer.Add(clear_btn, 0, wx.EXPAND|wx.ALL, 3)

self.SetSizer(main_sizer)
```

This is a decent chunk of code, so let's break it down a bit:

```
def create_ui(self):
    main_sizer = wx.BoxSizer(wx.VERTICAL)
    font = wx.Font(12, wx.MODERN, wx.NORMAL, wx.NORMAL)
```

Here you create the sizer that you will need to help organize the user interface. You will also create a wx.Font object, which is used to modifying the default font of widgets like wx.TextCtrl or wx.StaticText. This is helpful when you want a larger font size or a different font face for your widget than what comes as the default.

Now you can add the wx.TextCtrl that will represent your solution:

```
self.solution = wx.TextCtrl(self, style=wx.TE_RIGHT)
self.solution.SetFont(font)
self.solution.Disable()
main_sizer.Add(self.solution, 0, wx.EXPAND|wx.ALL, 5)
```

These lines create the wx.TextCtrl, set it to right-justified (wx.TE_RIGHT), set the font and Disable() the widget. The reason that you want to disable the widget is because you don't want the user to be able to type any string of text into the control.

As you may recall, you will be using eval() for evaluating the strings in that widget, so you can't allow the user to abuse that. Instead, you want fine-grained control over what the user can enter into that widget.

```
self.running_total = wx.StaticText(self)
main_sizer.Add(self.running_total, 0, wx.ALIGN_RIGHT)
```

Some calculator applications have a running total widget underneath the actual "display". One way to add this widget is via the wx.StaticText widget.

Now let's add main buttons you will need to use a calculator effectively:

```
buttons = [['7', '8', '9', '/'],
           ['4', '5', '6', '*'],
           ['1', '2', '3', '-'],
           ['.', '0', '', '+']]
for label_list in buttons:
    btn_sizer = wx.BoxSizer()
    for label in label_list:
        button = wx.Button(self, label=label)
        btn_sizer.Add(button, 1, wx.ALIGN_CENTER|wx.EXPAND, 0)
        button.Bind(wx.EVT_BUTTON, self.update_equation)
    main_sizer.Add(btn_sizer, 1, wx.ALIGN_CENTER|wx.EXPAND)
```

Here you create a list of lists. In this data structure, you have the primary buttons used by your calculator. There is a blank string in the last list that will be used to create a button that doesn't do anything. This is to keep the layout correct. Theoretically, you could update this calculator down the road such that that button could be percentage or do some other function.

The next step is to create the buttons, which you can do by looping over the list. Each nested list represents a row of buttons. So for each row of buttons, you will create a horizontally oriented wx.BoxSizer and then loop over the row of widgets to add them to that sizer. Once every button is added to the row sizer, you will add that sizer to your main sizer. Note that each of these button's is bound to the update_equation() event handler as well.

Now you need to add the equals button and the button that you may use to clear your calculator:

```
equals_btn = wx.Button(self, label='=')
equals_btn.Bind(wx.EVT_BUTTON, self.on_total)
main_sizer.Add(equals_btn, 0, wx.EXPAND|wx.ALL, 3)

clear_btn = wx.Button(self, label='Clear')
clear_btn.Bind(wx.EVT_BUTTON, self.on_clear)
main_sizer.Add(clear_btn, 0, wx.EXPAND|wx.ALL, 3)

self.SetSizer(main_sizer)
```

In this code snippet you create the "equals" button which you then bind to the on_total() event handler method. You also create the "Clear" button, for clearing your calculator and starting over. The last line sets the panel's sizer.

Let's move on and learn what most of the buttons in your calculator are bound to:

```python
def update_equation(self, event):
    operators = ['/', '*', '-', '+']
    btn = event.GetEventObject()
    label = btn.GetLabel()
    current_equation = self.solution.GetValue()

    if label not in operators:
        if self.last_button_pressed in operators:
            self.solution.SetValue(current_equation + ' ' + label)
        else:
            self.solution.SetValue(current_equation + label)
    elif label in operators and current_equation != '' \
            and self.last_button_pressed not in operators:
        self.solution.SetValue(current_equation + ' ' + label)

    self.last_button_pressed = label

    for item in operators:
        if item in self.solution.GetValue():
            self.update_solution()
            break
```

This is an example of binding multiple widgets to the same event handler. To get information about which widget has called the event handler, you can call the event object's GetEventObject() method. This will return whatever widget it was that called the event handler. In this case, you know you called it with a wx.Button instance, so you know that wx.Button has a GetLabel() method which will return the label on the button. Then you get the current value of the solution text control.

Next you want to check if the button's label is an operator (i.e. /, *, -, +). If it is, you will change the text controls value to whatever is currently in it plus the label. On the other hand, if the label is **not** an operator, then you want to put a space between whatever is currently in the text box and the new label. This is for presentation purposes. You could technically skip the string formatting if you wanted to.

The last step is to loop over the operands and check if any of them are currently in the equation string. If they are, then you will call the update_solution() method and break out of the loop.

Now you need to write the update_solution() method:

```
def update_solution(self):
    try:
        current_solution = str(eval(self.solution.GetValue()))
        self.running_total.SetLabel(current_solution)
        self.Layout()
        return current_solution
    except ZeroDivisionError:
        self.solution.SetValue('ZeroDivisionError')
    except:
        pass
```

Here is where the "evil" eval() makes its appearance. You will extract the current value of the equation from the text control and pass that string to eval(). Then convert that result back to a string so you can set the text control to the newly calculated solution. You want to wrap the whole thing in a try/except statement to catch errors, such as the ZeroDivisionError. The last except statement is known as a **bare except** and should really be avoided in most cases. For simplicity, I left it in there, but feel free to delete those last two lines if they offend you.

The next method you will want to take a look at is the on_clear() method:

```
def on_clear(self, event):
    self.solution.Clear()
    self.running_total.SetLabel('')
```

This code is pretty straight-forward. All you need to do is call your solution text control's Clear() method to empty it out. You will also want to clear the running_total widget, which is an instance of wx.StaticText. That widget does not have a Clear() method, so instead you will call SetLabel() and pass in an empty string.

The last method you will need to create is the on_total() event handler, which will calculate the total and also clear out your running total widget:

```
def on_total(self, event):
    solution = self.update_solution()
    if solution:
        self.solution.SetValue(solution)
        self.running_total.SetLabel('')
```

Here you can call the update_solution() method and get the result. Assuming that all went well, the solution will appear in the main text area and the running total will be emptied.

Here is what the calculator looks like when I ran it on a Mac:

Fig. 6-2: Calculator Created with wxPython on Mac OSX

And here is what the calculator looks like on Windows 10:

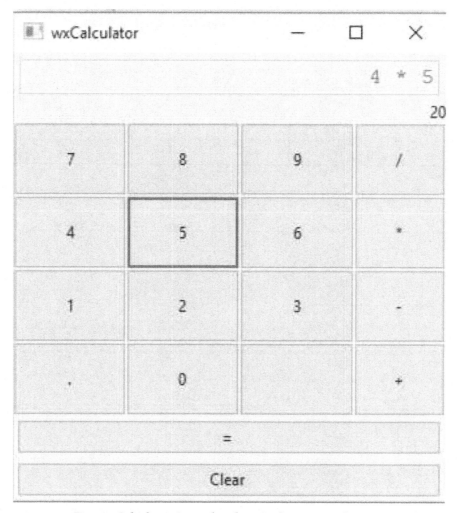

Fig. 6-1: Calculator Created with wxPython on Windows 10

Let's move on and learn how you might allow the user to use their keyboard in addition to your widgets to enter an equation.

Using a Validator

Most calculators will allow the user to use the keyboard when entering values. In this section, I will show you how to get started adding this ability to your code. The simplest method to make this work is to use a wx.PyValidator. I will be using this method for this example. However another way that you could do this would be to catch character or key events using wx.EVT_CHAR and wx.EVT_KEY_DOWN respectively and then analyze the key codes.

Let's start by adding a new class:

```python
# wxcalculator_validator.py

import string
import wx

class CharValidator(wx.PyValidator):
    '''
    Validates data as it is entered into the text controls.
    '''

    def __init__(self, flag):
        wx.PyValidator.__init__(self)
        self.flag = flag
        self.Bind(wx.EVT_CHAR, self.OnChar)

    def Clone(self):
        '''Required Validator method'''
        return CharValidator(self.flag)

    def Validate(self, win):
        return True

    def TransferToWindow(self):
        return True

    def TransferFromWindow(self):
        return True

    def OnChar(self, event):
        keycode = int(event.GetKeyCode())
        if keycode < 256:
            key = chr(keycode)
            if self.flag == 'no-alpha' and key in string.ascii_letters:
                return
            if self.flag == 'no-digit' and key in string.digits:
                return
        event.Skip()
```

Most of this code is boilerplate from the wx.PyValidator class that you don't need to think about.
The parts that are most important for this task are the __init__() and the __OnChar() methods. The
__init__() binds the validator to wx.EVT_CHAR. What that does is that with each key press in the
text control, it will call OnChar() and check to see if the key code is in the list of characters allow,
which in this case is represented by string.digits. I left in support for ignoring digits too, just so

you could see how that works.

The next item that you need to change is your CalcPanel's constructor:

```python
class CalcPanel(wx.Panel):

    def __init__(self, parent):
        super().__init__(parent)
        self.last_button_pressed = None
        self.whitelist = [['7', '8', '9', '/'],
                          ['4', '5', '6', '*'],
                          ['1', '2', '3', '-'],
                          ['.', '0', '', '+']]
        self.empty = True
        self.create_ui()
```

Here you add a whitelist attribute and a couple of flags, self.on_key_called and self.empty. The white list are the only characters that you will allow the user to type in your text control. You will learn about the flags when we actually get to the code that uses them.

But first, you will need to modify the create_ui() method of your panel class.

For brevity, I will only reproduce the first few lines of this method:

```python
def create_ui(self):
    main_sizer = wx.BoxSizer(wx.VERTICAL)
    font = wx.Font(12, wx.MODERN, wx.NORMAL, wx.NORMAL)

    # Replace Disable() with a Validator
    self.solution = wx.TextCtrl(self, style=wx.TE_RIGHT,
                                validator=CharValidator('no-alpha'))
    self.solution.SetFont(font)

    self.solution.Bind(wx.EVT_TEXT, self.on_key)
    main_sizer.Add(self.solution, 0, wx.EXPAND|wx.ALL, 5)
    self.running_total = wx.StaticText(self)
    main_sizer.Add(self.running_total, 0, wx.ALIGN_RIGHT)

    for label_list in self.whitelist:
        btn_sizer = wx.BoxSizer()
        for label in label_list:
            button = wx.Button(self, label=label)
            btn_sizer.Add(button, 1, wx.ALIGN_CENTER|wx.EXPAND, 0)
            button.Bind(wx.EVT_BUTTON, self.on_calculate)
        main_sizer.Add(btn_sizer, 1, wx.ALIGN_CENTER|wx.EXPAND)
```

Here you are no longer disabling the wx.TextCtrl, but binding it to an event instead: wx.EVT_TEXT. The other change is that you are looping over the whitelist here instead of a buttons list like you did in the previous version. You are also binding each button to the on_calculate() event handler instead of the update_equation() method.

Let's go ahead and write the on_calculate() event handler now:

```python
def on_calculate(self, event):
    btn = event.GetEventObject()
    label = btn.GetLabel()
    self.update_equation(label)
```

This code is extracted from the original update_equation() event handler. You are extracting the button that called this handler and getting its label. Then you call update_equation(), which is a method now instead of an event handler. It now accepts a string of text (i.e. the label) instead of an event object.

The next method you will need to update is update_equation():

```python
def update_equation(self, text):
    operators = ['/', '*', '-', '+']
    current_equation = self.solution.GetValue()

    if text not in operators:
        if self.last_button_pressed in operators:
            self.solution.SetValue(current_equation + ' ' + text)
        elif self.empty and current_equation:
            # The solution is not empty
            self.empty = False
        else:
            self.solution.SetValue(current_equation + text)
    elif text in operators and current_equation != '' \
        and self.last_button_pressed not in operators:
        self.solution.SetValue(current_equation + ' ' + text)

    self.last_button_pressed = text
    self.solution.SetInsertionPoint(-1)

    for item in operators:
        if item in self.solution.GetValue():
            self.update_solution()
            break
```

Here you add a new elif that checks if the self.empty flag is set and if the current_equation has anything in it. In other words, if it is supposed to be empty and it's not, then we set the flag to

`False` because it's not empty. This prevents a duplicate value when the keyboard key is pressed. So basically you need two flags to deal with duplicate values that can be caused because you decided to allow users to use their keyboard.

The other change to this method is to add a call to `SetInsertionPoint()` on your text control, which will put the insertion point at the end of the text control after each update.

The last required change to the panel class happens in the `on_clear()` method:

```python
def on_clear(self, event):
    self.solution.Clear()
    self.running_total.SetLabel('')
    self.empty = True
    self.solution.SetFocus()
```

This change was done by adding two new lines to the end of the method. The first is to reset self.empty back to `True`. The second is to call the text control's `SetFocus()` method so that the focus is reset to the text control after it has been cleared.

You could also add this `SetFocus()` call to the end of the `on_calculate()` and the `on_total()` methods. This should keep the text control in focus at all times. Feel free to play around with that on your own.

Creating a Better eval()

Now that you have looked at a couple of different methods of keeping the "evil" `eval()` under control, let's take a few moments to learn how you can create a custom version of `eval()` on your own. Python comes with a couple of handy built-in modules called ast and operator. The ast module is an acronym that stands for "Abstract Syntax Trees" and is used "for processing trees of the Python abstract syntax grammar" according to the documentation. You can think of it as a data structure that is a representation of code. You can use the ast module to create a compiler in Python.

The `operator` module is a set of functions that correspond to Python's operators. A good example would be `operator.add(x, y)` which is equivalent to the expression x+y. You can use this module along with the ast module to create a limited version of `eval()`.

Let's find out how:

```python
# not_eval.py

import ast
import operator

allowed_operators = {ast.Add: operator.add, ast.Sub: operator.sub,
                     ast.Mult: operator.mul, ast.Div: operator.truediv}

def noeval(expression):
    if isinstance(expression, ast.Num):
        return expression.n
    elif isinstance(expression, ast.BinOp):
        print('Operator: {}'.format(expression.op))
        print('Left operand: {}'.format(expression.left))
        print('Right operand: {}'.format(expression.right))
        op = allowed_operators.get(type(expression.op))
        if op:
            return op(noeval(expression.left),
                      noeval(expression.right))
    else:
        print('This statement will be ignored')

if __name__ == '__main__':
    print(ast.parse('1+4', mode='eval').body)
    print(noeval(ast.parse('1+4', mode='eval').body))
    print(noeval(ast.parse('1**4', mode='eval').body))
    print(noeval(ast.parse("__import__('os').remove(
        'path/to/file')", mode='eval').body))
```

Here you create a dictionary of allowed operators. You map ast.Add to operator.add, etc. Then you create a function called noeval() that accepts an ast object. If the expression is a number, you return it. However if it is a BinOp instance, than you print out the pieces of the expression.

A BinOp is made up of three parts:

- The left part of the expression
- The operator
- The right hand of the expression

What this code does when it finds a BinOp object is that it then attempts to get the type of ast operation. If it is one that is in our allowed_operators dictionary, then you call the mapped function with the left and right parts of the expression and return the result.

Finally if the expression is not a number or one of the approved operators, then you ignore it. Try playing around with this example a bit with various strings and expressions to see how it works.

Once you are done playing with this example, let's integrate it into your calculator code. For this version of the code, you can call the Python script **wxcalculator_no_eval.py**. The top part of your new file should look like this:

```python
# wxcalculator_no_eval.py

import ast
import operator

import wx


class CalcPanel(wx.Panel):

    def __init__(self, parent):
        super().__init__(parent)
        self.last_button_pressed = None
        self.create_ui()

        self.allowed_operators = {
            ast.Add: operator.add, ast.Sub: operator.sub,
            ast.Mult: operator.mul, ast.Div: operator.truediv}
```

The main differences here is that you now have a couple of new imports (i.e. ast and operator) and you will need to add a Python dictionary called self.allowed_operators.

Next you will want to create a new method called noeval():

```python
    def noeval(self, expression):
        if isinstance(expression, ast.Num):
            return expression.n
        elif isinstance(expression, ast.BinOp):
            return self.allowed_operators[
                type(expression.op)](self.noeval(expression.left),
                                     self.noeval(expression.right))
        return ''
```

This method is pretty much exactly the same as the function you created in the other script. It has been modified slightly to call the correct class methods and attributes however.

The other change you will need to make is in the update_solution() method:

```python
def update_solution(self):
    try:
        expression = ast.parse(self.solution.GetValue(),
                               mode='eval').body
        current_solution = str(self.noeval(expression))
        self.running_total.SetLabel(current_solution)
        self.Layout()
        return current_solution
    except ZeroDivisionError:
        self.solution.SetValue('ZeroDivisionError')
    except:
        pass
```

Now the calculator code will use your custom eval() method and keep you protected from the potentially harmfulness of eval(). The code that is in Github has the added protection of only allowing the user to use the onscreen UI to modify the contents of the text control. However you can easily change it to enable the text control and try out this code without worrying about eval() causing you any harm.

Wrapping Up

In this chapter you learned several different approaches to creating a calculator using wxPython. You also learned a little bit about the pros and cons of using Python's built-in eval() function. Finally, you learned that you can use Python's ast and operator modules to create a finely-grained version of eval() that is safe for you to use. Of course, since you are controlling all input into eval(), you can also control the real version quite easily though your UI that you generate with wxPython.

Take some time and play around with the examples in this chapter. There are many enhancements that could be made to make this application even better. When you find bugs or missing features, challenge yourself to try to fix or add them.

Chapter 7 - Creating a Tarball Archiver

When you start writing software, you will find yourself creating applications that require updates. Sometimes those updates happen within a few hours or days of the initial release. Other times your little application will work for years before an update is required. In this chapter, you will learn how to create a command line archive application and then you will learn how to add a graphical user interface to it.

Let's look at a fairly common scenario:

Today your employer comes up to you and tells you that they are giving you a fun new project. The new project is that the company needs a way for tech support to create tar files out of folders using a command line interface. They want the following features:

- Create a tarball by default (*.tar)
- Add multiple folders to be archived

Let's get started!

Creating a Command Line Interface

The first step when creating a new application is determining what libraries or packages you can use. If you do a quick search online, you will find that Python has a built-in library that you can use for creating an application that accepts command line arguments called argparse. There are many alternative packages you can download from the Python Packaging Index as well, but you can focus on using the built-in library for this application.

To keep things simple, you will start by only supporting a regular tarball. As a Python developer, you value explicit over implicit, so you should create an argument for specifying the archive type and an output path.

Let's go ahead and take a stab at writing the code:

```python
import argparse
import pathlib
import textwrap

import controller


def get_args():
    parser = argparse.ArgumentParser(
        description='Create a tar file',
        epilog=textwrap.dedent(
            '''
        Example Usage:
            archiver.py -t input_path
            archiver.py --tar input_path -o output_path
        ''')
    )
    parser.add_argument('-t', '--tar',
                        help='Create a tar file from the input path',
                        required=True, action='store',
                        dest='input_path')
    parser.add_argument('-o', '--output',
                        help='Output path',
                        action='store',
                        dest='output')
    return parser.parse_args()


def main():
    args = get_args()
    if args.output:
        output = pathlib.Path(args.output)
        input_path = pathlib.Path(args.input_path)
    else:
        temp = pathlib.Path(args.input_path)
        output = pathlib.Path(f'{temp}.tar')
        input_path = pathlib.Path(args.input_path)
    controller.create_tar(output, archive_objects=[input_path])
    print(f'Created tarball from {input_path} to {output}')


if __name__ == '__main__':
    main()
```

This is kind of long, so let's start by looking at the imports:

```python
import argparse
import pathlib
import textwrap

import controller
```

Here you will import the `argparse` module. You will also be using the `pathlib` and `textwrap` modules. The `pathlib` module is new in Python 3 and quite nice for working with file paths. The `textwrap` module is useful for dedenting help text in your argument parsing code.

Technically you do not need a `controller` module, but if you were to expand this example to support other archive types, such as zip files, you might find a controller handy. It's always nice to plan for the future when you can.

Now let's move on to the `get_args()` function:

```python
def get_args():
    parser = argparse.ArgumentParser(
        description='Create a tar file',
        epilog=textwrap.dedent(
            '''
        Example Usage:
            archiver.py -t input_path
            archiver.py --tar input_path -o output_path
        ''')
    )
    parser.add_argument('-t', '--tar',
                        help='Create a tar file from the input path',
                        required=True, action='store',
                        dest='input_path')
    parser.add_argument('-o', '--output',
                        help='Output path',
                        action='store',
                        dest='output')
    return parser.parse_args()
```

Here you create a parser using ArgumentParser. You can set its description and example usage via the epilog argument. This is also where you can use textwrap.dedent() to dedent or unindent your help text. Then you add two arguments that your application can handle via the call to `add_argument()`.

The first two arguments that you pass to `add_argument()` are the flags you can pass to your application on the command line. There is also a help string, whether or not the argument is required and where to save or store the argument. When you create an argument parser in Python, it creates an object. This object will have attributes that you can specify using the dest argument.

Finally you need to call parse_args(), which will parse any arguments passed to your application. It will raise errors if the user passes in an invalid argument or uses a specified argument incorrectly.

The last piece of the puzzle in this script is the main() function:

```python
def main():
    args = get_args()
    if args.output:
        output = pathlib.Path(args.output)
        input_path = pathlib.Path(args.input_path)
        controller.create_tar(output, archive_objects=[input_path])
        print(f'Created tarball from {input_path} to {output}')

if __name__ == '__main__':
    main()
```

In this example, you check if the user provided the -o or --output flag to your application. If they did, then you turn it into a Path object. You also turn the path to the file or folder to be tarred into a Path object too. If the user did not provide an output path, you will save the file or folder with the same name as the input path but with .tar appended to it. Finally you call the create_tar() function in the controller module with the items to be tarred.

Let's look at **controller.py** now:

```python
# controller.py


import tarfile


def create_tar(path, archive_objects):
    with tarfile.open(path, 'w') as tar:
        for archive_object in archive_objects:
            tar.add(archive_object,
                arcname=archive_object.name)
```

This code uses Python's pathlib module. It is also where the tarfile module from Python's standard library comes in. The function that you care about is the create_tar() function. It takes the output path and a list of Path objects. You open the output path via tarfile.open(). Then you loop over the archive_objects and add them to the tarball.

You can use the arcname parameter to set the name of the item in the tarball. This prevents the tarball from having a long nested path inside of it. Instead you will end up with the files and folders being at the top level within the tarball, which is what you will want most of the time.

Try running the code without parameters so you can see what kind of helpful information it will give you:

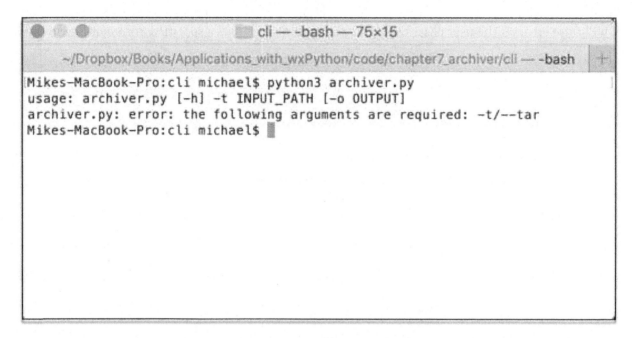

Fig. 7-1: Command Line Interface

You can also run your script with -h or --help to get help from your program:

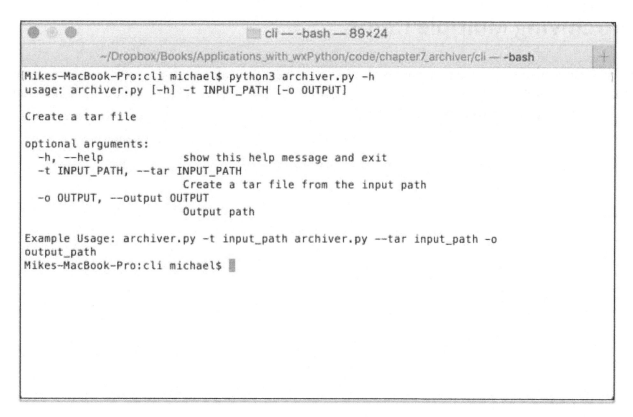

Fig. 7-2: Command Line Interface Help

The help text is automatically generated by the argparse package. The last line is the epilog that you created when you created your ArgumentParser.

If you happen to try to run the program with the wrong command line arguments, you will see a decent error message:

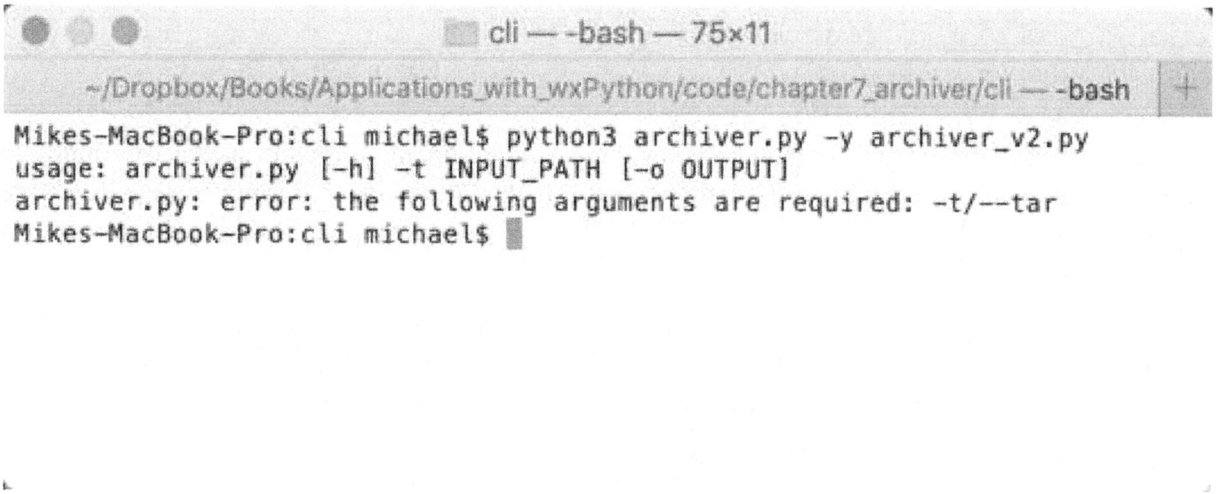

Fig. 7-3: Command Line Interface Error

Now you are ready to learn how to add multiple items to archive at once!

Archiving Multiple Items

The code you wrote in the previous section has a problem. It can only tar up one item. If you were to pass in multiple paths to your script, the script would fail. So let's take a minute and update the code so that it works with multiple paths.

Copy the code from the previous example into a new file that you can call **archiver_v2.py**.

Now you can update the get_args() function as follows:

```python
def get_args():
    parser = argparse.ArgumentParser(
        description='Create a tar file',
        epilog=textwrap.dedent(
        '''

    Example Usage:
        archiver.py -t input_path
        archiver.py --tar input_path -o output_path
    ''')
    )
    parser.add_argument('-t', '--tar',
                        help='Create a tar file from the input path',
                        required=True, action='store', nargs='+',
                        dest='input_path')
    parser.add_argument('-o', '--output',
                        help='Output path',
                        action='store',
                        required=True,
                        dest='output')
    return parser.parse_args()
```

The only thing that needs changing here is for the --tar argument. You want it to accept multiple arguments, so you add the nargs parameter and set it to +. This means that it now accepts multiple arguments. It would also be a good idea to make the --output parameter a required argument, so go ahead and do that too.

The next step is to create a new function for converting the input paths into pathlib objects. The reason is that while args.input_path will now contain a list of paths, it is a list of strings. You want it to be a list of pathlib.Path objects instead.

Here's the function you will need to create:

```
def get_paths(paths):
    path_objs = []
    for path in paths:
        path_objs.append(pathlib.Path(path))
    return path_objs
```

In this code, you loop over a list of strings and turn them into Path objects that are appended to a new list. Then you return the new list instead.

Now you need to update the main() function:

```
def main():
    args = get_args()
    if args.output:
        output = pathlib.Path(args.output)
        input_paths = get_paths(args.input_path)
    else:
        output = pathlib.Path(f'{temp}.tar')
        input_paths = get_paths(args.input_path)
    controller.create_tar(output, archive_objects=input_paths)
    print(f'Created tarball from {input_path} to {output}')


if __name__ == '__main__':
    main()
```

For this code, the change here is to call the get_paths() function with args.input_path to get it into the format that you want. This also allows you drop the temp variable that you had in the previous version of the script.

Give this version of the code a try and see how it works for yourself.

Now you are ready to design a graphical user interface!

Adding a GUI

Creating a GUI from scratch is always an interesting exercise. You can look at how other archiving tools are laid out. A good one to check out would be **7-Zip**, which is a popular archiving application on Windows.

Let's sketch out a simple tarball creation interface:

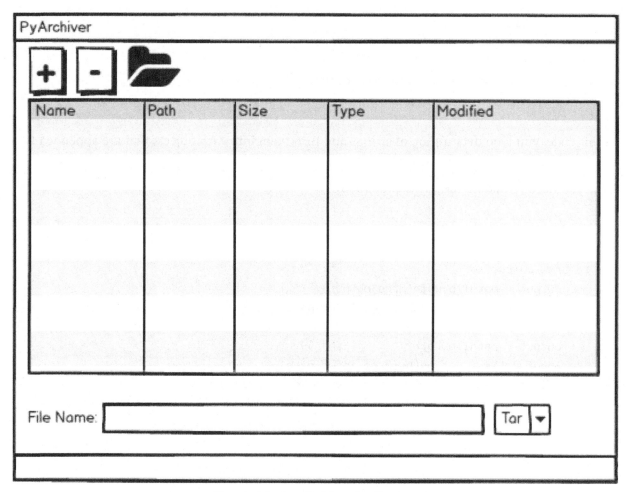

Fig. 7-4: Mockup Archiver Application

The sketch above is of the final version of the application that you will create. However, after looking at several different tools for creating archives, I noticed that most of them have several different methods for adding and removing items to the archive. You can add or remove items in one of three ways:

- Drag-and-drop
- Use a menu
- Use the toolbar

Let's create the user interface iteratively, adding each of these features as you go along. The drag-and-drop version will also be the first version of your application.

Using Drag-and-Drop

The wxPython toolkit provides several different methods for adding drag-and-drop to your applications. The class you will want to use in this case is wx.FileDropTarget. Go ahead and create a file named **archiver_gui.py** and add the following class to it:

```
# archiver_gui.py

class DropTarget(wx.FileDropTarget):

    def __init__(self, window):
        super().__init__()
        self.window = window

    def OnDropFiles(self, x, y, filenames):
        self.window.update_display(filenames)
        return True
```

All this code does is subclass wx.FileDropTarget and accept a widget instance (i.e. window) into the constructor. Then you override the OnDropFiles() method. This method accepts the x/y coordinates of the drop along with the paths to the filenames. Here you call the widget's update_display() method and pass along the paths that were dropped. You must also return True to make the method work correctly.

Let's go ahead and add the imports that you will need at the top of your script:

```
import controller

import os
import pathlib
import time
import wx

from ObjectListView import ObjectListView, ColumnDefn
```

These are the imports you will need to make the rest of the code work. These should already by familiar to you at this point in the book.

Now let's add a class to model the items to be archived:

```
class Items:

    def __init__(self, path, name, size, item_type,
                 modified):
        self.path = path
        self.name = name
        self.size = size
        self.item_type = item_type
        self.modified = modified
```

This class represents the paths that we can archive. The class attributes match up with the path's attributes. So when you add a path, you will record its path, the file name, its file size, whether or not it is a file or folder and the date it was modified.

Now let's get to the meat of the application and create a panel class:

```python
class ArchivePanel(wx.Panel):

    def __init__(self, parent):
        super().__init__(parent)
        font = wx.Font(12, wx.SWISS, wx.NORMAL, wx.NORMAL)
        drop_target = DropTarget(self)
        self.SetDropTarget(drop_target)
        self.archive_items = []
        paths = wx.StandardPaths.Get()
        self.current_directory = paths.GetDocumentsDir()
```

Here you instantiate the class and create an instance of the `DropTarget` class that you created earlier. Then you call the panel's `SetDropTarget()` method so that the panel accepts dropped files or folders. Since you will want to keep track of the current directory, you can use wxPython's `wx.StandardPaths` to access some of the standard paths on your operating system. In this case, you grab the documents folder using `GetDocumentsDir()`. This will return the equivalent of "My Documents" on Mac and Linux.

The `wx.StandardPaths` class supports getting many different common folders.

For example, you can use it to get any of the following:

- My Documents
- Desktop
- The executable path
- Temp directory
- Data directory
- and quite a few more

Be sure to check out https://wxpython.org/Phoenix/docs/html/wx.StandardPaths.html for more information.

Now let's add the code that will hold the files and folders to be archived:

```
# Create sizers
main_sizer = wx.BoxSizer(wx.VERTICAL)
h_sizer = wx.BoxSizer(wx.HORIZONTAL)

# Create input widget
self.archive_olv = ObjectListView(
    self, style=wx.LC_REPORT|wx.SUNKEN_BORDER)
self.archive_olv.SetEmptyListMsg("Add Files / Folders here")
self.update_archive()
main_sizer.Add(self.archive_olv, 1, wx.ALL|wx.EXPAND, 5)
```

This code goes into the ArchivePanel's __init__() as well. Take a look at the line where you call
SetEmptyListMsg(). This will show whatever custom message you give it in the middle of the widget
when it is empty.

The last piece of the puzzle here is that you need to call the update_archive() method, which will
update the ObjectListView widget. You will learn more about that shortly.

But first, you need to add a row of widgets that you will use for creating the output archive:

```
# Create output related widgets
label = wx.StaticText(self, label='File name:')
label.SetFont(font)
h_sizer.Add(label, 0, wx.CENTER)
self.archive_filename = wx.TextCtrl(self)
h_sizer.Add(self.archive_filename, 1, wx.EXPAND)
self.archive_types = wx.ComboBox(
    self, value='Tar',
    choices=['Tar'],
    size=(75, -1))
h_sizer.Add(self.archive_types, 0)
main_sizer.Add(h_sizer, 0, wx.EXPAND|wx.ALL, 5)
```

In the sketch that you saw earlier, you had a label, a text control for the archive filename and a
combo box widget for choosing the archive type. The code above create those three widgets and
adds them to a horizontally oriented sizer. The reason you created a combo box is because it allows
you to easily update the code with other archive types, such as Zip files.

It is always a good idea to keep future enhancements in mind when you are coding your applications.
The main thing you want to do is to make it easy for a future developer to edit and enhance your
code.

Now let's go ahead and add the archive button and you'll be done with the __init__() method:

```python
# Create archive button
create_archive_btn = wx.Button(self, label='Create Archive')
create_archive_btn.Bind(wx.EVT_BUTTON, self.on_create_archive)
main_sizer.Add(create_archive_btn, 0, wx.ALL|wx.CENTER, 5)


self.SetSizer(main_sizer)
```

This creates the button you need and binds its click event to the `on_create_archive()` method. Speaking of which, you should write that method next:

```python
def on_create_archive(self, event):
    if not self.archive_olv.GetObjects():
        self.show_message('No files / folders to archive',
                          'Error', wx.ICON_ERROR)
        return

    if not self.archive_filename.GetValue():
        self.show_message('File name is required!',
                          'Error', wx.ICON_ERROR)
        return

    with wx.DirDialog(
        self, "Choose a directory:",
        style=wx.DD_DEFAULT_STYLE,
        defaultPath=self.current_directory) as dlg:
        if dlg.ShowModal() == wx.ID_OK:
            path = dlg.GetPath()
            self.current_directory = path
            archive_filename = self.archive_filename.GetValue()
            archive_type = self.archive_types.GetValue()

            full_save_path = pathlib.Path(
                path, '{filename}.{type}'.format(
                    filename=archive_filename,
                    type=archive_type.lower()
                ))
            controller.create_archive(
                full_save_path,
                self.archive_olv.GetObjects(),
                archive_type)
            message = f'Archive created at {full_save_path}'
            self.show_message(message, 'Archive Created',
                              wx.ICON_INFORMATION)
```

The on_create_archive() method is also an event handler that is called when you press the "Create Archive" button. The first thing to do is to check whether or not there are any items actually listed in the ObjectListView instance. If not, then you will show a message dialog to the user letting them know that they clicked the button in error. You will also show an error if the user forgets to enter a filename.

If the widget does have some paths in it, then you will create a wx.DirDialog instance so that the user can choose an output folder for their archive file. Finally, if the user presses the OK button, then you will grab the folder path, the filename from your text control and the archive type from the combo control widget and create the archive via a call to controller.create_archive().

There isn't any handling of errors here. You can assume that it works for now and show a message to the user that the archive completed. You can always add error handling later as an enhancement.

The next method that you will be creating is update_archive(), which you will use to update your ObjectListView widget when you add new items to be archived.

Let's create the update_archive() method now:

```python
def update_archive(self):
    self.archive_olv.SetColumns([
                    ColumnDefn("Name", "left", 350, "name"),
                    ColumnDefn("Path", "left", 350, "path"),
                    ColumnDefn("Size", "left", 75, "size"),
                    ColumnDefn("Type", "right", 75, "item_type"),
                    ColumnDefn("Modified", "left", 150, "modified")
                ])
    self.archive_olv.SetObjects(self.archive_items)
```

All this method does is update your ObjectListView widget. Here you call the SetColumns() method and pass it some instances of ColumnDefn. These will create the columns in the widget.

The first four parameters for the ColumnDefn' are as follows:

- Title of column
- Alignment of column
- Column width
- valueGetter - The class attribute name for the item added to the widget

When you call the SetObjects(method, you will be passing it a list of instances of your Items class. That last parameter to ColumnDefn maps to the attribute in your Items class of the same name. If the list is empty, then the widget will also be empty.

Now let's create the update_display() method:

```python
def update_display(self, items):
    paths = [pathlib.Path(item) for item in items]
    for path in paths:
        basename = path.name
        size = self.get_size(path)
        if path.is_dir():
            item_type = 'folder'
        else:
            item_type = 'file'
        last_modified = time.ctime(path.stat().st_mtime)
        item = Items(path, basename, size, item_type,
                     last_modified)
        self.archive_items.append(item)

    self.update_archive()
```

The `update_display()` method is called when you drag and drop files onto the `ObjectListView` widget. When that happens, it will loop over the items and turn them into pathlib objects. Then you loop over the path objects and get the attributes of the file that you care about, such as the file size, whether it's a file or a folder, and when it was last modified.

To finish up, you create an instance of the `Items` class with the information you extracted from the path object, append it to the archive list and call `update_archive()` to update the `ObjectListView` widget.

Let's learn how to get the size of a file path:

```python
def get_size(self, path):
    size = path.stat().st_size

    suffixes = ['B', 'KB', 'MB', 'GB', 'TB']
    index = 0
    while size > 1024:
        index += 1
        size = size / 1024.0

    suffix = suffixes[index]
    return f'{size:.1f} {suffix}'
```

The nice thing about the `pathlib` module is that it provides a lot of convenient attributes. For example, you can call the `stat()` method on your pathlib object and it works just like `os.stat()` would. Then you can access st_size to get the size of the path in bytes.

Of course, most users don't expect files to be listed in bytes, so to be a bit more user friendly, I went and researched various ways to convert bytes to more normal formats, such as KB, MB, etc. Then

I modified that example for you. So in this example, you loop over the size variable, dividing it by 1024 until the result is less than 1024. Then you can take the result and find the correct suffix for the size and return the appropriate string.

You have been calling the show_message() method, but you haven't written it yet. Let's fix that:

```python
def show_message(self, message, caption, flag=wx.ICON_ERROR):
    """
    Show a message dialog
    """
    msg = wx.MessageDialog(None, message=message,
                            caption=caption, style=flag)
    msg.ShowModal()
    msg.Destroy()
```

Here you create an instance of wx.MessageDialog and set its message, caption and which flag to use. Then you show it modally to the user and Destroy() it when the user dismisses the dialog.

Now let's subclass the wx.Frame so we can run our code:

```python
class MainFrame(wx.Frame):

    def __init__(self):
        """Constructor"""
        super().__init__(
            None, title="PyArchiver",
            size=(800, 600))
        self.panel = ArchivePanel(self)

        self.Show()

if __name__ == "__main__":
    app = wx.App(False)
    frame = MainFrame()
    app.MainLoop()
```

Here you instantiate your frame and the ArchivePanel class you created at the beginning of this section. Then you Show() it to the user.

This is what the application looks like without files or folders added:

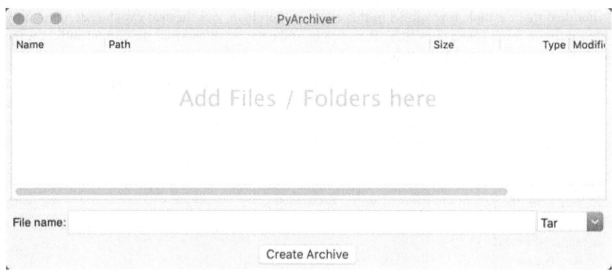

Fig. 7-5: Empty Early Version of PyArchiver

And here is what it looks like after you have added a file and a folder:

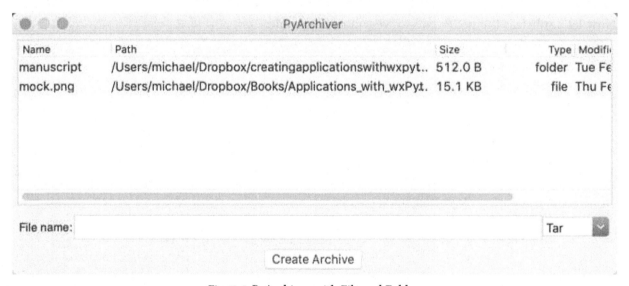

Fig. 7-6: PyArchiver with File and Folder

Now let's move on and learn how to add a menu!

Adding a Menu

Users like to have multiple ways to do common tasks. As was mentioned at the beginning of this chapter, you will now learn how to add a menu bar so that the user can add and remove items to your archive application.

Copy the code from the previous example and paste it into a new a file called **archiver_gui2.py**. Instead of reproducing the entire file here again, in this section you will focus on what has changed. You will be only editing the beginning of the file and the `MainFrame` class to add a menu.

Let's start by inserting a module level variable and editing the `MainFrame` class:

```python
open_wildcard = "All files (*.*)|*.*"


class MainFrame(wx.Frame):

    def __init__(self):
        """Constructor"""
        super().__init__(
            None, title="PyArchiver",
            size=(800, 600))
        self.panel = ArchivePanel(self)
        self.create_menu()

        self.Show()
```

Here the only change is that you add a variable at the top of the file (after the imports) and now call the `create_menu()` method after instantiating the panel class. This method holds all the code you will need to create a menu.

Since the `create_menu()` method is kind of long, let's take a look at it in smaller pieces:

```python
def create_menu(self):
    menu_bar = wx.MenuBar()

    # Create file menu
    file_menu = wx.Menu()

    exit_menu_item = file_menu.Append(
        wx.ID_ANY, "Exit",
        "Exit the application")
    menu_bar.Append(file_menu, '&File')
    self.Bind(wx.EVT_MENU, self.on_exit,
              exit_menu_item)
```

Here you need to create an instance of `wx.MenuBar`. This class will do the actual creation of the menu bar itself. Then to add a menu to the menu bar, you need to create an instance of `wx.Menu`. Once that is created, you will want to add a menu item to the menu.

To add a menu item, you can call the menu's `Append()` method. When you do that, you pass it the following parameters:

- A unique id

- The name of the menu item as a string
- Help text that will appear if you have a status bar

Once the menu item is appended to the menu, you can then add the menu to the MenuBar instance using the menu bar's Append() method. This method accepts the menu object and the name of the menu. In this case, you pass it the string &File, which tells wxPython that you want to associate the keyboard shortcut, **ALT+F**, to opening the File menu.

The ampersand in the string is what does the magic. Whatever letter it appears before becomes the keyboard shortcut.

Finally you need to bind the menu item to the wx.EVT_MENU event. At this point, you now have a **File** menu with one menu item that you may use to exit your application.

Let's add an **Edit** menu item to this method too:

```python
# Create edit menu
edit_menu = wx.Menu()

add_file_menu_item = edit_menu.Append(
    wx.ID_ANY, 'Add File',
    'Add a file to be archived')
self.Bind(wx.EVT_MENU, self.on_add_file,
        add_file_menu_item)

add_folder_menu_item = edit_menu.Append(
    wx.ID_ANY, 'Add Folder',
    'Add a folder to be archived')
self.Bind(wx.EVT_MENU, self.on_add_folder,
        add_folder_menu_item)

remove_menu_item = edit_menu.Append(
    wx.ID_ANY, 'Remove File/Folder',
    'Remove a file or folder')
self.Bind(wx.EVT_MENU, self.on_remove,
        remove_menu_item)
menu_bar.Append(edit_menu, 'Edit')

self.SetMenuBar(menu_bar)
```

For this example, you create another instance of wx.Menu and add three menu items:

- Add File
- Add folder

    • Remove File / Folder

For each of these menu items, you append them to the **Edit** menu and you bind them to different event handlers. Then you append the **Edit** menu to the menu bar as you did with the **File** menu. When appending menus to the menu bar, the menus will be added from left-to-right in the order in which they are appended.

The final step is to call the SetMenuBar() method on the frame instance and pass it the menu bar instance. This attaches the menu bar to the frame and shows it. If you don't call this method, the menu bar will not be displayed to the user.

Now let's learn how to add a file using the menu:

```python
def on_add_file(self, event):
    with wx.FileDialog(
        self, message="Choose a file",
        defaultDir=self.panel.current_directory,
        defaultFile="",
        wildcard=open_wildcard,
        style=wx.FD_OPEN | wx.FD_MULTIPLE | wx.FD_CHANGE_DIR
        ) as dlg:
        if dlg.ShowModal() == wx.ID_OK:
            paths = dlg.GetPaths()
            self.panel.update_display(paths)
```

Here you create an instance of the wx.FileDialog. You use the open_wildcard variable that you created earlier to make all the file types show up. Since you have access to the panel object, you can also set the defaultDir to the current_directory.

Finally you set a few flags for the dialog:

- wx.FD_OPEN - This is an open file dialog instead of a save file dialog
- wx.FD_MULTIPLE - Allows selecting of multiple files
- wx.FD_CHANGE_DIR - Allows changing of the current working directory

If the user chooses one or more files and presses the OK button, then you call the dialog's GetPaths() method. Then you pass the return value to the panel's update_display() method.

Let's find out how to add a folder next:

```python
def on_add_folder(self, event):
    with wx.DirDialog(
        self, message="Choose a directory:",
        defaultPath=self.panel.current_directory,
        style=wx.DD_DEFAULT_STYLE) as dlg:
        if dlg.ShowModal() == wx.ID_OK:
            paths = [dlg.GetPath()]
            self.panel.update_display(paths)
```

To add a folder to the archiving widget, you will create an instance of wx.DirDialog. This dialog also takes a defaultPath, so you can use the same trick you used for the wx.FileDialog here to set it. The wx.DirDialog doesn't allow you to select more than one directory. For that, you would need to use a different widget. The main reason to use this dialog is that it looks native cross platform.

When the user presses the OK button, you can call the dialog's GetPath() method. Since that method will only ever return one string, you need to put it into a Python list. Then call the panel's update_-display() with your list.

Now let's find out how to exit the application using the menu:

```python
def on_exit(self, event):
    self.Close()
```

This method is short and sweet. All you need to do is call the frame's Close() method. That method will tell wxPython to close the frame object and exit.

The final menu item event handler to create is on_remove():

```python
def on_remove(self, event):
    selected_items = self.panel.archive_olv.GetSelectedObjects()
    self.panel.archive_olv.RemoveObjects(selected_items)
```

The ObjectListView widget will allow the user to select multiple items at once. Because of this, you will need to call its GetSelectedObjects() method to acquire a list of all the selected items. Then you can call the widget's RemoveObject() method to remove the selected items.

One improvement that you could add here is to ask the user if they really want to remove the items from the list by opening up a dialog. Feel free to add that on your own.

Let's move on and learn how to add a tool bar!

Adding a Toolbar

I have always found toolbars to be more user friendly than menus. However this is only true when the toolbar icons make sense. There are some applications where they don't and figuring out what those buttons do can be difficult. The wxPython toolkit comes with a nice class called `wx.ArtProvider` that you can use to load up stock toolbar icons. You will be using that for this update to the application.

Once again, copy the previous example and save it into a new file with a new name: **archiver_- gui3.py**.

Now you can update the `MainFrame` class again:

```python
class MainFrame(wx.Frame):

    def __init__(self):
        """Constructor"""
        super().__init__(
            None, title="PyArchiver",
            size=(800, 600))
        self.panel = ArchivePanel(self)
        self.create_menu()
        self.create_toolbar()

        self.statusbar = self.CreateStatusBar()
        self.statusbar.SetStatusText('Welcome to PyArchiver!')

        self.Show()
```

In this example, you add a call to a new method called `create_toolbar()`. Just for fun, let's go ahead and add a status bar to the application too. To do that, you need to call the frame's `CreateStatusBar()` method. This will add a status bar to the bottom of the frame. Then to add some text to the status bar, you can call the status bar's `SetStatusText()` method.

Now let's learn how to create a toolbar:

```python
def create_toolbar(self):
    self.toolbar = self.CreateToolBar()

    add_ico = wx.ArtProvider.GetBitmap(
        wx.ART_PLUS, wx.ART_TOOLBAR, (16, 16))
    add_file_tool = self.toolbar.AddTool(
        wx.ID_ANY, 'Add File', add_ico,
        'Add a file to be archived')
    self.Bind(wx.EVT_MENU, self.on_add_file,
            add_file_tool)

    add_folder_ico = wx.ArtProvider.GetBitmap(
```

```
        wx.ART_FOLDER_OPEN, wx.ART_TOOLBAR, (16, 16))
    add_folder_tool = self.toolbar.AddTool(
        wx.ID_ANY, 'Add Folder', add_folder_ico,
        'Add a folder to be archived')
    self.Bind(wx.EVT_MENU, self.on_add_folder,
            add_folder_tool)

    remove_ico = wx.ArtProvider.GetBitmap(
        wx.ART_MINUS, wx.ART_TOOLBAR, (16, 16))
    remove_tool = self.toolbar.AddTool(
        wx.ID_ANY, 'Remove', remove_ico,
        'Remove selected item')
    self.Bind(wx.EVT_MENU, self.on_remove, remove_tool)

    self.toolbar.Realize()
```

The `create_toolbar()` method will create a toolbar with three toolbar buttons. To create the toolbar, you will need to call the frame's CreateToolBar() method. This won't actually show the toolbar on-screen. Much like the menu, you have to finish the toolbar by calling the toolbar's `Realize()` method at the end of our `create_toolbar()` method. One item of note here is that you do need to add tool bar buttons to the toolbar before calling Realize().

After you create the toolbar, you can add tool bar buttons by using the toolbar's `AddTool()` method.

This method accepts the following:

- The tool ID (`toolId`)
- A short help string (`shortHelpString`)
- A bitmap object (`bitmap`)
- A long help string (`longHelpString`)

The bitmap object can be made using `wx.StaticBitmap`, but in this case it is simpler to use `wx.ArtProvider.GetBitmap()`. The wxPython demo has a nice demo of `wx.ArtProvider` that shows you the various built-in icons that you can use.

The long help string is a tooltip that will appear when you mouse over the toolbar button.

After adding a toolbar button to the toolbar, you can bind the button to `wx.EVT_MENU` in the same manner as you did with the menu items in the previous section.

Here is what the application looks like with the toolbar and statusbar:

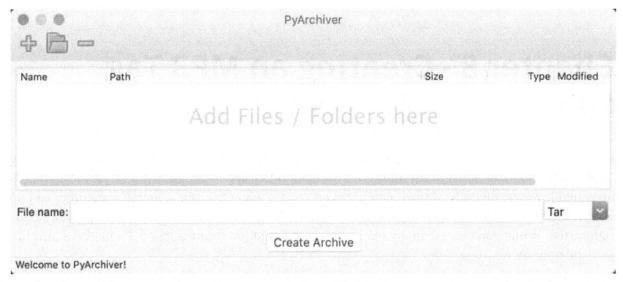

Fig. 7-7: PyArchiver Final Version

Adding toolbars and menus can add a lot of repetitious code to your source. You may want to move the menu and toolbar code to separate modules if you have a complex toolbar or menu system.

Wrapping Up

Creating an application that can archive files is fun. You learned some of the tricks needed to keep your code extendable. There are definitely parts of the code that could be refactored or changed to make it better. Feel free to do those kinds of changes as you will learn a lot more from editing the examples yourself.

In this chapter you learned how to add menus, toolbars and status bars. You also learned more about how the ObjectListView widget works.

Now let's get ready to create something new in the next chapter!

Chapter 8 - Creating an MP3 Tag Editor

I don't know about you, but I enjoy listening to music. As an avid music fan, I also like to rip my CDs to MP3 so I can listen to my music on the go a bit easier. There is still a lot of music that is unavailable to buy digitally. Unfortunately, when you rip a lot of music, you will sometimes end up with errors in the MP3 tags. Usually there is a mis-spelling in a title or a track isn't tagged with the right artist. While you can use many open source and paid programs to tag MP3 files, it's also fun to write your own.

That is the topic of this chapter. In this chapter, you will write a simple MP3 tagging application. This application will allow you to view an MP3 file's current tags as well as edit the following tags:

- Artist
- Album
- Track Name
- Track Number

The first step in your adventure is finding the right Python package for the job!

Finding an MP3 Package

There are several Python packages that you can use for editing MP3 tags. Here are a few that I found when I did a Google search:

- eyeD3
- mutagen
- mp3-tagger
- pytaglib

You will be using **eyeD3** for this chapter. It has a nice API that is fairly straight-forward. Frankly, I found most of the APIs for these packages to be brief and not all that helpful. However eyeD3 seemed a bit more natural in the way it worked than the others that I tried, which is why it was chosen.

By the way, the package name, eyeD3, refers to the ID3 specification for metadata related to MP3 files.

However the **mutagen** package is definitely a good fall back option because it supports many other types of audio metadata. If you happen to be working with other audio file types beside MP3, then you should definitely give mutagen a try.

Installing eyeD3

The eyeD3 package can be installed with pip. If you have been using a virtual environment (`venv` or `virtualenv`) for this book, make sure you have it activated before you install eyeD3:

```
pip install eyeD3
```

Once you have eyeD3 installed, you might want to check out its documentation:

- https://pypi.org/project/eyeD3/[1]

Now let's get started and make a neat application!

Designing the MP3 Tagger

Your first step is to figure out what you want the user interface to look like. You will need the following features to make a useful application:

- Some way to import MP3s
- A way to display some of the metadata of the files
- A method of editing the metadata

Here is a simple mockup of what the main interface might look like:

---

[1]https://pypi.org/project/eyeD3/

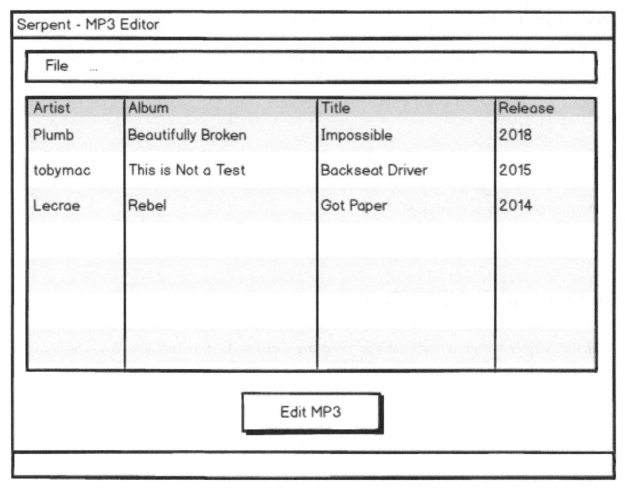

Fig. 8-1: Mockup MP3 Tagger

This user interface doesn't show how to actually edit the MP3, but it implies that the user would need to press the button at the bottom to start editing. This seems like a reasonable way to start.

Let's code the main interface first!

Creating the Main Application

Now comes the fun part, which is writing the actual application. You will be using `ObjectListView` again for this example for displaying the MP3's metadata. Technically you could use one of wxPython's list control widgets. If you'd like a challenge, you should try changing the code in this chapter to using one of those.

Anyway, you can start by creating a file named **main.py** and entering the following:

```python
# main.py

import eyed3
import editor
import glob
import wx

from ObjectListView import ObjectListView, ColumnDefn

class Mp3:

    def __init__(self, id3):
        self.artist = ''
        self.album = ''
        self.title = ''
        self.year = ''

        # Attempt to extract MP3 tags
        if not isinstance(id3.tag, type(None)):
            id3.tag.artist = self.normalize_mp3(
                id3.tag.artist)
            self.artist = id3.tag.artist
            id3.tag.album = self.normalize_mp3(
                id3.tag.album)
            self.album = id3.tag.album
            id3.tag.title = self.normalize_mp3(
                id3.tag.title)
            self.title = id3.tag.title
            if hasattr(id3.tag, 'best_release_date'):
                if not isinstance(
                        id3.tag.best_release_date, type(None)):
                    self.year = self.normalize_mp3(
                        id3.tag.best_release_date.year)
                else:
                    id3.tag.release_date = 2019
                    self.year = self.normalize_mp3(
                        id3.tag.best_release_date.year)
        else:
            tag = id3.initTag()
            tag.release_date = 2019
            tag.artist = 'Unknown'
            tag.album = 'Unknown'
            tag.title = 'Unknown'
```

```
self.id3 = id3
self.update()
```

Here you have the imports you need. You also created a class called Mp3 which will be used by the ObjectListView widget. The first four instance attributes in this class are the metadata that will be displayed in your application and are defaulted to strings. The last instance attribute, id3, will be the object returned from eyed3 when you load an MP3 file into it.

Not all MP3s are created equal. Some have no tags whatsoever and others may have only partial tags. Because of those issues, you will check to see if id3.tag exists. If it does not, then the MP3 has no tags and you will need to call id3.initTag() to add blank tags to it. If id3.tag does exist, then you will want to make sure that the tags you are interested in also exist. That is what the first part of the if statement attempts to do when it calls the normalize_mp3() function.

The other item here is that if there are no dates set, then the best_release_date attribute will return None. So you need to check that and set it to some default if it happens to be None.

Let's go ahead and create the normalize_mp3() method now:

```
def normalize_mp3(self, tag):
    try:
        if tag:
            return tag
        else:
            return 'Unknown'
    except:
        return 'Unknown'
```

This will check to see if the specified tag exists. If it does, it simply returns the tag's value. If it does not, then it returns the string: 'Unknown'

The last method you need to implement in the Mp3 class is update():

```
def update(self):
    self.artist = self.id3.tag.artist
    self.album = self.id3.tag.album
    self.title = self.id3.tag.title
    self.year = self.id3.tag.best_release_date.year
```

This method is called at the end of the outer else in the class's __init__() method. It is used to update the instance attributes after you have initialized the tags for the MP3 file.

There may be some edge cases that this method and the __init__() method will not catch. You are encouraged to enhance this code yourself to see if you can figure out how to fix those kinds of issues.

Now let's go ahead and create a subclass of wx.Panel called TaggerPanel:

```python
class TaggerPanel(wx.Panel):

    def __init__(self, parent):
        super().__init__(parent)
        self.mp3s = []
        main_sizer = wx.BoxSizer(wx.VERTICAL)

        self.mp3_olv = ObjectListView(
            self, style=wx.LC_REPORT | wx.SUNKEN_BORDER)
        self.mp3_olv.SetEmptyListMsg("No Mp3s Found")
        self.update_mp3_info()
        main_sizer.Add(self.mp3_olv, 1, wx.ALL | wx.EXPAND, 5)

        edit_btn = wx.Button(self, label='Edit Mp3')
        edit_btn.Bind(wx.EVT_BUTTON, self.edit_mp3)
        main_sizer.Add(edit_btn, 0, wx.ALL | wx.CENTER, 5)

        self.SetSizer(main_sizer)
```

The TaggerPanel is nice and short. Here you set up an instance attribute called mp3s that is initialized as an empty list. This list will eventually hold a list of instances of your Mp3 class. You also create you ObjectListView instance here and add a button for editing MP3 files.

Speaking of editing, let's create the event handler for editing MP3s:

```python
def edit_mp3(self, event):
    selection = self.mp3_olv.GetSelectedObject()
    if selection:
        with editor.Mp3TagEditorDialog(selection.id3) as dlg:
            dlg.ShowModal()
            self.update_mp3_info()
```

Here you will use the GetSelectedObject() method from the ObjectListView widget to get the selected MP3 that you want to edit. Then you make sure that you got a valid selection and open up an editor dialog which is contained in your editor module that you will write soon. The dialog accepts a single argument, the eyed3 object, which you are calling id3 here.

Note that you will need to call update_mp3_info() to apply any updates you made to the MP3's tags in the editor dialog.

Now let's learn how to load a folder that contains MP3 files:

```python
def load_mp3s(self, path):
    if self.mp3s:
        # clear the current contents
        self.mp3s = []
    mp3_paths = glob.glob(path + '/*.mp3')
    for mp3_path in mp3_paths:
        id3 = eyed3.load(mp3_path)
        mp3_obj = Mp3(id3)
        self.mp3s.append(mp3_obj)
    self.update_mp3_info()
```

In this example, you take in a folder path and use Python's `glob` module to search it for MP3 files. Assuming that you find the files, you then loop over the results and load them into `eyed3`. Then you create an instance of your `Mp3` class so that you can show the user the MP3's metadata. To do that, you call the `update_mp3_info()` method. The `if` statement at the beginning of the method is there to clear out the `mp3s` list so that you do not keep appending to it indefinitely.

Let's go ahead and create the `update_mp3_info()` method now:

```python
def update_mp3_info(self):
    self.mp3_olv.SetColumns([
        ColumnDefn("Artist", "left", 100, "artist"),
        ColumnDefn("Album", "left", 100, "album"),
        ColumnDefn("Title", "left", 150, "title"),
        ColumnDefn("Year", "left", 100, "year")
    ])
    self.mp3_olv.SetObjects(self.mp3s)
```

The `update_mp3_info()` method is used for displaying MP3 metadata to the user. In this case, you will be showing the user the Artist, Album title, Track name (title) and the Year the song was released. To actually update the widget, you call the `SetObjects()` method at the end.

Now let's move on and create the `TaggerFrame` class:

```python
class TaggerFrame(wx.Frame):

    def __init__(self):
        super().__init__(
            None, title="Serpent - MP3 Editor")
        self.panel = TaggerPanel(self)
        self.create_menu()
        self.Show()
```

Here you create an instance of the aforementioned `TaggerPanel` class, create a menu and show the frame to the user. This is also where you would set the initial size of the application and the title of the application. Just for fun, I am calling it **Serpent**, but you can name the application whatever you want to.

Let's learn how to create the menu next:

```python
def create_menu(self):
    menu_bar = wx.MenuBar()
    file_menu = wx.Menu()
    open_folder_menu_item = file_menu.Append(
        wx.ID_ANY, 'Open Mp3 Folder', 'Open a folder with MP3s'
    )
    menu_bar.Append(file_menu, '&File')
    self.Bind(wx.EVT_MENU, self.on_open_folder,
              open_folder_menu_item)
    self.SetMenuBar(menu_bar)
```

In this small piece of code, you create a menubar object. Then you create the file menu with a single menu item that you will use to open a folder on your computer. This menu item is bound to an event handler called `on_open_folder()`. To show the menu to the user, you will need to call the frame's `SetMenuBar()` method.

The last piece of the puzzle is to create the `on_open_folder()` event handler:

```python
def on_open_folder(self, event):
    with wx.DirDialog(self, "Choose a directory:",
                      style=wx.DD_DEFAULT_STYLE,
                      ) as dlg:
        if dlg.ShowModal() == wx.ID_OK:
            self.panel.load_mp3s(dlg.GetPath())
```

You will want to open a `wx.DirDialog` here using Python's `with` statement and show it modally to the user. This prevents the user from interacting with your application while they choose a folder. If the user presses the OK button, you will call the panel instance's `load_mp3s()` method with the path that they have chosen.

For completeness, here is how you will run the application:

```
if __name__ == '__main__':
    app = wx.App(False)
    frame = TaggerFrame()
    app.MainLoop()
```

You are always required to create a wx.App instance so that your application can respond to events.

Your application won't run yet as you haven't created the editor module yet.

Let's learn how to do that next!

Editing MP3s

Editing MP3s is the point of this application, so you definitely need to have a way to accomplish that. You could modify the ObjectListView widget so that you can edit the data there or you can open up a dialog with editable fields. Both are valid approaches. For this version of the application, you will be doing the latter.

Let's get started by creating the Mp3TagEditorDialog class:

```
# editor.py

import wx

class Mp3TagEditorDialog(wx.Dialog):

    def __init__(self, mp3):
        title = f'Editing "{mp3.id3.tag.title}"'
        super().__init__(parent=None, title=title)

        self.mp3 = mp3
        self.create_ui()
```

Here you instantiate your class and grab the MP3's title from its tag to make the title of the dialog refer to which MP3 you are editing. Then you set an instance attribute and call the create_ui() method to create the dialog's user interface.

Let's create the dialog's UI now:

```python
def create_ui(self):
    self.main_sizer = wx.BoxSizer(wx.VERTICAL)

    size = (200, -1)
    track_num = str(self.mp3.id3.tag.track_num[0])
    year = str(self.mp3.id3.tag.best_release_date.year)

    self.track_number = wx.TextCtrl(
        self, value=track_num, size=size)
    self.create_row('Track Number', self.track_number)

    self.artist = wx.TextCtrl(self, value=self.mp3.id3.tag.artist,
                              size=size)
    self.create_row('Artist', self.artist)

    self.album = wx.TextCtrl(self, value=self.mp3.id3.tag.album,
                             size=size)
    self.create_row('Album', self.album)

    self.title = wx.TextCtrl(self, value=self.mp3.id3.tag.title,
                             size=size)
    self.create_row('Title', self.title)

    btn_sizer = wx.BoxSizer()
    save_btn = wx.Button(self, label="Save")
    save_btn.Bind(wx.EVT_BUTTON, self.save)

    btn_sizer.Add(save_btn, 0, wx.ALL, 5)
    btn_sizer.Add(wx.Button(self, id=wx.ID_CANCEL), 0, wx.ALL, 5)
    self.main_sizer.Add(btn_sizer, 0, wx.CENTER)

    self.SetSizerAndFit(self.main_sizer)
```

Here you create a series of `wx.TextCtrl` widgets that you pass to a function called `create_row()`. You also add the "Save" button at the end and bind it to the `save()` event handler. Finally you add a "Cancel" button. The way you create the Cancel button is kind of unique. All you need to do is pass `wx.Button` a special id: `wx.ID_CANCEL`. This will add the right label to the button and automatically make it close the dialog for you without actually binding it to a function.

This is one of the convenience functions built-in to the wxPython toolkit. As long as you don't need to do anything special, this functionality is great.

Now let's learn what to put into the `create_row()` method:

```
def create_row(self, label, text):
    sizer = wx.BoxSizer(wx.HORIZONTAL)
    row_label = wx.StaticText(self, label=label, size=(50, -1))
    widgets = [(row_label, 0, wx.ALL, 5),
               (text, 0, wx.ALL, 5)]
    sizer.AddMany(widgets)
    self.main_sizer.Add(sizer)
```

In this example, you create a horizontal sizer and an instance of wx.StaticText with the label that you passed in. Then you add both of these widgets to a list of tuples where each tuple contains the arguments you need to pass to the main sizer. This allows you to add multiple widgets to a sizer at once via the AddMany() method.

The last piece of code you need to create is the save() event handler:

```
def save(self, event):
    current_track_num = self.mp3.id3.tag.track_num
    if current_track_num:
        new_track_num = (int(self.track_number.GetValue()),
                         current_track_num[1])
    else:
        new_track_num = (int(self.track_number.GetValue()), 0)

    self.mp3.id3.tag.artist = self.artist.GetValue()
    self.mp3.id3.tag.album = self.album.GetValue()
    self.mp3.id3.tag.title = self.title.GetValue()
    self.mp3.id3.tag.track_num = new_track_num
    self.mp3.id3.tag.save()
    self.mp3.update()
    self.Close()
```

Here you check if the track number was set in the MP3's tag. If it was, then you update it to the new value you set it to. On the other hand, if the track number is not set, then you need to create the tuple yourself. The first number in the tuple is the track number and the second number is the total number of tracks on the album. If the track number is not set, then you can't know the total number of track reliably programmatically, so you just set it to zero by default.

The rest of the function is setting the various MP3 object's tag attributes to what is in the dialog's text controls. Once all the attributes are set, you can call the save() method on the eyed3 MP3 object, tell the Mp3 class instance to update itself and close the dialog.

Now you have all the pieces that you need and you should be able to run the program.

Here is what the main application looked like on my machine:

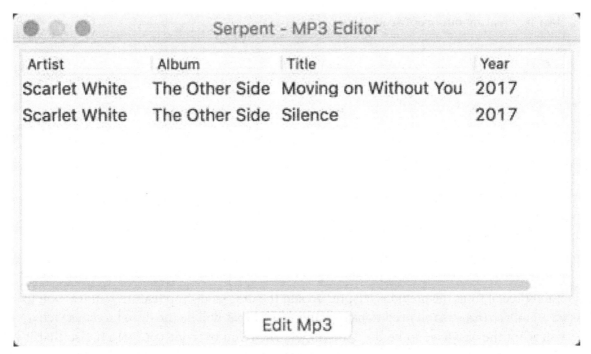

Fig. 8-2: MP3 Tagger

And here is what the editor dialog looked like:

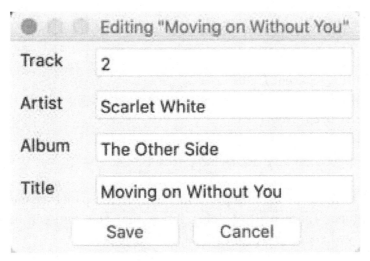

Fig. 8-3: MP3 Editor Dialog

Now let's learn how to add a few enhancements to your program!

Adding New Features

Most applications of this type will allow the user to drag-and-drop files or folders onto them. They also usually have a toolbar for opening folders in addition to the menu. You learned how to do both of these in the previous chapter. You will now add these features to this program as well

Let's start by creating our `DropTarget` class:

```python
import os

class DropTarget(wx.FileDropTarget):

    def __init__(self, window):
        super().__init__()
        self.window = window

    def OnDropFiles(self, x, y, filenames):
        self.window.update_on_drop(filenames)
        return True
```

As you may recall from the previous chapter, to add the drag-and-drop feature requires you to sub-class `wx.FileDropTarget`. You need to pass in the widget that will be the drop target as well. In this case, you want the `wx.Panel` to be the drop target. Then you override `OnDropFiles` so that it calls the `update_on_drop()` method. This is a new method that you will be adding shortly.

But before you do that, you need to update the beginning of your `TaggerPanel` class:

```python
class TaggerPanel(wx.Panel):

    def __init__(self, parent):
        super().__init__(parent)
        self.mp3s = []
        drop_target = DropTarget(self)
        self.SetDropTarget(drop_target)
        main_sizer = wx.BoxSizer(wx.VERTICAL)
```

Here you create an instance of `DropTarget` and then set the panel as the drop target via the `SetDropTarget()` method. The benefit of doing this is that now you can drag and drop files or folder pretty much anywhere on your application and it will work.

Note that the above code is not the full code for the `__init__()` method, but only shows the changes in context. See the source code on Github for the full version.

The first new method to look at is `add_mp3()`:

```
def add_mp3(self, path):
    id3 = eyed3.load(path)
    mp3_obj = Mp3(id3)
    self.mp3s.append(mp3_obj)
```

Here you pass in the path of the MP3 file that you want to add to the user interface. It will take that path and load it with eyed3 and add that to your mp3s list.

The edit_mp3() method is unchanged for this version of the application, so it is not reproduced here.

Now let's move on and create another new method called find_mp3s():

```
def find_mp3s(self, folder):
    mp3_paths = glob.glob(folder + '/*.mp3')
    for mp3_path in mp3_paths:
        self.add_mp3(mp3_path)
```

This code and the code in the add_mp3s() method might look a bit familiar to you. It is originally from the load_mp3() method that you created earlier. You are moving this bit of code into its own function. This is known as **refactoring** your code. There are many reasons to refactor your code. In this case, you are doing so because you will need to call this function from multiple places. Rather than copying this code into multiple functions, it is almost always better to separate it into its own function that you can call.

Now let's update the load_mp3s() method so that it calls the new one above:

```
def load_mp3s(self, path):
    if self.mp3s:
        # clear the current contents
        self.mp3s = []
    self.find_mp3s(path)
    self.update_mp3_info()
```

This method has been reduced to two lines of code. The first calls the find_mp3s() method that you just wrote while the second calls the update_mp3_info(), which will update the user interface (i.e. the ObjectListView widget).

The DropTarget class is calling the update_on_drop() method, so let's write that now:

```
def update_on_drop(self, paths):
    for path in paths:
        if os.path.isdir(path):
            self.load_mp3s(path)
        elif os.path.isfile(path):
            self.add_mp3(mp3_path)
            self.update_mp3_info()
```

The `update_on_drop()` method is the reason you did the refactoring earlier. It also needs to call the `load_mp3s()`, but only when the path that is passed in is determined to be a directory. Otherwise you check to see if the path is a file and load it up.

But wait! There's an issue with the code above. Can you tell what it is?

The problem is that when the path is a file, you aren't checking to see if it is an MP3. If you run this code as is, you will cause an exception to be raised at the `eyed3` package will not be able to turn all file types into Mp3 objects.

Let's fix that issue:

```
def update_on_drop(self, paths):
    for path in paths:
        _, ext = os.path.splitext(path)
        if os.path.isdir(path):
            self.load_mp3s(path)
        elif os.path.isfile(path) and ext.lower() == '.mp3':
            self.add_mp3(path)
            self.update_mp3_info()
```

You can use Python's `os` module to get the extension of files using the `splitext()` function. It will return a tuple that contains two items: The path to the file and the extension.

Now that you have the extension, you can check to see if it is `.mp3` and only update the UI if it is. By the way, the `splitext()` function returns an empty string when you pass it a directory path.

The next bit of code that you need to update is the `TaggerFrame` class so that you can add a toolbar:

```python
class TaggerFrame(wx.Frame):

    def __init__(self):
        super().__init__(
            None, title="Serpent - MP3 Editor")
        self.panel = TaggerPanel(self)
        self.create_menu()
        self.create_tool_bar()
        self.Show()
```

The only change to the code above is to add a call to the `create_tool_bar()` method. You will almost always want to create the toolbar in a separate method as there is typically several lines of code per toolbar button. For applications with many buttons in the toolbar, you should probably separate that code out even more and put it into a class or module of its own.

Let's go ahead and write that method:

```python
def create_tool_bar(self):
    self.toolbar = self.CreateToolBar()

    add_folder_ico = wx.ArtProvider.GetBitmap(
        wx.ART_FOLDER_OPEN, wx.ART_TOOLBAR, (16, 16))
    add_folder_tool = self.toolbar.AddTool(
        wx.ID_ANY, 'Add Folder', add_folder_ico,
        'Add a folder to be archived')
    self.Bind(wx.EVT_MENU, self.on_open_folder,
              add_folder_tool)
    self.toolbar.Realize()
```

To keep things simple, you add a single toolbar button that will open a directory dialog via the `on_open_folder()` method.

When you run this code, your updated application should now look like this:

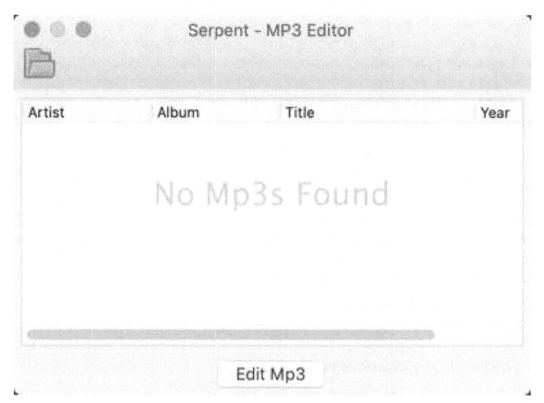

Fig. 8-4: MP3 Tagger with New Features

Feel free to add more toolbar buttons, menu items, a status bar or other fun enhancements to this application.

Wrapping Up

This chapter taught you a little about some of Python's MP3 related packages that you can use to edit MP3 tags as well as other tags for other music file formats. You learned how to create a nice main application that opens an editing dialog. The main application can be used to display relevant MP3 metadata to the user. It also serves to show the user their updates should they decide to edit one or more tags.

The wxPython tookit has support for playing back certain types of audio file formats including MP3. You could create an MP3 player using these capabilities and make this application a part of that.

Chapter 9 - Creating an Application for NASA's API

Growing up, I have always found the universe and space in general to be exciting. It is fun to dream about what worlds remain unexplored. I also enjoy seeing photos from other worlds or thinking about the vastness of space. What does this have to do with Python though? Well, the National Aeronautics and Space Administration (NASA) has a web API that allows you to search their image library.

You can read all about it here:

- https://api.nasa.gov/

The NASA website recommends getting an Application Programming Interface (API) key. You can get one here:

- https://api.nasa.gov/index.html#apply-for-an-api-key

If you go to that website, the form that you will fill out is nice and short:

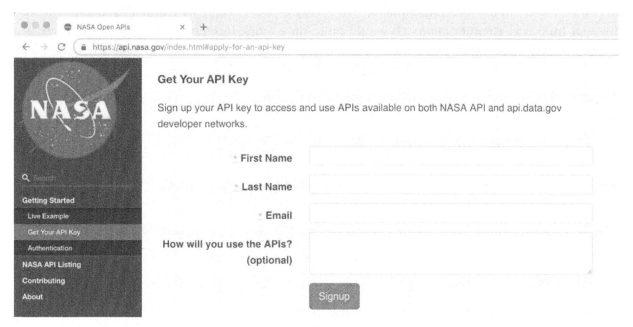

Fig. 9-1: NASA API Signup Form

Technically, you do not need an API key to make requests against NASA's services. However they do have rate limiting in place for developers who access their site without an API key. Even with a key, you are limited to a default of 1000 requests per hour. If you go over your allocation, you will be temporarily blocked from making requests. You can contact NASA to request a higher rate limit though.

Interestingly, the documentation doesn't really say how many requests you can make without an API key.

The API documentation disagrees with NASA's Image API documentation about which endpoints to hit, which makes working with their website a bit confusing.

For example, you will see the API documentation talking about this URL:

- https://api.nasa.gov/planetary/apod?api_key=API_KEY_GOES_HERE

But in the Image API documentation, the API root is:

- https://images-api.nasa.gov

For the purposes of this chapter, you will be using the latter.

Using NASA's API

When you start out using an unfamiliar API, it is always best to begin by reading the documentation for that interface. Another approach would be to do a quick Internet search and see if there is a Python package that wraps your target API. Unfortunately, there do not seem to be any maintained NASA libraries for Python. When this happens, you get to create your own.

To get started, try reading the NASA Images API document:

- https://images.nasa.gov/docs/images.nasa.gov_api_docs.pdf

Their API documentation isn't very long, so it shouldn't take you very long to read or at least skim it.

The next step is to take that information and try playing around with their API.

Here are the first few lines of an experiment at accessing their API:

```python
# simple_api_request.py

import requests

from urllib.parse import urlencode, quote_plus


base_url = 'https://images-api.nasa.gov/search'
search_term = 'apollo 11'
desc = 'moon landing'
media = 'image'
query = {'q': search_term, 'description': desc, 'media_type': media}
full_url = base_url + '?' + urlencode(query, quote_via=quote_plus)

r = requests.get(full_url)
data = r.json()
```

If you run this in a debugger, you can print out the JSON that is returned.
Here is a snippet of what was returned:

```
'items': [{'data':
          [{'center': 'HQ',
            'date_created': '2009-07-18T00:00:00Z',
            'description': 'On the eve of the '
                          'fortieth anniversary of '
                          "Apollo 11's first human "
                          'landing on the Moon, '
                          'Apollo 11 crew member, '
                          'Buzz Aldrin speaks during '
                          'a lecture in honor of '
                          'Apollo 11 at the National '
                          'Air and Space Museum in '
                          'Washington, Sunday, July '
                          '19, 2009. Guest speakers '
                          'included Former NASA '
                          'Astronaut and U.S. '
                          'Senator John Glenn, NASA '
                          'Mission Control creator '
                          'and former NASA Johnson '
                          'Space Center director '
                          'Chris Kraft and the crew '
                          'of Apollo 11.  Photo '
```

```
                              'Credit: (NASA/Bill '
                              'Ingalls)',
               'keywords': ['Apollo 11',
                            'Apollo 40th Anniversary',
                            'Buzz Aldrin',
                            'National Air and Space '
                            'Museum (NASM)',
                            'Washington, DC'],
               'location': 'National Air and Space '
                           'Museum',
               'media_type': 'image',
               'nasa_id': '200907190008HQ',
               'photographer': 'NASA/Bill Ingalls',
               'title': 'Glenn Lecture With Crew of '
                        'Apollo 11'}],
       'href': 'https://images-assets.nasa.gov/image/200907190008HQ/collection.json',
       'links': [{'href': 'https://images-assets.nasa.gov/image/200907190008HQ/20090\
7190008HQ~thumb.jpg',
                  'rel': 'preview',
                  'render': 'image'}]}
```

Now that you know what the format of the JSON is, you can try parsing it a bit.

Let's add the following lines of code to your Python script:

```
item = data['collection']['items'][0]
nasa_id = item['data'][0]['nasa_id']
asset_url = 'https://images-api.nasa.gov/asset/' + nasa_id
image_request = requests.get(asset_url)
image_json = image_request.json()
image_urls = [url['href'] for url in image_json['collection']['items']]
print(image_urls)
```

This will extract the first item in the list of items from the JSON response. Then you can extract the nasa_id, which is required to get all the images associated with this particular result. Now you can add that nasa_id to a new URL end point and make a new request.

The request for the image JSON returns this:

```
{'collection': {'href': 'https://images-api.nasa.gov/asset/200907190008HQ',
                'items': [{'href': 'http://images-assets.nasa.gov/image/200907190008\
HQ/200907190008HQ~orig.tif'},
                          {'href': 'http://images-assets.nasa.gov/image/200907190008\
HQ/200907190008HQ~large.jpg'},
                          {'href': 'http://images-assets.nasa.gov/image/200907190008\
HQ/200907190008HQ~medium.jpg'},
                          {'href': 'http://images-assets.nasa.gov/image/200907190008\
HQ/200907190008HQ~small.jpg'},
                          {'href': 'http://images-assets.nasa.gov/image/200907190008\
HQ/200907190008HQ~thumb.jpg'},
                          {'href': 'http://images-assets.nasa.gov/image/200907190008\
HQ/metadata.json'}],
                'version': '1.0'}}
```

The last two lines in your Python code will extract the URLs from the JSON. Now you have all the pieces you need to write a basic user interface!

Designing the User Interface

There are many different ways you could design your image downloading application. You will be doing what is simplest as that is almost always the quickest way to create a prototype. The nice thing about prototyping is that you end up with all the pieces you will need to create a useful application. Then you can take your knowledge and either enhance the prototype or create something new with the knowledge you have gained.

Here's a mockup of what you will be attempting to create:

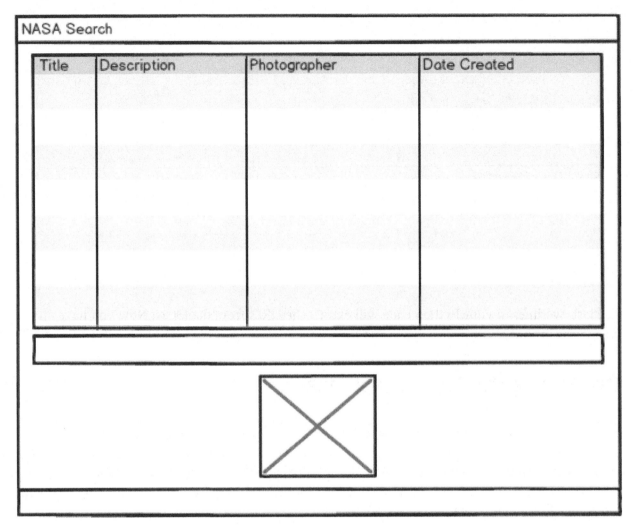

Fig. 9-2: NASA Image Search Mockup

As you can see, you will want an application with the following features:

- A search bar
- A widget to hold the search results
- A way to display an image when a result is chosen
- The ability to download the image

Let's learn how to create this user interface now!

Creating the NASA Search Application

Rapid prototyping is an idea in which you will create a small, runnable application as quickly as you can. Rather than spending a lot of time getting all the widgets laid out, let's add them from top to bottom in the application. This will give you something to work with more quickly than creating a series of nested sizers will.

Let's start by creating a script called **nasa_search_ui.py**:

```python
# nasa_search_ui.py

import os
import requests
import wx

from download_dialog import DownloadDialog
from ObjectListView import ObjectListView, ColumnDefn
from urllib.parse import urlencode, quote_plus


base_url = 'https://images-api.nasa.gov/search'
```

Here you import a few new items that you haven't seen as of yet. The first is the requests package. This is a handy package for downloading files and doing things on the Internet with Python. Many developers feel that it is better than Python's own urllib. You will need to install it to use it though.

Here is how you can do that with pip:

```
pip install requests
```

The other piece that is new are the imports from urllib.parse. You will be using this module for encoding URL parameters. Lastly, the DownloadDialog is a class for a small dialog that you will be creating for downloading NASA images.

Since you will be using ObjectListView in this application, you will need a class to represent the objects in that widget:

```python
class Result:

    def __init__(self, item):
        data = item['data'][0]
        self.title = data['title']
        self.location = data.get('location', '')
        self.nasa_id = data['nasa_id']
        self.description = data['description']
        self.photographer = data.get('photographer', '')
        self.date_created = data['date_created']
        self.item = item
```

```
if item.get('links'):
    try:
        self.thumbnail = item['links'][0]['href']
    except BaseException:
        self.thumbnail = ''
```

The `Result` class is what you will be using to hold that data that makes up each row in your `ObjectListView`. The `item` parameter is a portion of JSON that you are receiving from NASA as a response to your query. In this class, you will need to parse out the information you require.

In this case, you want the following fields:

- Title
- Location of image
- NASA's internal ID
- Description of the photo
- The photographer's name
- The date the image was created
- The thumbnail URL

Some of these items aren't always included in the JSON response, so you will use the dictionary's `get()` method to return an empty string in those cases.

Now let's start working on the UI:

```
class MainPanel(wx.Panel):

    def __init__(self, parent):
        super().__init__(parent)
        self.search_results = []
        self.max_size = 300
        self.paths = wx.StandardPaths.Get()
        font = wx.Font(12, wx.SWISS, wx.NORMAL, wx.NORMAL)

        main_sizer = wx.BoxSizer(wx.VERTICAL)
```

The `MainPanel` is where the bulk of your code will be. Here you do some housekeeping and create a `search_results` to hold a list of `Result` objects when the user does a search. You also set the `max_size` of the thumbnail image, the font to be used, the sizer and you get some `StandardPaths` as well.

Now let's add the following code to the `__init__()`:

```
txt = 'Search for images on NASA'
label = wx.StaticText(self, label=txt)
main_sizer.Add(label, 0, wx.ALL, 5)
self.search = wx.SearchCtrl(
    self, style=wx.TE_PROCESS_ENTER, size=(-1, 25))
self.search.Bind(wx.EVT_SEARCHCTRL_SEARCH_BTN, self.on_search)
self.search.Bind(wx.EVT_TEXT_ENTER, self.on_search)
main_sizer.Add(self.search, 0, wx.EXPAND)
```

Here you create a header label for the application using wx.StaticText. Then you add a wx.SearchCtrl, which is very similar to a wx.TextCtrl except that it has special buttons built into it. You also bind the search button's click event (EVT_SEARCHCTRL_SEARCH_BTN) and EVT_TEXT_ENTER to a search related event handler (on_search).

The next few lines add the search results widget:

```
self.search_results_olv = ObjectListView(
    self, style=wx.LC_REPORT | wx.SUNKEN_BORDER)
self.search_results_olv.SetEmptyListMsg("No Results Found")
self.search_results_olv.Bind(wx.EVT_LIST_ITEM_SELECTED,
                             self.on_selection)
main_sizer.Add(self.search_results_olv, 1, wx.EXPAND)
self.update_search_results()
```

This code sets up the ObjectListView in much the same way as some of the other chapters use it. You customize the empty message by calling SetEmptyListMsg() and you also bind the widget to EVT_LIST_ITEM_SELECTED so that you do something when the user selects a search result.

Now let's add the rest of the code to the __init__() method:

```
main_sizer.AddSpacer(30)
self.title = wx.TextCtrl(self, style=wx.TE_READONLY)
self.title.SetFont(font)
main_sizer.Add(self.title, 0, wx.ALL|wx.EXPAND, 5)
img = wx.Image(240, 240)
self.image_ctrl = wx.StaticBitmap(self,
                                  bitmap=wx.Bitmap(img))
main_sizer.Add(self.image_ctrl, 0, wx.CENTER|wx.ALL, 5
              )
download_btn = wx.Button(self, label='Download Image')
download_btn.Bind(wx.EVT_BUTTON, self.on_download)
main_sizer.Add(download_btn, 0, wx.ALL|wx.CENTER, 5)

self.SetSizer(main_sizer)
```

These final few lines of code add a `title` text control and an image widget that will update when a result is selected. You also add a download button to allow the user to select which image size they would like to download. NASA usually gives several different versions of the image from thumbnail all the way up to the original TIFF image.

The first event handler to look at is `on_download()`:

```
def on_download(self, event):
    selection = self.search_results_olv.GetSelectedObject()
    if selection:
        with DownloadDialog(selection) as dlg:
            dlg.ShowModal()
```

Here you call `GetSelectedObject()` to get the user's selection. If the user hasn't selected anything, then this method exits. On the other hand, if the user has selected an item, then you instantiate the `DownloadDialog` and show it to the user to allow them to download something.

Now let's learn how to do a search:

```
def on_search(self, event):
    search_term = event.GetString()
    if search_term:
        query = {'q': search_term, 'media_type': 'image'}
        full_url = base_url + '?' + urlencode(query, quote_via=quote_plus)
        r = requests.get(full_url)
        data = r.json()
        self.search_results = []
        for item in data['collection']['items']:
            if item.get('data') and len(item.get('data')) > 0:
                data = item['data'][0]
                if data['title'].strip() == '':
                    # Skip results with blank titles
                    continue
                result = Result(item)
                self.search_results.append(result)
        self.update_search_results()
```

The `on_search()` event handler will get the string that the user has entered into the search control or return an empty string. Assuming that the user actually enters something to search for, you use NASA's general search query, `q` and hard code the `media_type` to `image`. Then you encode the query into a properly formatted URL and use `requests.get()` to request a JSON response.

Next you attempt to loop over the results of the search. Note that if no `data` is returned, this code will fail and cause an exception to be thrown. But if you do get data, then you will need to parse it to get the bits and pieces you need.

You will skip items that don't have the `title` field set. Otherwise you will create a `Result` object and add it to the `search_results` list. At the end of the method, you tell your UI to update the search results.

Before we get to that function, you will need to create `on_selection()`:

```python
def on_selection(self, event):
    selection = self.search_results_olv.GetSelectedObject()
    self.title.SetValue(f'{selection.title}')
    if selection.thumbnail:
        self.update_image(selection.thumbnail)
    else:
        img = wx.Image(240, 240)
        self.image_ctrl.SetBitmap(wx.Bitmap(img))
        self.Refresh()
        self.Layout()
```

Once again, you get the selected item, but this time you take that selection and update the `title` text control with the selection's `title` text. Then you check to see if there is a thumbnail and update that accordingly if there is one. When there is no thumbnail, you set it back to an empty image as you do not want it to keep showing a previously selected image.

The next method to create is `update_image()`:

```python
def update_image(self, url):
    filename = url.split('/')[-1]
    tmp_location = os.path.join(self.paths.GetTempDir(), filename)
    r = requests.get(url)
    with open(tmp_location, "wb") as thumbnail:
        thumbnail.write(r.content)

    if os.path.exists(tmp_location):
        img = wx.Image(tmp_location, wx.BITMAP_TYPE_ANY)
        W = img.GetWidth()
        H = img.GetHeight()
        if W > H:
            NewW = self.max_size
            NewH = self.max_size * H / W
        else:
            NewH = self.max_size
            NewW = self.max_size * W / H
        img = img.Scale(NewW, NewH)
    else:
        img = wx.Image(240, 240)
```

```
self.image_ctrl.SetBitmap(wx.Bitmap(img))
self.Refresh()
self.Layout()
```

The update_image() accepts a url as its sole argument. It takes this URL and splits off the filename. Then it creates a new download location, which is the computer's temp directory. Your code then downloads the image and checks to be sure the file saved correctly. If it did, then the thumbnail is loaded using the max_size that you set; otherwise you set it to use a blank image.

The last couple of lines Refresh() and Layout() the panel so that the widget appears correctly.

Finally you need to create the last method:

```
def update_search_results(self):
    self.search_results_olv.SetColumns([
        ColumnDefn("Title", "left", 250, "title"),
        ColumnDefn("Description", "left", 350, "description"),
        ColumnDefn("Photographer", "left", 100, "photographer"),
        ColumnDefn("Date Created", "left", 150, "date_created")
    ])
    self.search_results_olv.SetObjects(self.search_results)
```

This is the method you call when you need to update your search results. It will set the columns in your ObjectListView and then use SetObjects() to set the new list to the widget, which causes the widget to update its contents.

The last piece of code is your SearchFrame:

```
class SearchFrame(wx.Frame):

    def __init__(self):
        super().__init__(None, title='NASA Search',
                         size=(1200, 800))
        panel = MainPanel(self)
        self.Show()


if __name__ == '__main__':
    app = wx.App(False)
    frame = SearchFrame()
    app.MainLoop()
```

Here you create the frame, set the title and initial size and add the panel. Then you show the frame. This is what the main UI will look like:

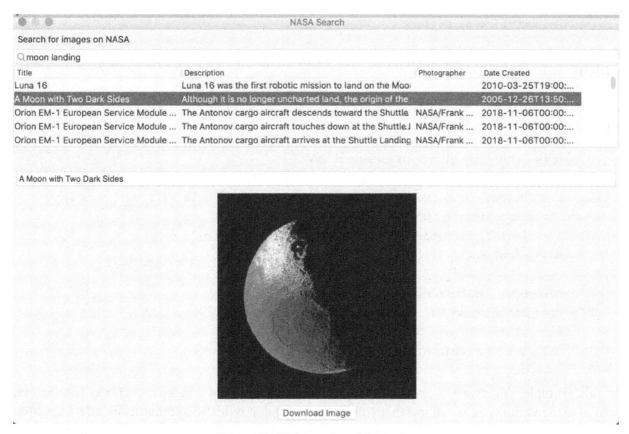

Fig. 9-3: NASA Image Search Main App

Now let's learn what goes into making a download dialog!

The Download Dialog

The download dialog will allow the user to download one or more of the images that they have selected. There are almost always at least two versions of every image and sometimes five or six.

The first piece of code to learn about is the first few lines:

```
# download_dialog.py

import requests
import wx


wildcard = "All files (*.*)|*.*"
```

Here you once again import `requests` and set up a `wildcard` that you will use when saving the images.

Now let's create the dialog's __init__():

```python
class DownloadDialog(wx.Dialog):

    def __init__(self, selection):
        super().__init__(None, title='Download images')
        self.paths = wx.StandardPaths.Get()
        main_sizer = wx.BoxSizer(wx.VERTICAL)
        self.list_box = wx.ListBox(self, choices=[], size=wx.DefaultSize)
        urls = self.get_image_urls(selection)
        if urls:
            choices = {url.split('/')[-1]: url for url in urls if 'jpg' in url}
            for choice in choices:
                self.list_box.Append(choice, choices[choice])
        main_sizer.Add(self.list_box, 1, wx.EXPAND|wx.ALL, 5)

        save_btn = wx.Button(self, label='Save')
        save_btn.Bind(wx.EVT_BUTTON, self.on_save)
        main_sizer.Add(save_btn, 0, wx.ALL|wx.CENTER, 5)
        self.SetSizer(main_sizer)
```

In this example, you create a new reference to `StandardPaths` and add a `wx.ListBox`. The list box will hold the variants of the photos that you can download. It will also automatically add a scrollbar should there be too many results to fit on-screen at once. You call `get_image_urls` with the passed-in `selection` object to get a list of `urls`. Then you loop over the `urls` and extract the ones that have `jpg` in their name. This does result in you missing out on alternate image files types, such as PNG or TIFF.

This gives you an opportunity to enhance this code and improve it. The reason that you are filtering the URLs is that the results usually have non-image URLs in the mix and you probably don't want to show those as potentially downloadable as that would be confusing to the user.

The last widget to be added is the "Save" button. You could add a "Cancel" button as well, but the dialog has an exit button along the top that works, so it's not required.

Now it's time to learn what `get_image_urls()` does:

```python
def get_image_urls(self, item):
    asset_url = f'https://images-api.nasa.gov/asset/{item.nasa_id}'
    image_request = requests.get(asset_url)
    image_json = image_request.json()
    try:
        image_urls = [url['href'] for url in image_json['collection']['items']]
    except BaseException:
        image_urls = []
    return image_urls
```

The `get_image_urls()` method will use NASA's asset endpoint to get the image assets for the specified NASA ID. This uses the `requests` library to request a JSON response. You then use a list comprehension to extract the image URLs. If an error occurs, then you set the list to an empty list instead.

The next step is to create `on_save()`:

```
def on_save(self, event):
    selection = self.list_box.GetSelection()
    if selection != -1:
        with wx.FileDialog(
                self, message="Save file as ...",
                defaultDir=self.paths.GetDocumentsDir(),
                defaultFile=self.list_box.GetString(selection),
                wildcard=wildcard,
                style=wx.FD_SAVE
                ) as dlg:
            if dlg.ShowModal() == wx.ID_OK:
                path = dlg.GetPath()
                self.save(path)
    else:
        message = 'No image selected'
        with wx.MessageDialog(None, message=message,
                        caption='Cannot Save',
                        style=wx.ICON_ERROR) as dlg:
            dlg.ShowModal()
```

This event handler is activated when the user presses the "Save" button. When the user tries to save something without selecting an item in the list box, it will return -1. Should that happen, you show them a `MessageDialog` to tell them that they might want to select something. When they do select something, you will show them a `wx.FileDialog` that allows them to choose where to save the file and what to call it.

The event handler calls the `save()` method, so that is your next project:

```python
def save(self, path):
    selection = self.list_box.GetSelection()
    r = requests.get(
        self.list_box.GetClientData(selection))
    try:
        with open(path, "wb") as image:
            image.write(r.content)

        message = 'File saved successfully'
        with wx.MessageDialog(None, message=message,
                              caption='Save Successful',
                              style=wx.ICON_INFORMATION) as dlg:
            dlg.ShowModal()
    except BaseException:
        message = 'File failed to save!'
        with wx.MessageDialog(None, message=message,
                              caption='Save Failed',
                              style=wx.ICON_ERROR) as dlg:
            dlg.ShowModal()
```

Here you get the selection again and use the `requests` package to download the image. Note that there is no check to make sure that the user has added an extension, let along the right extension. You can add that yourself when you get a chance.

Anyway, when the file is finished downloading, you will show the user a message letting them know.

If an exception occurs, you can show them a dialog that lets them know that too!

Here is what the download dialog looks like:

Fig. 9-4: NASA Image Download Dialog

Now let's add some new functionality!

Adding Advanced Search

There are several fields that you can use to help narrow your search. However you don't want to clutter your user interface with them unless the user really wants to use those filters. To allow for that, you can add an "Advanced Search" option.

Adding this option requires you to rearrange your code a bit, so let's copy your **nasa_search_ui.py** file and your **download_dialog.py** module to a new folder called **version_2**.

Now rename **nasa_search_ui.py** to **main.py** to make it more obvious which script is the main entry point for your program. To make things more modular, you will be extracting your search results into its own class and have the advanced search in a separate class. This means that you will have three panels in the end:

- The main panel
- The search results panel
- The advanced search panel

Here is what the main dialog will look like when you are finished:

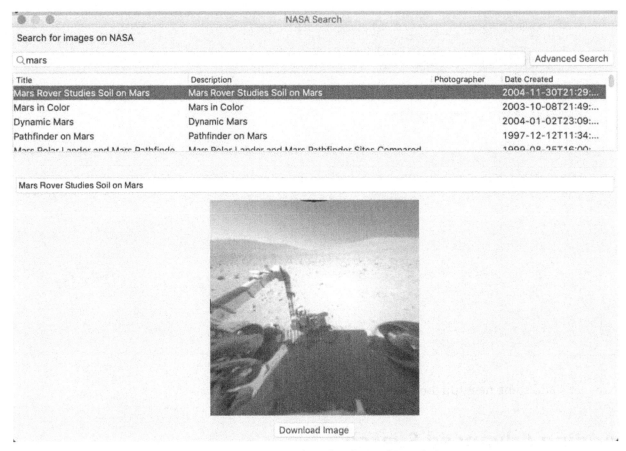

Fig. 9-5: NASA Image Search with Advanced Search Option

Let's go over each of these separately.

The main.py Script

The **main** module is your primary entry point for your application. An entry point is the code that your user will run to launch your application. It is also the script that you would use if you were to bundle up your application into an executable.

Let's take a look at how your **main** module starts out:

```python
# main.py

import wx

from advanced_search import AdvancedSearch
from regular_search import RegularSearch
from pubsub import pub


class MainPanel(wx.Panel):

    def __init__(self, parent):
        super().__init__(parent)
        pub.subscribe(self.update_ui, 'update_ui')

        self.main_sizer = wx.BoxSizer(wx.VERTICAL)
        search_sizer = wx.BoxSizer()
```

This example imports both of your search-related panels:

- AdvancedSearch
- RegularSearch

It also uses pubsub to subscribe to an update topic.

Let's find out what else is in the __init__():

```python
txt = 'Search for images on NASA'
label = wx.StaticText(self, label=txt)
self.main_sizer.Add(label, 0, wx.ALL, 5)
self.search = wx.SearchCtrl(
    self, style=wx.TE_PROCESS_ENTER, size=(-1, 25))
self.search.Bind(wx.EVT_SEARCHCTRL_SEARCH_BTN, self.on_search)
self.search.Bind(wx.EVT_TEXT_ENTER, self.on_search)
search_sizer.Add(self.search, 1, wx.EXPAND)

self.advanced_search_btn = wx.Button(self, label='Advanced Search',
                          size=(-1, 25))
self.advanced_search_btn.Bind(wx.EVT_BUTTON, self.on_advanced_search)
search_sizer.Add(self.advanced_search_btn, 0, wx.ALL, 5)
self.main_sizer.Add(search_sizer, 0, wx.EXPAND)
```

Here you add the title for the page along with the search control widget as you did before. You also add the new **Advanced Search** button and use a new sizer to contain the search widget and the button. You then add that sizer to your main sizer.

Now let's add the panels:

```
self.search_panel = RegularSearch(self)
self.advanced_search_panel = AdvancedSearch(self)
self.advanced_search_panel.Hide()
self.main_sizer.Add(self.search_panel, 1, wx.EXPAND)
self.main_sizer.Add(self.advanced_search_panel, 1, wx.EXPAND)

self.SetSizer(self.main_sizer)
```

In this example, you instantiate the `RegularSearch` and the `AdvancedSearch` panels. Since the `RegularSearch` is the default, you hide the `AdvancedSearch` from the user on startup.

Now let's update `on_search()`:

```
def on_search(self, event):
    search_results = []
    search_term = event.GetString()
    if search_term:
        query = {'q': search_term, 'media_type': 'image'}
        pub.sendMessage('search_results', query=query)
```

The `on_search()` method will get called when the user presses "Enter / Return" on their keyboard or when they press the search button icon in the search control widget. If the user has entered a search string into the search control, a search query will be constructed and then sent off using `pubsub`.

Let's find out what happens when the user presses the **Advanced Search** button:

```
def on_advanced_search(self, event):
    self.search.Hide()
    self.search_panel.Hide()
    self.advanced_search_btn.Hide()
    self.advanced_search_panel.Show()
    self.main_sizer.Layout()
```

When `on_advanced_search()` fires, it hides the search widget, the regular search panel and the advanced search button. Next, it shows the advanced search panel and calls `Layout()` on the `main_-sizer`. This will cause the panels to switch out and resize to fit properly within the frame.

The last method to create is `update_ui()`:

```
def update_ui(self):
    """

    Hide advanced search and re-show original screen

    Called by pubsub when advanced search is invoked
    """
    self.advanced_search_panel.Hide()
    self.search.Show()
    self.search_panel.Show()
    self.advanced_search_btn.Show()
    self.main_sizer.Layout()
```

The update_ui() method is called when the user does an **Advanced Search**. This method is invoked by pubsub. It will do the reverse of on_advanced_search() and un-hide all the widgets that were hidden when the advanced search panel was shown. It will also hide the advanced search panel.

The frame code is the same as it was before, so it is not shown here.

Let's move on and learn how the regular search panel is created!

The regular_search.py Script

The **regular_search** module is your refactored module that contains the ObjectListView that will show your search results. It also has the **Download** button on it.

The following methods / classes will not be covered as they are the same as in the previous iteration:

- on_download()
- on_selection()
- update_image()
- update_search_results()
- The Result class

Let's get started by seeing how the first few lines in the module are laid out:

```
# regular_search.py

import os
import requests
import wx

from download_dialog import DownloadDialog
from ObjectListView import ObjectListView, ColumnDefn
from pubsub import pub
from urllib.parse import urlencode, quote_plus


base_url = 'https://images-api.nasa.gov/search'
```

Here you have all the imports you had in the original **nasa_search_ui.py** script from **version_1**. You also have the base_url that you need to make requests to NASA's image API. The only new import is for pubsub.

Let's go ahead and create the RegularSearch class:

```
class RegularSearch(wx.Panel):

    def __init__(self, parent):
        super().__init__(parent)
        self.search_results = []
        self.max_size = 300
        font = wx.Font(12, wx.SWISS, wx.NORMAL, wx.NORMAL)
        main_sizer = wx.BoxSizer(wx.VERTICAL)
        self.paths = wx.StandardPaths.Get()
        pub.subscribe(self.load_search_results, 'search_results')

        self.search_results_olv = ObjectListView(
            self, style=wx.LC_REPORT | wx.SUNKEN_BORDER)
        self.search_results_olv.SetEmptyListMsg("No Results Found")
        self.search_results_olv.Bind(wx.EVT_LIST_ITEM_SELECTED,
                                     self.on_selection)
        main_sizer.Add(self.search_results_olv, 1, wx.EXPAND)
        self.update_search_results()
```

This code will initialize the search_results list to an empty list and set the max_size of the image. It also sets up a sizer and the ObjectListView widget that you use for displaying the search results to the user. The code is actually quite similar to the first iteration of the code when all the classes were combined.

Here is the rest of the code for the __init__():

```
main_sizer.AddSpacer(30)
self.title = wx.TextCtrl(self, style=wx.TE_READONLY)
self.title.SetFont(font)
main_sizer.Add(self.title, 0, wx.ALL|wx.EXPAND, 5)
img = wx.Image(240, 240)
self.image_ctrl = wx.StaticBitmap(self,
                                    bitmap=wx.Bitmap(img))
main_sizer.Add(self.image_ctrl, 0, wx.CENTER|wx.ALL, 5
            )
download_btn = wx.Button(self, label='Download Image')
download_btn.Bind(wx.EVT_BUTTON, self.on_download)
main_sizer.Add(download_btn, 0, wx.ALL|wx.CENTER, 5)


self.SetSizer(main_sizer)
```

The first item here is to add a spacer to the main_sizer. Then you add the title and the img related widgets. The last widget to be added is still the download button.

Next, you will need to write a new method:

```
def reset_image(self):
    img = wx.Image(240, 240)
    self.image_ctrl.SetBitmap(wx.Bitmap(img))
    self.Refresh()
```

The reset_image() method is for resetting the wx.StaticBitmap back to an empty image. This can happen when the user uses the regular search first, selects an item and then decides to do an advanced search. Resetting the image prevents the user from seeing a previously selected item and potentially confusing the user.

The last method you need to add is load_search_results():

```
def load_search_results(self, query):
    full_url = base_url + '?' + urlencode(query, quote_via=quote_plus)
    r = requests.get(full_url)
    data = r.json()
    self.search_results = []
    for item in data['collection']['items']:
        if item.get('data') and len(item.get('data')) > 0:
            data = item['data'][0]
            if data['title'].strip() == '':
                # Skip results with blank titles
                continue
            result = Result(item)
```

```
            self.search_results.append(result)
        self.update_search_results()
        self.reset_image()
```

The `load_search_results()` method is called using `pubsub`. Both the `main` and the `advanced_search` modules call it by passing in a query dictionary. Then you encode that dictionary into a formatted URL. Next you use `requests` to send a JSON request and you then extract the results. This is also where you call `reset_image()` so that when a new set of results loads, there is no result selected.

Now you are ready to create an advanced search!

The advanced_search.py Script

The **advanced_search** module is a `wx.Panel` that has all the widgets you need to do an advanced search against NASA's API. If you read their documentation, you will find that there are around a dozen filters that can be applied to a search.

Let's start at the top:

```python
# advanced_search.py

import wx

from pubsub import pub
```

Surprisingly, this module has the shortest set of imports of any of the modules. All you need is `wx` and `pubsub`.

So let's move on and add the all the widgets in the __init__():

```python
class AdvancedSearch(wx.Panel):

    def __init__(self, parent):
        super().__init__(parent)

        self.main_sizer = wx.BoxSizer(wx.VERTICAL)

        self.free_text = wx.TextCtrl(self)
        self.ui_helper('Free text search:', self.free_text)
        self.nasa_center = wx.TextCtrl(self)
        self.ui_helper('NASA Center:', self.nasa_center)
        self.description = wx.TextCtrl(self)
        self.ui_helper('Description:', self.description)
        self.description_508 = wx.TextCtrl(self)
```

```
self.ui_helper('Description 508:', self.description_508)
self.keywords = wx.TextCtrl(self)
self.ui_helper('Keywords (separate with commas):',
               self.keywords)
```

The code to set up the various filters is all pretty similar. You create a text control for the filter, then you pass it into `ui_helper()` along with a string that is a label for the text control widget. Repeat until you have all the filters in place.

Here are the rest of the filters:

```
self.location = wx.TextCtrl(self)
self.ui_helper('Location:', self.location)
self.nasa_id = wx.TextCtrl(self)
self.ui_helper('NASA ID:', self.nasa_id)
self.photographer = wx.TextCtrl(self)
self.ui_helper('Photographer:', self.photographer)
self.secondary_creator = wx.TextCtrl(self)
self.ui_helper('Secondary photographer:', self.secondary_creator)
self.title = wx.TextCtrl(self)
self.ui_helper('Title:', self.title)
search = wx.Button(self, label='Search')
search.Bind(wx.EVT_BUTTON, self.on_search)
self.main_sizer.Add(search, 0, wx.ALL | wx.CENTER, 5)


self.SetSizer(self.main_sizer)
```

At the end, you set the sizer to the `main_sizer`. Note that not all the filters that are in NASA's API are implemented in this code. For example, I didn't add `media_type` because this application will be hard-coded to only look for images. However if you wanted audio or video, you could update this application for that. I also didn't include the `year_start` and `year_end` filters. Feel free to add those if you wish.

Now let's move on and create the `ui_helper()` method:

```
def ui_helper(self, label, textctrl):
    sizer = wx.BoxSizer()
    lbl = wx.StaticText(self, label=label, size=(150, -1))
    sizer.Add(lbl, 0, wx.ALL, 5)
    sizer.Add(textctrl, 1, wx.ALL | wx.EXPAND, 5)
    self.main_sizer.Add(sizer, 0, wx.EXPAND)
```

The `ui_helper()` takes in label text and the text control widget. It then creates a `wx.BoxSizer` and a `wx.StaticText`. The `wx.StaticText` is added to the sizer, as is the passed-in text control widget.

Finally the new sizer is added to the `main_sizer` and then you're done. This is a nice way to reduce repeated code.

The last item to create in this class is `on_search()`:

```
def on_search(self, event):
    query = {'q': self.free_text.GetValue(),
             'media_type': 'image',
             'center': self.nasa_center.GetValue(),
             'description': self.description.GetValue(),
             'description_508': self.description_508.GetValue(),
             'keywords': self.keywords.GetValue(),
             'location': self.location.GetValue(),
             'nasa_id': self.nasa_id.GetValue(),
             'photographer': self.photographer.GetValue(),
             'secondary_creator': self.secondary_creator.GetValue(),
             'title': self.title.GetValue()}
    pub.sendMessage('update_ui')
    pub.sendMessage('search_results', query=query)
```

When the user presses the **Search** button, this event handler gets called. It creates the search query based on what the user has entered into each of the fields. Then the handler will send out two messages using `pubsub`. The first message will update the UI so that the advanced search is hidden and the search results are shown. The second message will actually execute the search against NASA's API.

Here is what the advanced search page looks like:

Fig. 9-6: NASA Image Search with Advanced Search Page

Now let's update the download dialog.

The download_dialog.py Script

The download dialog has a couple of minimal changes to it. Basically you need to add an import of Python's os module and then update the save() function.

Add the following lines to the beginning of the function:

```python
def save(self, path):
    _, ext = os.path.splitext(path)
    if ext.lower() != '.jpg':
        path = f'{path}.jpg'
```

This code was added to account for the case where the user does not specify the extension of the image in the saved file name.

Wrapping Up

This chapter covered a lot of fun new information. You learned one approach for working with an open API that doesn't have a Python wrapper already around it. You discovered the importance of reading the API documentation and then added a user interface to that API. Then you learned how to parse JSON and download images from the Internet.

While it is not covered here, Python has a `json` module that you could use as well.

Here are some ideas for enhancing this application:

- Caching search results
- Downloading thumbnails in the background
- Downloading links in the background

You could use threads to download the thumbnails and the larger images as well as for doing the web requests in general. This would improve the performance of your application. You may have noticed that the application became slightly unresponsive, depending on your Internet connectivity. This is because when it is doing a web request or downloading a file, it blocks the UI's main loop. You should give threads a try if you find that sort of thing bothersome.

You will learn about using threads in your application in the next chapter!

Chapter 10 - Creating a PDF Merger / Splitter Utility

The Portable Document Format (PDF) is a well-known format popularized by Adobe. It purports to create a document that should render the same across platforms.

Python has several libraries that you can use to work with PDFs:

- ReportLab - Creating PDFs
- PyPDF2 - Manipulating preexisting PDFs
- pdfrw - Also for manipulating preexisting PDFs, but also works with ReportLab
- PDFMiner - Extracts text from PDFs

There are several more Python PDF-related packages, but those four are probably the most well known. One common task of working with PDFs is the need for merging or concatenating multiple PDFs into one PDF. Another common task is taking a PDF and splitting out one or more of its pages into a new PDF.

You will be creating a graphical user interface that does both of these tasks using **PyPDF2**.

Installing PyPDF2

The PyPDF2 package can be installed using pip:

```
pip install pypdf2
```

This package is pretty small, so the installation should be quite quick.

Now that PyPDF2 is installed, you can design your UI!

Designing the Interface

This application is basically two programs contained in one window. You need a way of displaying a merging application and a splitting application. Having an easy way to switch between the two would be nice. You can design your own panel swapping code or you can use one of wxPython's many notebook widgets.

To keep things simpler, let's use a wx.Notebook for this application.

Here is a mockup of the merging tab:

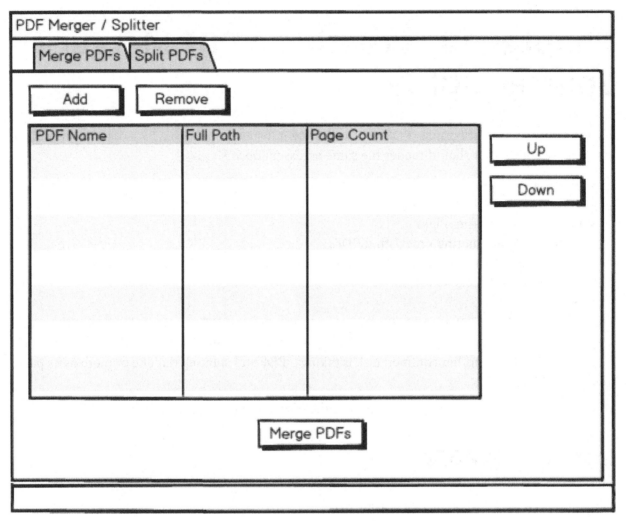

Fig. 10-1: The PDF Merger Mockup

You will be loading up PDF files into a list control type widget. You also want a way to re-order the PDFs. And you need a way to remove items from the list. This mockup shows all the pieces you need to accomplish those goals.

Next is a mockup of the splitting tab:

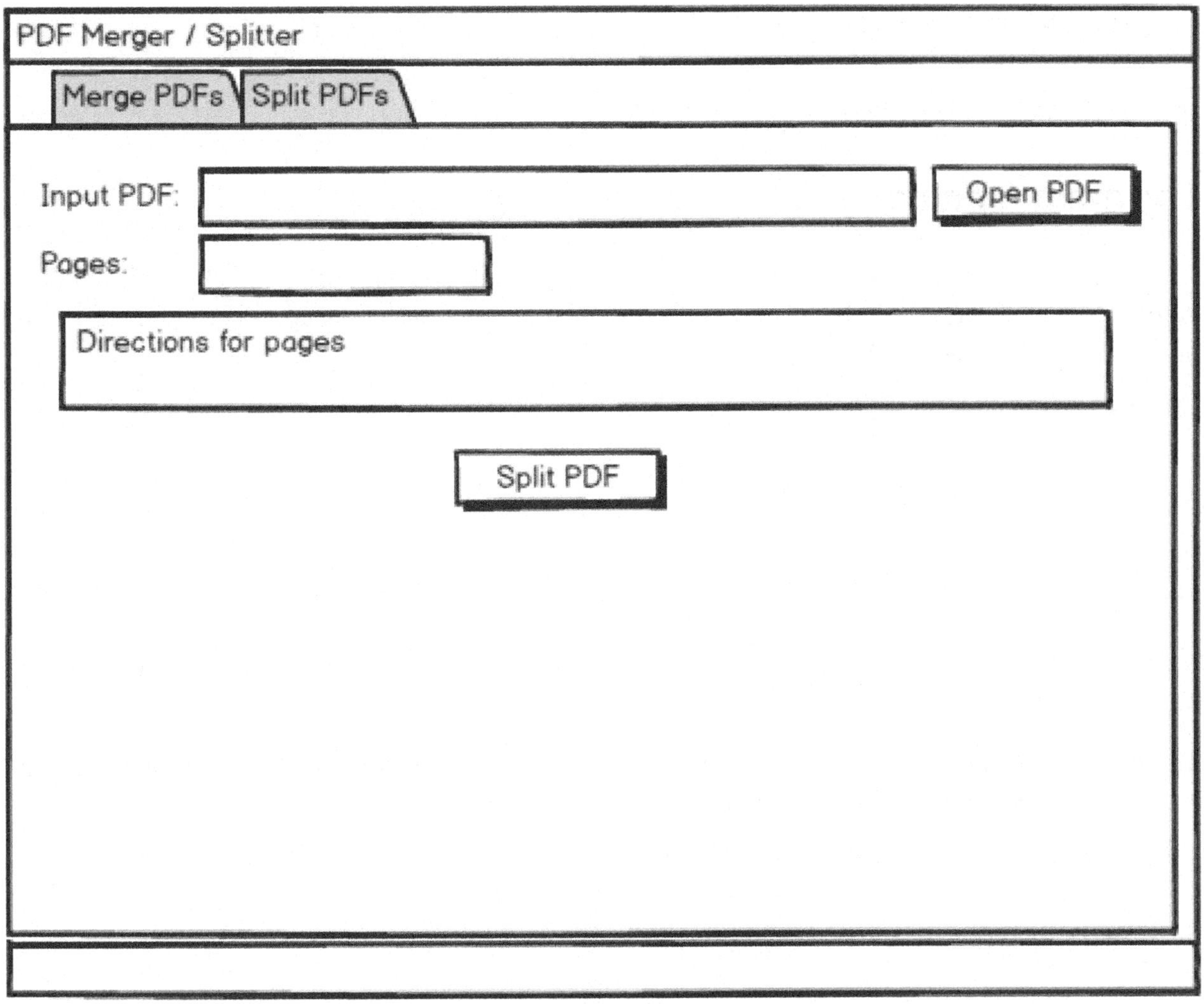

Fig. 10-2: The PDF Splitter Mockup

Basically what you want is a tool that shows what the input PDF is and what page(s) are to be split off. The user interface for this is pretty plain, but it should work for your needs.

Now let's create this application!

Creating the Application

Let's put some thought into your code's organization. Each tab should probably be in its own module. You should also have a main entry point to run your application. That means you can reasonably have at least three Python files.

Here is what you will be creating:

- The main module
- The merge panel module

- The split panel module

Let's start with the main module!

The main Module

As the main entry point of your application, the **main** module has a lot of responsibility. It will hold your other panels and could be a hub between the panels should they need to communicate. Most of the time, you would use pubsub for that though.

Let's go ahead and write your first version of the code:

```python
# main.py

import wx

from merge_panel import MergePanel
from split_panel import SplitPanel
```

The imports for the **main** module are nice and short. All you need is wx, the MergePanel and the SplitPanel. The latter two are ones that you will write soon.

Let's go ahead and write the MainPanel code though:

```python
class MainPanel(wx.Panel):

    def __init__(self, parent):
        super().__init__(parent)

        main_sizer = wx.BoxSizer(wx.VERTICAL)
        notebook = wx.Notebook(self)
        merge_tab = MergePanel(notebook)
        notebook.AddPage(merge_tab, 'Merge PDFs')
        split_tab = SplitPanel(notebook)
        notebook.AddPage(split_tab, 'Split PDFs')
        main_sizer.Add(notebook, 1, wx.ALL | wx.EXPAND, 5)
        self.SetSizer(main_sizer)
```

The MainPanel is where all the action is. Here you instantiate a wx.Notebook and add the MergePanel and the SplitPanel to it. Then you add the notebook to the sizer and you're done!

Here's the frame code that you will need to add:

```
class MainFrame(wx.Frame):

    def __init__(self):
        super().__init__(None, title='PDF Merger / Splitter',
                          size=(800, 600))
        self.panel = MainPanel(self)
        self.Show()

if __name__ == '__main__':
    app = wx.App(False)
    frame = MainFrame()
    app.MainLoop()
```

As usual, you construct your frame, add a panel and show it to the user. You also set the size of the frame. You might want to experiment with the initial size as it may be too big or too small for your setup.

Now let's move on and learn how to merge PDFs!

The merge_panel Module

The **merge_panel** module contains all the code you need for creating a user interface around merging PDF files. The user interface for merging is a bit more involved than it is for splitting.

Let's get started!

```
# merge_panel.py

import os
import glob
import wx

from ObjectListView import ObjectListView, ColumnDefn
from PyPDF2 import PdfFileReader, PdfFileWriter


wildcard = "PDFs (*.pdf)|*.pdf"
```

Here you need to import Python's os module for some path-related activities and the glob module for searching duty. You will also need ObjectListView for displaying PDF information and PyPDF2 for merging the PDFs together.

The last item here is the wildcard which is used when adding files to be merged as well as when you save the merged file.

To make the UI more friendly, you should add drag-and-drop support:

```python
class DropTarget(wx.FileDropTarget):

    def __init__(self, window):
        super().__init__()
        self.window = window

    def OnDropFiles(self, x, y, filenames):
        self.window.update_on_drop(filenames)
        return True
```

You may recognize this code from the Archiver chapter. In fact, it's pretty much unchanged. You still need to subclass `wx.FileDropTarget` and pass it the widget that you want to add drag-and-drop support to. You also need to override `OnDropFile()` to have it call a method using the widget you passed in. For this example, you are passing in the panel object itself.

You will also need to create a class for holding information about the PDFs. This class will be used by your `ObjectListView` widget.

Here it is:

```python
class Pdf:

    def __init__(self, pdf_path):
        self.full_path = pdf_path
        self.filename = os.path.basename(pdf_path)
        try:
            with open(pdf_path, 'rb') as f:
                pdf = PdfFileReader(f)
                number_of_pages = pdf.getNumPages()
        except:
            number_of_pages = 0
        self.number_of_pages = str(number_of_pages)
```

The `Pdf` class takes in the full path to the PDF that you want to merge and stores that path in `full_path`. It also extracts the `filename` from the path. Lastly, it attempts to get the number of pages contained within the PDF by opening the PDF using `PdfFileReader` and calling its `getNumPages()` method. Should that fail, you set the number of pages to zero.

Now you are ready to create the `MergePanel`:

```
class MergePanel(wx.Panel):

    def __init__(self, parent):
        super().__init__(parent)
        self.pdfs = []
        drop_target = DropTarget(self)
        self.SetDropTarget(drop_target)
        self.main_sizer = wx.BoxSizer(wx.VERTICAL)
        self.create_ui()
```

The __init__() is nice and short this time around. You set up a list of pdfs for holding the PDF objects to be merged. You also instantiate and add the DropTarget to the panel. Then you create the main_sizer and call create_ui(), which will add all the widgets you need.

Speaking of which, let's add create_ui() next:

```
def create_ui(self):
    btn_sizer = wx.BoxSizer()
    add_btn = wx.Button(self, label='Add')
    add_btn.Bind(wx.EVT_BUTTON, self.on_add_file)
    btn_sizer.Add(add_btn, 0, wx.ALL, 5)
    remove_btn = wx.Button(self, label='Remove')
    remove_btn.Bind(wx.EVT_BUTTON, self.on_remove)
    btn_sizer.Add(remove_btn, 0, wx.ALL, 5)
    self.main_sizer.Add(btn_sizer)
```

The create_ui() method is a bit long. The code will be broken up to make it easier to digest. The code above will add two buttons:

- An Add file button
- A Remove file button

These buttons go inside of a horizontally-oriented sizer along the top of the merge panel. You also bind each of these buttons to their own event handlers.

Now let's add the widget for displaying PDFs to be merged:

```
move_btn_sizer = wx.BoxSizer(wx.VERTICAL)
row_sizer = wx.BoxSizer()

self.pdf_olv = ObjectListView(
    self, style=wx.LC_REPORT | wx.SUNKEN_BORDER)
self.pdf_olv.SetEmptyListMsg("No PDFs Loaded")
self.update_pdfs()
row_sizer.Add(self.pdf_olv, 1, wx.ALL | wx.EXPAND)
```

Here you add the `ObjectListView` widget to the `row_sizer` and call `update_pdfs()` to update it so that it has column labels.

You need to add support for reordering the PDFs in the `ObjectListView` widget, so let's add that next:

```
move_up_btn = wx.Button(self, label='Up')
move_up_btn.Bind(wx.EVT_BUTTON, self.on_move)
move_btn_sizer.Add(move_up_btn, 0, wx.ALL, 5)
move_down_btn = wx.Button(self, label='Down')
move_down_btn.Bind(wx.EVT_BUTTON, self.on_move)
move_btn_sizer.Add(move_down_btn, 0, wx.ALL, 5)
row_sizer.Add(move_btn_sizer)
self.main_sizer.Add(row_sizer, 1, wx.ALL | wx.EXPAND, 5)
```

Here you add two more buttons. One for moving items up and one for moving items down. These two buttons are added to a vertically-oriented sizer, `move_btn_sizer`, which in turn is added to the `row_sizer`. Finally the `row_sizer` is added to the `main_sizer`.

Here's the last few lines of the __init():

```
merge_pdfs = wx.Button(self, label='Merge PDFs')
merge_pdfs.Bind(wx.EVT_BUTTON, self.on_merge)
self.main_sizer.Add(merge_pdfs, 0, wx.ALL | wx.CENTER, 5)

self.SetSizer(self.main_sizer)
```

These last four lines add the merge button and get it hooked up to an event handler. It also sets the panel's sizer to the `main_sizer`.

Now let's create `add_pdf()`:

```python
def add_pdf(self, path):
    self.pdfs.append(Pdf(path))
```

You will be calling this method with a path to a PDF that you wish to merge with another PDF. This method will create an instance of the Pdf class and append it to the pdfs list.

Now you're ready to create load_pdfs():

```python
def load_pdfs(self, path):
    pdf_paths = glob.glob(path + '/*.pdf')
    for path in pdf_paths:
        self.add_pdf(path)
    self.update_pdfs()
```

This method takes in a folder rather than a file. It then uses glob to find all the PDFs in that folder. You will loop over the list of files that glob returns and use add_pdf() to add them to the pdfs list. Then you call update_pdfs() which will update the UI with the newly added PDF files.

Let's find out what happens when you press the merge button:

```python
def on_merge(self, event):
    """
    TODO - Move this into a thread
    """
    objects = self.pdf_olv.GetObjects()
    if len(objects) < 2:
        with wx.MessageDialog(
            None,
            message='You need 2 or more files to merge!',
            caption='Error',
            style= wx.ICON_INFORMATION) as dlg:
            dlg.ShowModal()
        return
    with wx.FileDialog(
        self, message="Choose a file",
        defaultDir='~',
        defaultFile="",
        wildcard=wildcard,
        style=wx.FD_SAVE | wx.FD_CHANGE_DIR
        ) as dlg:
        if dlg.ShowModal() == wx.ID_OK:
            path = dlg.GetPath()
    if path:
        _, ext = os.path.splitext(path)
```

```
    if '.pdf' not in ext.lower():
        path = f'{path}.pdf'
self.merge(path)
```

The `on_merge()` method is the event handler that is called by your merge button. The docstring contains a TODO message to remind you to move the merging code to a thread. Technically the code you will be moving is actually in the `merge()` function, but as long as you have some kind of reminder, it doesn't matter all that much.

Anyway, you use `GetObjects()` to get all the PDFs in the `ObjectListView` widget. Then you check to make sure that there are at least two PDF files. If not, you will let the user know that they need to add more PDFs! Otherwise you will open up a `wx.FileDialog` and have the user choose the name and location for the merged PDF.

Finally you check if the user added the `.pdf` extension and add it if they did not. Then you call `merge()`.

The `merge()` method is conveniently the next method you should create:

```
def merge(self, output_path):
    pdf_writer = PdfFileWriter()

    objects = self.pdf_olv.GetObjects()

    for obj in objects:
        pdf_reader = PdfFileReader(obj.full_path)
        for page in range(pdf_reader.getNumPages()):
            pdf_writer.addPage(pdf_reader.getPage(page))

    with open(output_path, 'wb') as fh:
        pdf_writer.write(fh)

    with wx.MessageDialog(None, message='Save completed!',
                          caption='Save Finished',
                          style= wx.ICON_INFORMATION) as dlg:
        dlg.ShowModal()
```

Here you create a `PdfFileWriter()` object for writing out the merged PDF. Then you get the list of objects from the `ObjectListView` widget rather than the `pdfs` list. This is because you can reorder the UI so the list may not be in the correct order. The next step is to loop over each of the objects and get its full path out. You will open the path using `PdfFileReader` and loop over all of its pages, adding each page to the `pdf_writer`.

Once all the PDFs and all their respective pages are added to the `pdf_writer`, you can write out the merged PDF to disk. Then you open up a `wx.MessageDialog` that lets the user know that the PDFs have merged.

While this is happening, you may notice that your UI is frozen. That is because it can take a while to read all those pages into memory and then write them out. This is the reason why this part of your code should be done in a thread. You will be learning about that refactor later on in this chapter.

Now let's create `on_add_file()`:

```python
def on_add_file(self, event):
    paths = None
    with wx.FileDialog(
        self, message="Choose a file",
        defaultDir='~',
        defaultFile="",
        wildcard=wildcard,
        style=wx.FD_OPEN | wx.FD_MULTIPLE
        ) as dlg:
        if dlg.ShowModal() == wx.ID_OK:
            paths = dlg.GetPaths()
    if paths:
        for path in paths:
            self.add_pdf(path)
        self.update_pdfs()
```

This code will open up a `wx.FileDialog` and let the user choose one or more files. Then it returns them as a list of paths. You can then loop over those paths and use `add_path()` to add them to the `pdfs` list.

Now let's find out how to reorder the items in the `ObjectListView` widget:

```python
def on_move(self, event):
    btn = event.GetEventObject()
    label = btn.GetLabel()
    current_selection = self.pdf_olv.GetSelectedObject()
    data = self.pdf_olv.GetObjects()
    if current_selection:
        index = data.index(current_selection)
        new_index = self.get_new_index(
            label.lower(), index, data)
        data.insert(new_index, data.pop(index))
        self.pdfs = data
        self.update_pdfs()
        self.pdf_olv.Select(new_index)
```

Both the up and down buttons are bound to the `on_move()` event handler. You can get access to which button called this handler via `event.GetEventObject()`, which will return the button object.

Then you can get the button's label. Next you need to get the `current_selection` and a list of the objects, which is assigned to `data`. Now you can use the `index` attribute of the list object to find the index of the `current_selection`.

Once you have that information, you pass the button label, the `index` and the `data` list to `get_new_-index()` to calculate which direction the item should go. Once you have the `new_index`, you can `insert` it and remove the old index using the `pop()` method. Then reset the `pdfs` list to the `data` list so they match. The last two steps are to update the widget and re-select the item that you moved.

Let's take a look at how to get that new index now:

```python
def get_new_index(self, direction, index, data):
    if direction == 'up':
        if index > 0:
            new_index = index - 1
        else:
            new_index = len(data)-1
    else:
        if index < len(data) - 1:
            new_index = index + 1
        else:
            new_index = 0
    return new_index
```

Here you use the button label, `direction`, to determine which way to move the item. If it's "up", then you check if the index is greater than zero and subtract one. If it is zero, then you take the entire length of the list and subtract one, which should move the item back to the other end of the list.

If you user hit the "down" button, then you check to see if the `index` is less than the length of the `data` minus one. In that case, you add one to it. Otherwise you set the `new_index` to zero.

The code is a bit confusing to look at, so feel free to add some `print` functions in there and then run the code to see how it works.

The next new thing to learn is how to remove an item:

```python
def on_remove(self, event):
    current_selection = self.pdf_olv.GetSelectedObject()
    if current_selection:
        index = self.pdfs.index(current_selection)
        self.pdfs.pop(index)
        self.pdf_olv.RemoveObject(current_selection)
```

This method will get the `current_selection`, `pop()` it from the `pdfs` list and then use the `RemoveObject()` method to remove it from the `ObjectListView` widget.

Now let's take a look at the code that is called when you drag-and-drop items onto your application:

```
def update_on_drop(self, paths):
    for path in paths:
        _, ext = os.path.splitext(path)
        if os.path.isdir(path):
            self.load_pdfs(path)
        elif os.path.isfile(path) and ext.lower() == '.pdf':
            self.add_pdf(path)
            self.update_pdfs()
```

In this case, you loop over the paths and check to see if the path is a directory or a file. They could also be a link, but you will ignore those. If the path is a directory, then you call load_pdfs() with it. Otherwise you check to see if the file has an extension of .pdf and if it does, you call add_pdf() with it.

The last method to create is update_pdfs():

```
def update_pdfs(self):
    self.pdf_olv.SetColumns([
        ColumnDefn("PDF Name", "left", 200, "filename"),
        ColumnDefn("Full Path", "left", 250, "full_path"),
        ColumnDefn("Page Count", "left", 100, "number_of_pages")
    ])
    self.pdf_olv.SetObjects(self.pdfs)
```

This method adds or resets the column names and widths. It also adds the pdf list via SetObjects().

Here is what the merge panel looks like:

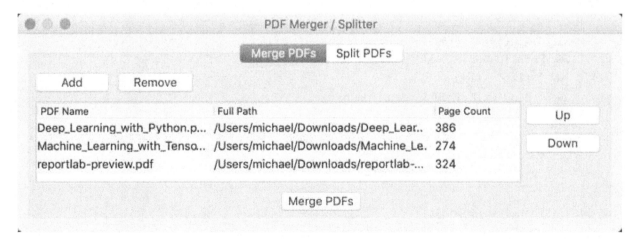

Fig. 10-3: The PDF Merger Tab

Now you are ready to create the split_panel!

The split_panel Module

The **split_panel** module is a bit simpler than the **merge_panel** was. You really only need a couple of text controls, some labels and a button.

Let's see how all of that ends up laying out:

```python
# split_panel.py

import os
import string
import wx

from PyPDF2 import PdfFileReader, PdfFileWriter

wildcard = "PDFs (*.pdf)|*.pdf"
```

Here you import Python's os and string modules. You will also be needing PyPDF2 again and the wildcard variable will be useful for opening and saving PDFs.

You will also need the CharValidator class from the calculator chapter.

It is reproduced for you again here:

```python
class CharValidator(wx.PyValidator):
    '''
    Validates data as it is entered into the text controls.
    '''

    def __init__(self, flag):
        wx.PyValidator.__init__(self)
        self.flag = flag
        self.Bind(wx.EVT_CHAR, self.OnChar)

    def Clone(self):
        '''Required Validator method'''
        return CharValidator(self.flag)

    def Validate(self, win):
        return True

    def TransferToWindow(self):
        return True
```

```python
    def TransferFromWindow(self):
        return True

    def OnChar(self, event):
        keycode = int(event.GetKeyCode())
        if keycode < 256:
            key = chr(keycode)
            if self.flag == 'no-alpha' and key in string.ascii_letters:
                return
            if self.flag == 'no-digit' and key in string.digits:
                return
        event.Skip()
```

The CharValidator class is useful for validating that the user is not entering any letters into a text control. You will be using it for splitting options, which will allow the user to choose which pages they want to split out of the input PDF.

But before we get to that, let's create the SplitPanel:

```python
class SplitPanel(wx.Panel):

    def __init__(self, parent):
        super().__init__(parent)
        font = wx.Font(12, wx.SWISS, wx.NORMAL, wx.NORMAL)
        main_sizer = wx.BoxSizer(wx.VERTICAL)
```

The first few lines of the __init__() create a wx.Font instance and the main_sizer.

Here's the next few lines of the __init__():

```python
row_sizer = wx.BoxSizer()
lbl = wx.StaticText(self, label='Input PDF:')
lbl.SetFont(font)
row_sizer.Add(lbl, 0, wx.ALL | wx.CENTER, 5)
self.pdf_path = wx.TextCtrl(self, style=wx.TE_READONLY)
row_sizer.Add(self.pdf_path, 1, wx.EXPAND | wx.ALL, 5)
pdf_btn = wx.Button(self, label='Open PDF')
pdf_btn.Bind(wx.EVT_BUTTON, self.on_choose)
row_sizer.Add(pdf_btn, 0, wx.ALL, 5)
main_sizer.Add(row_sizer, 0, wx.EXPAND)
```

This bit of code adds a row of widgets that will be contained inside of row_sizer. Here you have a nice label, a text control for holding the input PDF path and the "Open PDF" button. After adding each of these to the row_sizer, you will then add that sizer to the main_sizer.

Now let's add a second row of widgets:

```
# split PDF
row_sizer = wx.BoxSizer()
page_lbl = wx.StaticText(self, label='Pages:')
page_lbl.SetFont(font)
row_sizer.Add(page_lbl, 0, wx.ALL | wx.CENTER, 5)
self.pdf_split_options = wx.TextCtrl(
    self, validator=CharValidator('no-alpha'))
row_sizer.Add(self.pdf_split_options, 0, wx.ALL, 5)
main_sizer.Add(row_sizer)
```

You create a new `row_sizer` here and add another label and a text control. The text control holds the `pdf_split_options` that the user can use. This control uses the `CharValidator` to prevent the user from using letters inside of page numbers.

You also need to add some directions for how to use `pdf_split_options`:

```
msg = 'Type page numbers and/or page ranges separated by commas.' \
    ' For example: 1, 3 or 4-10. Note you cannot use both commas ' \
    'and dashes.'
directions_txt = wx.TextCtrl(
    self, value=msg,
    style=wx.TE_MULTILINE | wx.NO_BORDER)
directions_txt.SetFont(font)
directions_txt.Disable()
main_sizer.Add(directions_txt, 0, wx.ALL | wx.EXPAND, 5)
```

These lines of code create a multi-line text control that has no border. It contains the directions of use for the `pdf_split_options` text control and appears beneath that widget as well. You also `Disable()` the `directions_txt` to prevent the user from changing the directions.

There are four more lines to add to the __init__():

```
split_btn = wx.Button(self, label='Split PDF')
split_btn.Bind(wx.EVT_BUTTON, self.on_split)
main_sizer.Add(split_btn, 0, wx.ALL | wx.CENTER, 5)
self.SetSizer(main_sizer)
```

These last few lines will add the "Split PDF" button, bind it to an event handler and add the button to a sizer. Then you set the sizer for the panel.

Now that you have the UI itself written, you need to start writing the other methods:

```
def on_choose(self, event):
    path = None
    with wx.FileDialog(
        self, message="Choose a file",
        defaultDir='~',
        defaultFile="",
        wildcard=wildcard,
        style=wx.FD_OPEN | wx.FD_CHANGE_DIR
        ) as dlg:
        if dlg.ShowModal() == wx.ID_OK:
            path = dlg.GetPath()
    if path:
        self.pdf_path.SetValue(path)
```

The on_choose() event handler is called when the user presses the "Open PDF" button. It will load a wx.FileDialog and if the user chooses a PDF, it will set the pdf_path text control with that user's choice.

Now let's get to the meat of the code:

```
def on_split(self, event):
    output_path = None
    input_pdf = self.pdf_path.GetValue()
    split_options = self.pdf_split_options.GetValue()
    if not input_pdf:
        message='You must choose an input PDF!'
        self.show_message(message)
        return
```

When the user presses the "Split PDF" button, on_split() is called. You will start off by checking if the user has chosen a PDF to split at all. If they haven't, tell them to do so using the show_message() method and return.

Next you need to check to see if the PDF path that the user chose still exists:

```
if not os.path.exists(input_pdf):
    message = f'Input PDF {input_pdf} does not exist!'
    self.show_message(message)
    return
```

If the PDF does not exist, let the user know of the error and don't do anything.

Now you need to check if the user put anything into split_options:

```
if not split_options:
    message = 'You need to choose what page(s) to split off'
    self.show_message(message)
    return
```

If the user didn't set the `split_options` then your application won't know what pages to split off. So tell the user.

The next check is to make sure the user does not have both commas and dashes:

```
if ',' in split_options and '-' in split_options:
    message = 'You cannot have both commas and dashes in options'
    self.show_message(message)
    return
```

You could theoretically support both commas and dashes, but that will make the code more complex. If you want to add that, feel free. For now, it is not supported.

Another item to check is if there is more than one dash:

```
if split_options.count('-') > 1:
    message = 'You can only use one dash'
    self.show_message(message)
    return
```

Users are tricky and it is easy to bump a button twice, so make sure to let the user know that this is not allowed.

The user could also enter a single negative number:

```
if '-' in split_options:
    page_begin, page_end = split_options.split('-')
    if not page_begin or not page_end:
        message = 'Need both a beginning and ending page'
        self.show_message(message)
        return
```

In that case, you can check to make sure it `splits` correctly or you can try to figure out where in the string the negative number is. In this case, you use the `split` method to figure it out.

The last check is to make sure that the user has entered a number and not just a dash or comma:

```
if not any(char.isdigit() for char in split_options):
    message = 'You need to enter a page number to split off'
    self.show_message(message)
    return
```

You can use Python's any builtin for this. You loop over all the characters in the string and ask them if they are a digit. If they aren't, then you show a message to the user.

Now you are ready to create the split PDF:

```
with wx.FileDialog(
    self, message="Choose a file",
    defaultDir='~',
    defaultFile="",
    wildcard=wildcard,
    style=wx.FD_SAVE | wx.FD_CHANGE_DIR
    ) as dlg:
    if dlg.ShowModal() == wx.ID_OK:
        output_path = dlg.GetPath()
```

This bit of code will open the save version of the wx.FileDialog and let the user pick a name and location to save the split PDF.

The last piece of code for this function is below:

```
if output_path:
    _, ext = os.path.splitext(output_path)
    if '.pdf' not in ext.lower():
        output_path = f'{output_path}.pdf'
    split_options = split_options.strip()
    self.split(input_pdf, output_path, split_options)
```

Once you have the output_path, you will check to make sure the user added the .pdf extension. If they didn't, then you will add it for them. Then you will strip off any leading or ending white space in split_options and call split().

Now let's create the code used to actually split a PDF:

```python
def split(self, input_pdf, output_path, split_options):
    pdf = PdfFileReader(input_pdf)
    pdf_writer = PdfFileWriter()
    if ',' in split_options:
        pages = [page for page in split_options.split(',')
                 if page]
        for page in pages:
            pdf_writer.addPage(pdf.getPage(int(page)))
    elif '-' in split_options:
        page_begin, page_end = split_options.split('-')
        page_begin = int(page_begin)
        page_end = int(page_end)
        page_begin = self.get_actual_beginning_page(page_begin)

        for page in range(page_begin, page_end):
            pdf_writer.addPage(pdf.getPage(page))
    else:
        # User only wants a single page
        page_begin = int(split_options)
        page_begin = self.get_actual_beginning_page(page_begin)
        pdf_writer.addPage(pdf.getPage(page_begin))
```

Here you create a `PdfFileReader` object called `pdf` and a `PdfFileWriter` object called `pdf_writer`. Then you check `split_options` to see if the user used commas or dashes. If the user went with a comma separated list, then you loop over the pages and add them to the writer.

If the user used dashes, then you need to get the beginning page and the ending page. Then you call the `get_actual_beginning_page()` method to do a bit of math because page one when using PyPDF is actually page zero. Once you have the normalized numbers figured out, you can loop over the range of pages using Python's `range` function and add the pages to the writer object.

The `else` statement is only used when the user enters a single page number that they want to split off. For example, they might just want page 2 out of a 20 page document.

The last step is to write the new PDF to disk:

```python
# Write PDF to disk
with open(output_path, 'wb') as out:
    pdf_writer.write(out)

# Let user know that PDF is split
message = f'PDF split successfully to {output_path}'
self.show_message(message, caption='Split Finished',
                            style=wx.ICON_INFORMATION)
```

This code will create a new file using the path the user provided. Then it will write out the pages that were added to `pdf_writer` and display a dialog to the user letting them know that they now have a new PDF.

Let's take a quick look at the logic you need to add to the `get_actual_beginning_page()` method:

```python
def get_actual_beginning_page(self, page_begin):
    if page_begin < 0 or page_begin == 1:
        page_begin = 0
    if page_begin > 1:
        # Take off by one error into account
        page_begin -= 1
    return page_begin
```

Here you take in the beginning page and check if the page number is zero, one or greater than one. Then you do a bit of math to avoid off-by-one errors and return the actual beginning page number.

Now let's create `show_message()`:

```python
def show_message(self, message, caption='Error', style=wx.ICON_ERROR):
    with wx.MessageDialog(None, message=message,
                          caption=caption,
                          style=style) as dlg:
        dlg.ShowModal()
```

This is a helpful function for wrapping the creation and destruction of a `wx.MessageDialog`. It accepts the following arguments:

- `message`
- `caption`
- `style` flag

Then it uses Python's `with` statement to create an instance of the dialog and show it to the user.

Here is what the split panel looks like when you are finished coding:

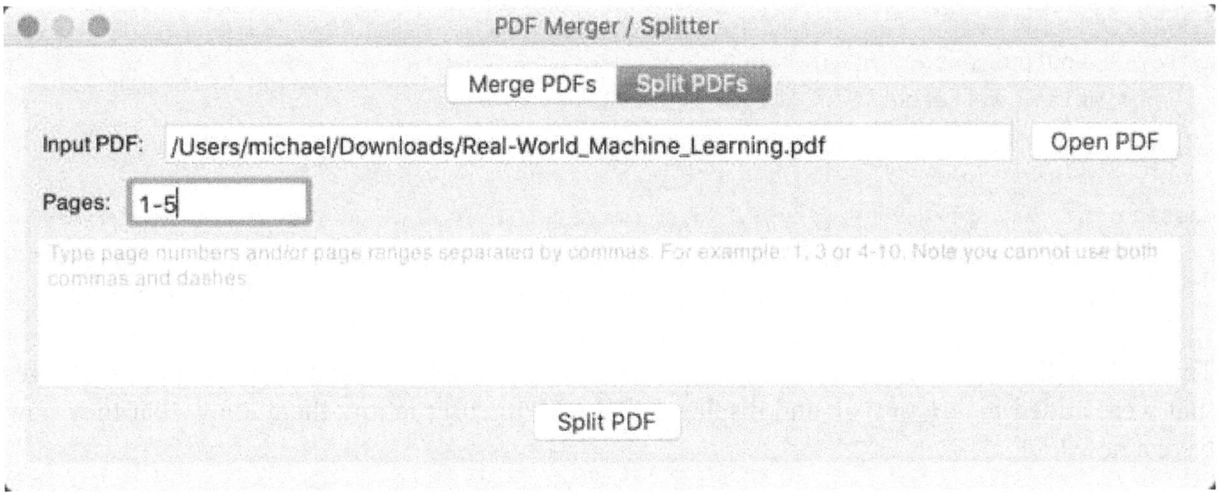

Fig. 10-4: The PDF Splitter Tab

Now you are ready to learn about threads and wxPython!

Using Threads in wxPython

Every GUI toolkit handles threads differently. The wxPython GUI toolkit has three thread-safe methods that you should use if you want to use threads:

- `wx.CallAfter`
- `wx.CallLater`
- `wx.PostEvent`

You can use these methods to post information from the thread back to wxPython.

Let's update the **merge_panel** so that it uses threads!

Enhancing PDF Merging with Threads

Python comes with several concurrency-related modules. You will be using the `threading` module here. Take the original code and copy it into a new folder called **version_2_threaded** or refer to the pre-made folder in the Github repository for this chapter.

Let's start by updating the imports in **merge_panel**:

```
# merge_panel.py

import os
import glob
import wx

from ObjectListView import ObjectListView, ColumnDefn
from pubsub import pub
from PyPDF2 import PdfFileReader, PdfFileWriter
from threading import Thread

wildcard = "PDFs (*.pdf)|*.pdf"
```

The only differences here are this import line: `from threading import Thread` and the addition of `pubsub`. That gives us ability to subclass `Thread`.

Let's do that next:

```
class MergeThread(Thread):

    def __init__(self, objects, output_path):
        super().__init__()
        self.objects = objects
        self.output_path = output_path
        self.start()
```

The `MergeThread` class will take in the list of `objects` from the `ObjectListView` widget as well as the `output_path`. At the end of the `__init__()` you tell the thread to `start()`, which actually causes the `run()` method to execute.

Let's override that:

```
def run(self):
    pdf_writer = PdfFileWriter()
    page_count = 1

    for obj in self.objects:
        pdf_reader = PdfFileReader(obj.full_path)
        for page in range(pdf_reader.getNumPages()):
            pdf_writer.addPage(pdf_reader.getPage(page))
            wx.CallAfter(pub.sendMessage, 'update',
                         msg=page_count)
            page_count += 1
```

```
    # All pages are added, so write it to disk
    with open(self.output_path, 'wb') as fh:
        pdf_writer.write(fh)


    wx.CallAfter(pub.sendMessage, 'close')
```

Here you create a `PdfFileWriter` class and then loop over the various PDFs, extracting their pages and adding them to the writer object as you did before. After a page is added, you use `wx.CallAfter` to send a message using `pubsub` back to the GUI thread. In this message, you send along the current page count of added pages. This will update a dialog that has a progress bar on it.

After the file is finished writing out, you send another message via `pubsub` to tell the progress dialog to close.

Let's create a progress widget:

```
class MergeGauge(wx.Gauge):

    def __init__(self, parent, range):
        super().__init__(parent, range=range)

        pub.subscribe(self.update_progress, "update")

    def update_progress(self, msg):
        self.SetValue(msg)
```

To create a progress widget, you can use wxPython's `wx.Gauge`. In the code above, you subclass that widget and subscribe it to the update message. Whenever it receives an update, it will change the gauge's value accordingly.

You will need to put this gauge into a dialog, so let's create that next:

```
class MergeProgressDialog(wx.Dialog):

    def __init__(self, objects, path):
        super().__init__(None, title='Merging Progress')
        pub.subscribe(self.close, "close")

        sizer = wx.BoxSizer(wx.VERTICAL)
        lbl = wx.StaticText(self, label='Merging PDFS')
        sizer.Add(lbl, 0, wx.ALL | wx.CENTER, 5)
        total_page_count = sum([int(obj.number_of_pages)
                                for obj in objects])
        gauge = MergeGauge(self, total_page_count)
```

```
        sizer.Add(gauge, 0, wx.ALL | wx.EXPAND, 5)

        MergeThread(objects, output_path=path)
        self.SetSizer(sizer)

    def close(self):
        self.Close()
```

The `MergeProgressDialog` subscribes the dialog to the "close" message. It also adds a label and the gauge / progress bar to itself. Then it starts the `MergeThread`. When the "close" message gets emitted, the `close()` method is called and the dialog will be closed.

The other change you will need to make is in the `MergePanel` class, specifically the `merge()` method:

```
def merge(self, output_path, objects):
    with MergeProgressDialog(objects, output_path) as dlg:
        dlg.ShowModal()

    with wx.MessageDialog(None, message='Save completed!',
                          caption='Save Finished',
                          style= wx.ICON_INFORMATION) as dlg:
        dlg.ShowModal()
```

Here you update the method to accept the `objects` parameter and create the `MergeProgressDialog` with that and the `output_path`. Note that you will need to change `on_merge()` to pass in the `objects` list in addition to the `path` to make this work. Once the merge is finished, the dialog will automatically close and destroy itself. Then you will create the same `wx.MessageDialog` as before and show that to the user to let them know the merged PDF is ready.

You can use the code here to update the **split_panel** to use threads too if you would like to. This doesn't have to happen necessarily unless you think you will be splitting off dozens or hundreds of pages. Most of the time, it should be quick enough that the user wouldn't notice or care much when splitting the PDF.

Wrapping Up

Splitting and merging PDFs can be done using **PyPDF2**. You could also use **pdfrw** if you wanted to. There are plenty of ways to improve this application as well.

Here are a few examples:

- Put splitting into a thread
- Add toolbar buttons

- Add keyboard shortcuts
- Add a statusbar

However you learned a lot in this chapter. You learned how to merge and split PDFs. You also learned how to use threads with wxPython. Finally this code demonstrated adding some error handling to your inputs, specifically in the **split_panel** module.

Chapter 11 - Creating a File Search Utility

Have you ever needed to search for a file on your computer? Most operating systems have a way to do this. Windows Explorer has a search function and there's also a search built-in to the Start Menu now. Other operating systems like Mac and Linux are similar. There are also applications that you can download that are sometimes faster at searching your hard drive than the built-in ones are.

In this chapter, you will be creating a simple file search utility and a text search utility using wxPython.

You will want to support the following tasks for the file search tool:

- Search by file type
- Case sensitive searches
- Search in sub-directories

Let's get started!

Designing Your File Search Utility

It is always fun to try to recreate a tool that you use yourself. However in this case, you will just take the features mentioned above and create a straight-forward user interface. You can use a `wx.SearchCtrl` for searching for files and an `ObjectListView` for displaying the results. For this particular utility, a `wx.CheckBox` or two will work nicely for telling your application to search in sub-directories or if the search term is case-sensitive or not.

Here is a mockup of what the application will eventually look like:

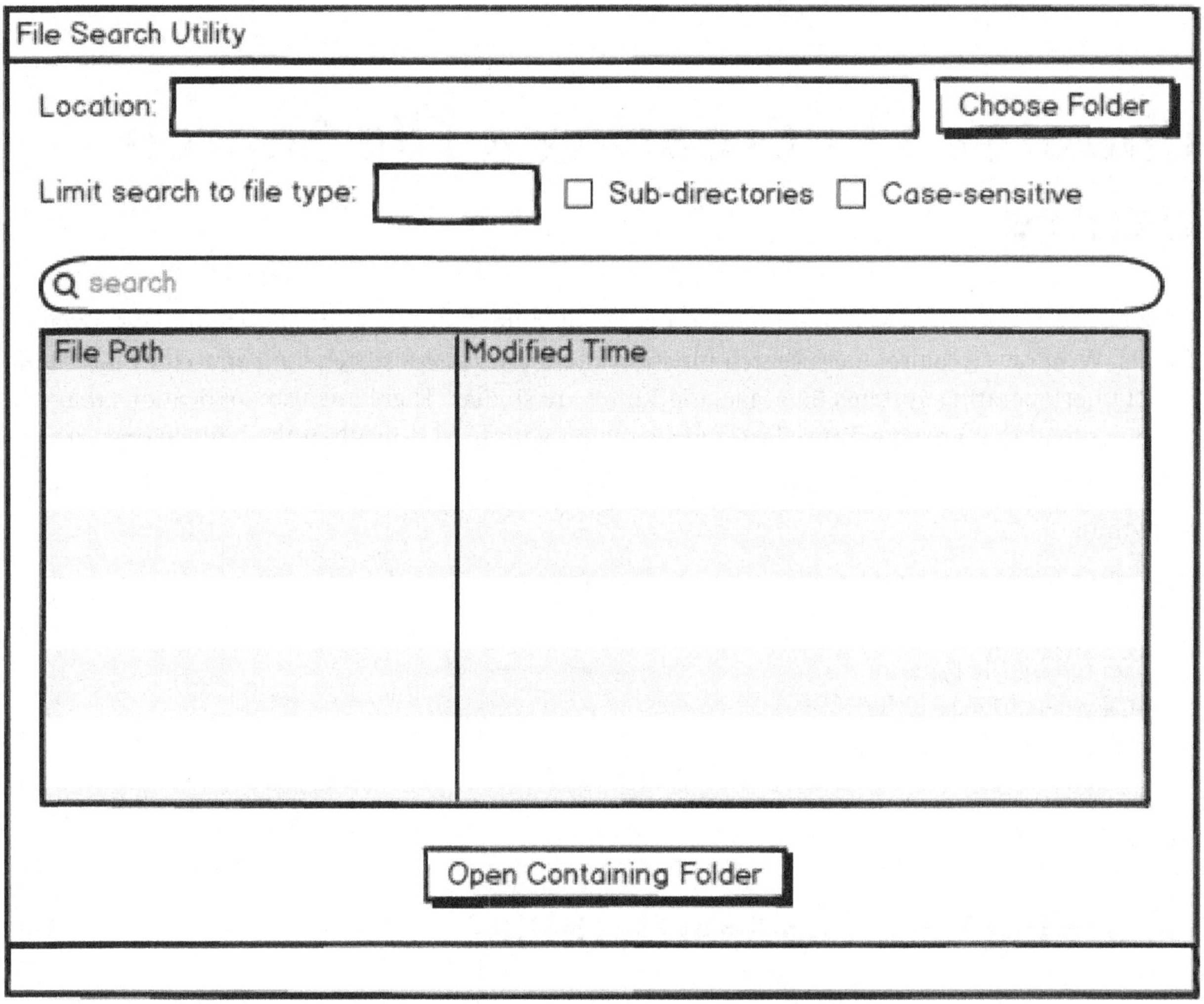

Fig. 11-1: File Search Utility Mockup

Now that you have a goal in mind, let's go ahead and start coding!

Creating the File Search Utility

Your search utility will need two modules. The first module will be called **main** and it will hold your user interface and most of the application's logic. The second module is named **search_threads** and it will contain the logic needed to search your file system using Python's threading module. You will use pubsub to update the **main** module as results are found.

The main script

The **main** module has the bulk of the code for your application. If you go on and enhance this application, the search portion of the code could end up having the majority of the code since that is where a lot of the refinement of your code should probably go though.

Regardless, here is the beginning of **main**:

```python
# main.py

import os
import sys
import subprocess
import time
import wx

from ObjectListView import ObjectListView, ColumnDefn
from pubsub import pub
from search_threads import SearchFolderThread, SearchSubdirectoriesThread
```

This time around, you will be using a few more built-in Python modules, such as os, sys, subprocess and time. The other imports are pretty normal, with the last one being a couple of classes that you will be creating based around Python's Thread class from the threading module.

For now though, let's just focus on the **main** module.

Here's the first class you need to create:

```python
class SearchResult:

    def __init__(self, path, modified_time):
        self.path = path
        self.modified = time.strftime('%D %H:%M:%S',
                                      time.gmtime(modified_time))
```

The SearchResult class is used for holding information about the results from your search. It is also used by the ObjectListView widget. Currently, you will use it to hold the full path to the search result as well as the file's modified time. You could easily enhance this to also include file size, creation time, etc.

Now let's create the MainPanel which houses most of UI code:

```python
class MainPanel(wx.Panel):

    def __init__(self, parent):
        super().__init__(parent)
        self.search_results = []
        self.main_sizer = wx.BoxSizer(wx.VERTICAL)
        self.create_ui()
        self.SetSizer(self.main_sizer)
        pub.subscribe(self.update_search_results, 'update')
```

The __init__() method gets everything set up. Here you create the main_sizer, an empty list of search_results and a listener or subscription using pubsub. You also call create_ui() to add the user interface widgets to the panel.

Let's see what's in create_ui() now:

```python
def create_ui(self):
    # Create the widgets for the search path
    row_sizer = wx.BoxSizer()
    lbl = wx.StaticText(self, label='Location:')
    row_sizer.Add(lbl, 0, wx.ALL | wx.CENTER, 5)
    self.directory = wx.TextCtrl(self, style=wx.TE_READONLY)
    row_sizer.Add(self.directory, 1, wx.ALL | wx.EXPAND, 5)
    open_dir_btn = wx.Button(self, label='Choose Folder')
    open_dir_btn.Bind(wx.EVT_BUTTON, self.on_choose_folder)
    row_sizer.Add(open_dir_btn, 0, wx.ALL, 5)
    self.main_sizer.Add(row_sizer, 0, wx.EXPAND)
```

There are quite a few widgets to add to this user interface. To start off, you add a row of widgets that consists of a label, a text control and a button. This series of widgets allows the user to choose which directory they want to search using the button. The text control will hold their choice.

Now let's add another row of widgets:

```python
# Create search filter widgets
row_sizer = wx.BoxSizer()
lbl = wx.StaticText(self, label='Limit search to filetype:')
row_sizer.Add(lbl, 0, wx.ALL|wx.CENTER, 5)

self.file_type = wx.TextCtrl(self)
row_sizer.Add(self.file_type, 0, wx.ALL, 5)

self.sub_directories = wx.CheckBox(self, label='Sub-directories')
row_sizer.Add(self.sub_directories, 0, wx.ALL | wx.CENTER, 5)
```

```
self.case_sensitive = wx.CheckBox(self, label='Case-sensitive')
row_sizer.Add(self.case_sensitive, 0, wx.ALL | wx.CENTER, 5)
self.main_sizer.Add(row_sizer)
```

This row of widgets contains another label, a text control and two instances of `wx.Checkbox`. These are the filter widgets which control what you are searching for. You can filter based on any of the following:

- The file type
- Search sub-directories (when checked) or just the chosen directory
- The search term is case-sensitive

The latter two options are represented by using the `wx.Checkbox` widget.

Let's add the search control next:

```
# Add search bar
self.search_ctrl = wx.SearchCtrl(
    self, style=wx.TE_PROCESS_ENTER, size=(-1, 25))
self.search_ctrl.Bind(wx.EVT_SEARCHCTRL_SEARCH_BTN, self.on_search)
self.search_ctrl.Bind(wx.EVT_TEXT_ENTER, self.on_search)
self.main_sizer.Add(self.search_ctrl, 0, wx.ALL | wx.EXPAND, 5)
```

The `wx.SearchCtrl` is the widget to use for searching. You could quite easily use a `wx.TextCtrl` instead though. Regardless, in this case you bind to the press of the Enter key and to the mouse click of the magnifying class within the control. If you do either of these actions, you will call `search()`.

Now let's add the last two widgets and you will be done with the code for `create_ui()`:

```
# Search results widget
self.search_results_olv = ObjectListView(
    self, style=wx.LC_REPORT | wx.SUNKEN_BORDER)
self.search_results_olv.SetEmptyListMsg("No Results Found")
self.main_sizer.Add(self.search_results_olv, 1, wx.ALL | wx.EXPAND, 5)
self.update_ui()

show_result_btn = wx.Button(self, label='Open Containing Folder')
show_result_btn.Bind(wx.EVT_BUTTON, self.on_show_result)
self.main_sizer.Add(show_result_btn, 0, wx.ALL | wx.CENTER, 5)
```

The results of your search will appear in your `ObjectListView` widget. You also need to add a button that will attempt to show the result in the containing folder, kind of like how Mozilla Firefox has a right-click menu called "Open Containing Folder" for opening downloaded files.

The next method to create is `on_choose_folder()`:

```python
def on_choose_folder(self, event):
    with wx.DirDialog(self, "Choose a directory:",
                      style=wx.DD_DEFAULT_STYLE,
                      ) as dlg:
        if dlg.ShowModal() == wx.ID_OK:
            self.directory.SetValue(dlg.GetPath())
```

You need to allow the user to select a folder that you want to conduct a search in. You could let the user type in the path, but that is error-prone and you might need to add special error checking. Instead, you opt to use a wx.DirDialog, which prevents the user from entering a non-existent path. It is possible for the user to select the folder, then delete the folder before executing the search, but that would be an unlikely scenario.

Now you need a way to open a folder with Python:

```python
def on_show_result(self, event):
    """
    Attempt to open the folder that the result was found in
    """
    result = self.search_results_olv.GetSelectedObject()
    if result:
        path = os.path.dirname(result.path)
        try:
            if sys.platform == 'darwin':
                subprocess.check_call(['open', '--', path])
            elif 'linux' in sys.platform:
                subprocess.check_call(['xdg-open', path])
            elif sys.platform == 'win32':
                subprocess.check_call(['explorer', path])
        except:
            if sys.platform == 'win32':
                # Ignore error on Windows as there seems to be
                # a weird return code on Windows
                return

            message = f'Unable to open file manager to {path}'
            with wx.MessageDialog(None, message=message,
                                  caption='Error',
                                  style= wx.ICON_ERROR) as dlg:
                dlg.ShowModal()
```

The on_show_result() method will check what platform the code is running under and then attempt to launch that platform's file manager. Windows uses **Explorer** while Linux uses **xdg-open** for example.

During testing, it was noticed that on Windows, Explorer returns a non-zero result even when it opens Explorer successfully, so in that case you just ignore the error. But on other platforms, you can show a message to the user that you were unable to open the folder.

The next bit of code you need to write is the on_search() event handler:

```python
def on_search(self, event):
    search_term = self.search_ctrl.GetValue()
    file_type = self.file_type.GetValue()
    file_type = file_type.lower()
    if '.' not in file_type:
        file_type = f'.{file_type}'

    if not self.sub_directories.GetValue():
        # Do not search sub-directories
        self.search_current_folder_only(search_term, file_type)
    else:
        self.search(search_term, file_type)
```

When you click the "Search" button, you want it to do something useful. That is where the code above comes into play. Here you get the search_term and the file_type. To prevent issues, you put the file type in lower case and you will do the same thing during the search.

Next you check to see if the sub_directories check box is checked or not. If it is, then you call search_current_folder_only(); otherwise you call search().

Let's see what goes into search() first:

```python
def search(self, search_term, file_type):
    """

    Search for the specified term in the directory and its
    sub-directories
    """
    folder = self.directory.GetValue()
    if folder:
        self.search_results = []
        SearchSubdirectoriesThread(folder, search_term, file_type,
                                   self.case_sensitive.GetValue())
```

Here you grab the folder that the user has selected. In the event that the user has not chosen a folder, the search button will not do anything. But if they have chosen something, then you call the SearchSubdirectoriesThread thread with the appropriate parameters. You will see what the code in that class is in a later section.

But first, you need to create the search_current_folder_only() method:

```
def search_current_folder_only(self, search_term, file_type):
    """
    Search for the specified term in the directory only. Do
    not search sub-directories
    """
    folder = self.directory.GetValue()
    if folder:
        self.search_results = []
        SearchFolderThread(folder, search_term, file_type,
                           self.case_sensitive.GetValue())
```

This code is pretty similar to the previous function. Its only difference is that it executes `SearchFolderThread` instead of `SearchSubdirectoriesThread`.

The next function to create is `update_search_results()`:

```
def update_search_results(self, result):
    """
    Called by pubsub from thread
    """
    if result:
        path, modified_time = result
        self.search_results.append(SearchResult(path, modified_time))
    self.update_ui()
```

When a search result is found, the thread will post that result back to the main application using a thread-safe method and `pubsub`. This method is what will get called assuming that the topic matches the subscription that you created in the `__init__()`. Once called, this method will append the result to `search_results` and then call `update_ui()`.

Speaking of which, you can code that up now:

```
def update_ui(self):
    self.search_results_olv.SetColumns([
        ColumnDefn("File Path", "left", 300, "path"),
        ColumnDefn("Modified Time", "left", 150, "modified")
    ])
    self.search_results_olv.SetObjects(self.search_results)
```

The `update_ui()` method defines the columns that are shown in your `ObjectListView` widget. It also calls `SetObjects()` which will update the contents of the widget and show your search results to the user.

To wrap up the **main** module, you will need to write the `Search` class:

```python
class Search(wx.Frame):

    def __init__(self):
        super().__init__(None, title='Search Utility',
                         size=(600, 600))
        pub.subscribe(self.update_status, 'status')
        panel = MainPanel(self)
        self.statusbar = self.CreateStatusBar(1)
        self.Show()

    def update_status(self, search_time):
        msg = f'Search finished in {search_time:5.4} seconds'
        self.SetStatusText(msg)

if __name__ == '__main__':
    app = wx.App(False)
    frame = Search()
    app.MainLoop()
```

This class creates the MainPanel which holds most of the widgets that the user will see and interact with. It also sets the initial size of the application along with its title. There is also a status bar that will be used to communicate to the user when a search has finished and how long it took for said search to complete.

Here is what the application will look like:

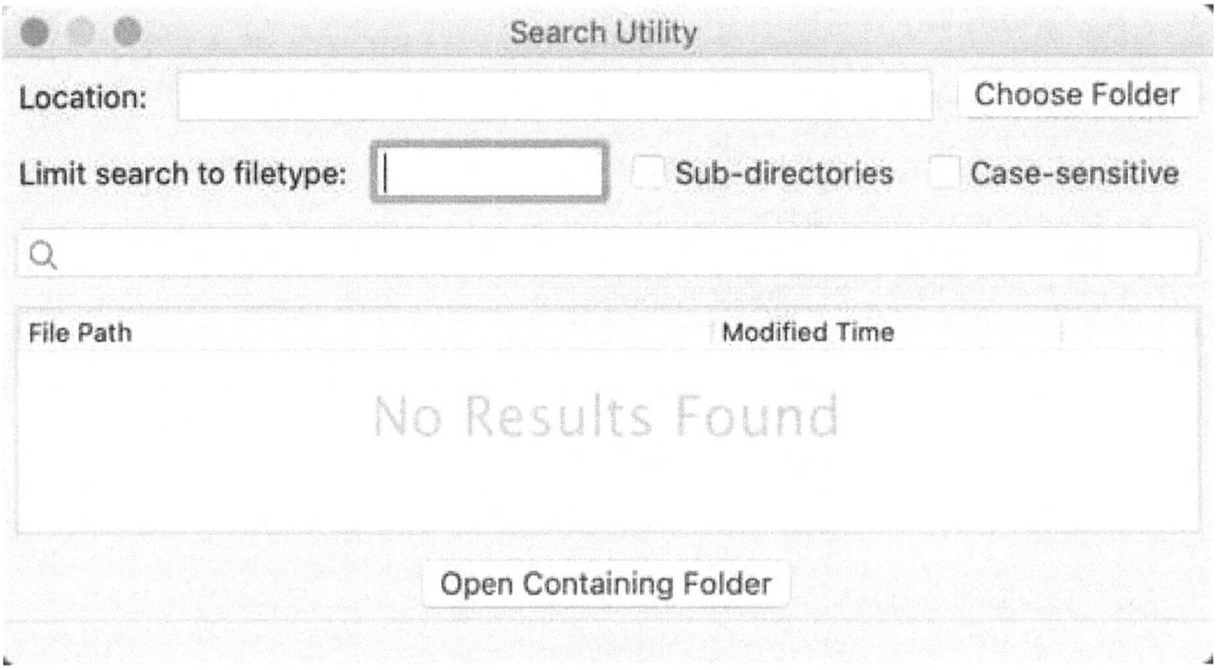

Fig. 11-2: File Search Utility

Now let's move on and create the module that holds your search threads.

The search_threads Module

The **search_threads** module contains the two `Thread` classes that you will use for searching your file system. The thread classes are actually quite similar in their form and function.

Let's get started:

```python
# search_threads.py

import os
import time
import wx

from pubsub import pub
from threading import Thread
```

These are the modules that you will need to make this code work. You will be using the `os` module to check paths, traverse the file system and get statistics from files. You will use `pubsub` to communicate with your application when your search returns results.

Here is the first class:

```
class SearchFolderThread(Thread):

    def __init__(self, folder, search_term, file_type, case_sensitive):
        super().__init__()
        self.folder = folder
        self.search_term = search_term
        self.file_type = file_type
        self.case_sensitive = case_sensitive
        self.start()
```

This thread takes in the `folder` to search in, the `search_term` to look for, a `file_type` filter and whether or not the search term is `case_sensitive`. You take these in and assign them to instance variables of the same name. The point of this thread is only to search the contents of the folder that is passed-in, not its sub-directories.

You will also need to override the thread's `run()` method:

```
def run(self):
    start = time.time()
    for entry in os.scandir(self.folder):
        if entry.is_file():
            if self.case_sensitive:
                path = entry.name
            else:
                path = entry.name.lower()

            if self.search_term in path:
                _, ext = os.path.splitext(entry.path)
                data = (entry.path, entry.stat().st_mtime)
                wx.CallAfter(pub.sendMessage, 'update', result=data)
    end = time.time()
    # Always update at the end even if there were no results
    wx.CallAfter(pub.sendMessage, 'update', result=[])
    wx.CallAfter(pub.sendMessage, 'status', search_time=end-start)
```

Here you collect the start time of the thread. Then you use `os.scandir()` to loop over the contents of the `folder`. If the path is a file, you will check to see if the `search_term` is in the path and has the right `file_type`. Should both of those return `True`, then you get the requisite data and send it to your application using `wx.CallAfter()`, which is a thread-safe method.

Finally you grab the `end_time` and use that to calculate the total run time of the search and then send that back to the application. The application will then update the status bar with the search time.

Now let's check out the other class:

```python
class SearchSubdirectoriesThread(Thread):

    def __init__(self, folder, search_term, file_type, case_sensitive):
        super().__init__()
        self.folder = folder
        self.search_term = search_term
        self.file_type = file_type
        self.case_sensitive = case_sensitive
        self.start()
```

The `SearchSubdirectoriesThread` thread is used for searching not only the passed-in `folder` but also its sub-directories. It accepts the same arguments as the previous class.

Here is what you will need to put in its `run()` method:

```python
def run(self):
    start = time.time()
    for root, dirs, files in os.walk(self.folder):
        for f in files:
            full_path = os.path.join(root, f)
            if not self.case_sensitive:
                full_path = full_path.lower()

            if self.search_term in full_path and os.path.exists(full_path):
                _, ext = os.path.splitext(full_path)
                data = (full_path, os.stat(full_path).st_mtime)
                wx.CallAfter(pub.sendMessage, 'update', result=data)

    end = time.time()
    # Always update at the end even if there were no results
    wx.CallAfter(pub.sendMessage, 'update', result=[])
    wx.CallAfter(pub.sendMessage, 'status', search_time=end-start)
```

For this thread, you need to use `os.walk()` to search the passed in `folder` and its sub-directories. Besides that, the conditional statements are virtually the same as the previous class.

Now let's find out how to create a search utility for text searches!

The Text Search Utility

A text search utility is a tool that can search inside of other files for words or phrases, like the popular GNU **grep** tool. There are some tools that can also search Microsoft Word, PDF file contents and more. You will focus only on searching text files. These include files like XML, HTML, Python files and other code files in addition to regular text files.

There is a nice Python package that does the text search for us called `grin`. Since this book is using Python 3, you will want to use `grin3` as that is the version of `grin` that is compatible with Python 3.

You can read all about this package here:

- https://pypi.org/project/grin3/

You will add a light-weight user interface on top of this package that allows you to use it to search text files.

Installing the Dependencies

You can install `grin3` by using `pip`:

```
pip install grin3
```

Once installed, you will be able to run `grin` or `grind` from the command line on Mac or Linux. You may need to add it to your path if you are on Windows.

Warning: The previous version of `grin3` is `grin`. If you install that into Python 3 and attempt to run it, you will see errors raised as `grin` is **NOT** Python 3 compatible. You will need to uninstall `grin` and install `grin3` instead.

Now you can design your user interface!

Designing a Text Search Utility

You can take the code from the file search utility earlier in this chapter and modify the user interface for use with the text search. You don't care about the search term being case-sensitive right now, so you can remove that widget. You can also remove the sub-directories check box since `grin` will search sub-directories by default and that's what you want anyway.

You could filter by file-type still, but to keep things simple, let's remove that too. However you will need a way to display the files that were found along with the lines that contain the found text. To do that, you will need to add a multi-line text control in addition to the `ObjectListView` widget.

With all that in mind, here is the mockup:

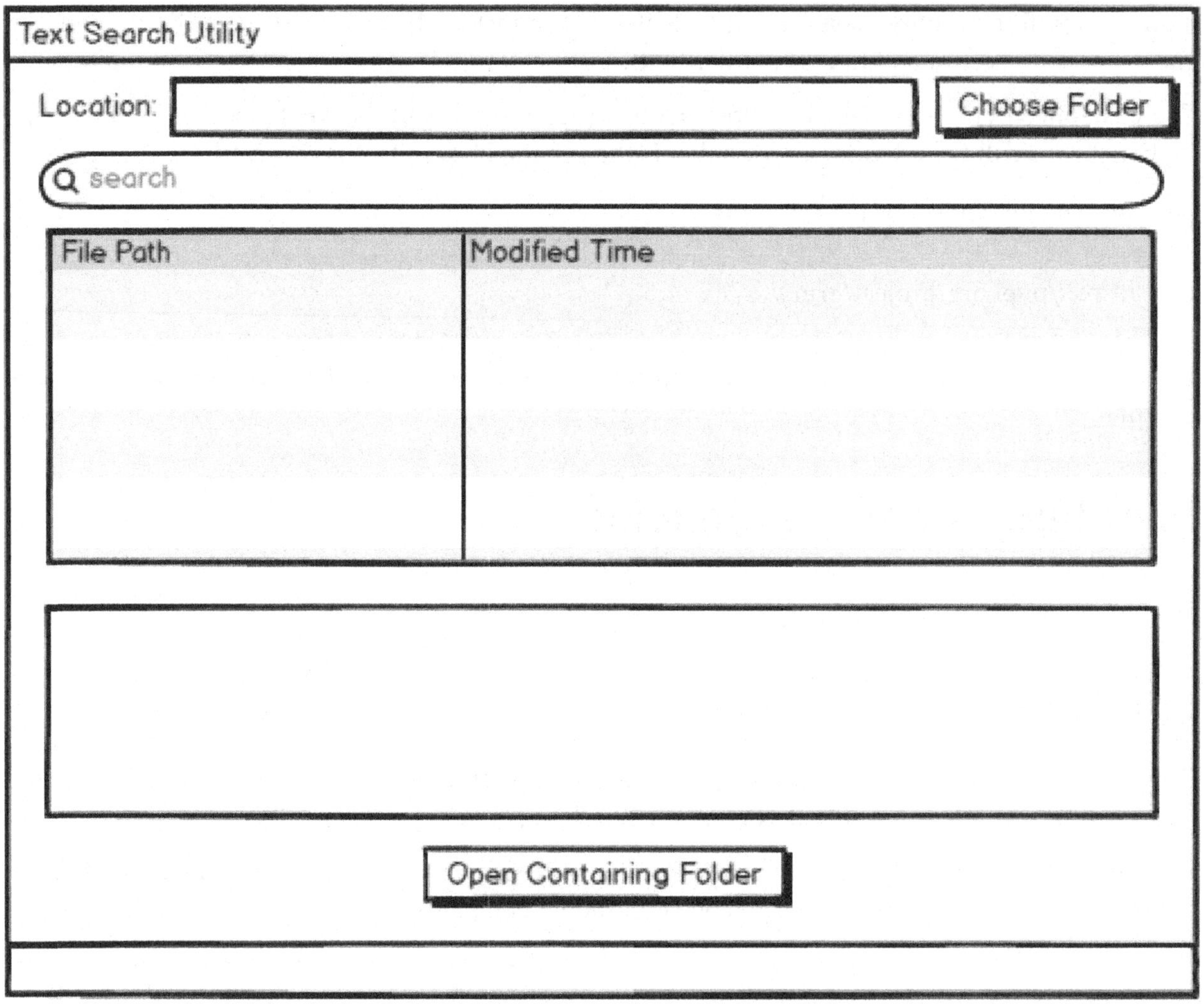

Fig. 11-3: Text Search Utility Mockup

It's time to start coding!

Creating a Text Search Utility

Your new text searching utility will be split up into three modules:

- The main module
- The search_thread module
- The preference module

The **main** module will contain the code for the main user interface. The **search_thread** module will contain the logic for searching for text using grin. And lastly, the **preferences** will be used for creating a dialog that you can use to save the location of the grin executable.

You can start by creating the **main** module now.

The main Module

The **main** module not only holds the user interface, but it will also check to make sure you have grin installed so that it will work. It will also launch the preferences dialog and show the user the search results, if any.

Here are the first few lines of code:

```python
# main.py

import os
import sys
import subprocess
import time
import wx

from configparser import ConfigParser, NoSectionError
from ObjectListView import ObjectListView, ColumnDefn
from preferences import PreferencesDialog
from pubsub import pub
from search_thread import SearchThread
```

This **main** module has many of the same imports as the previous version of the **main** module. However in this one, you will be using Python's configparser module as well as creating a PreferencesDialog and a SearchThread. The rest of the imports should be pretty self-explanatory.

You will need to copy the SearchResult class over and modify it like this:

```python
class SearchResult:

    def __init__(self, path, modified_time, data):
        self.path = path
        self.modified = time.strftime('%D %H:%M:%S',
                                      time.gmtime(modified_time))
        self.data = data
```

The class now accepts a new argument, data, which holds a string that contains references to all the places where the search term was found in the file. You will show that information to the user when the user selects a search result.

But first, you need to create the UI:

```
class MainPanel(wx.Panel):

    def __init__(self, parent):
        super().__init__(parent)
        self.search_results = []
        self.main_sizer = wx.BoxSizer(wx.VERTICAL)
        self.create_ui()
        self.SetSizer(self.main_sizer)
        pub.subscribe(self.update_search_results, 'update')

        module_path = os.path.dirname(os.path.abspath( __file__ ))
        self.config = os.path.join(module_path, 'config.ini')
        if not os.path.exists(self.config):
            message = 'Unable to find grin3 for text searches. ' \
                      'Install grin3 and open preferences to ' \
                      'configure it:  pip install grin3'
            self.show_error(message)
```

The `MainPanel` sets up an empty `search_results` list as before. It also creates the UI via a call to `create_ui()` and adds a `pubsub` subscription. But there is some new code added for getting the script's path and checking for a config file. If the config file does not exist, you show a message to the user letting them know that they need to install `grin3` and configure the application using the **Preferences** menu.

Now let's see how the user interface code has changed:

```
def create_ui(self):
    # Create a widgets for the search path
    row_sizer = wx.BoxSizer()
    lbl = wx.StaticText(self, label='Location:')
    row_sizer.Add(lbl, 0, wx.ALL | wx.CENTER, 5)
    self.directory = wx.TextCtrl(self, style=wx.TE_READONLY)
    row_sizer.Add(self.directory, 1, wx.ALL | wx.EXPAND, 5)
    open_dir_btn = wx.Button(self, label='Choose Folder')
    open_dir_btn.Bind(wx.EVT_BUTTON, self.on_choose_folder)
    row_sizer.Add(open_dir_btn, 0, wx.ALL, 5)
    self.main_sizer.Add(row_sizer, 0, wx.EXPAND)
```

This code will create a horizontal `row_sizer` and add three widgets: a label, a text control that holds the folder to search in and a button for choosing said folder. This series of widgets are the same as the previous ones in the other code example.

In fact, so is the following search control code:

```
# Add search bar
self.search_ctrl = wx.SearchCtrl(
    self, style=wx.TE_PROCESS_ENTER, size=(-1, 25))
self.search_ctrl.Bind(wx.EVT_SEARCHCTRL_SEARCH_BTN, self.on_search)
self.search_ctrl.Bind(wx.EVT_TEXT_ENTER, self.on_search)
self.main_sizer.Add(self.search_ctrl, 0, wx.ALL | wx.EXPAND, 5)
```

Once again, you create an instance of `wx.SearchCtrl` and bind it to the same events and the same event handler. The event handler's code will be different, but you will see how that changes soon.

Let's finish out the widget code first:

```
# Search results widget
self.search_results_olv = ObjectListView(
    self, style=wx.LC_REPORT | wx.SUNKEN_BORDER)
self.search_results_olv.SetEmptyListMsg("No Results Found")
self.search_results_olv.Bind(wx.EVT_LIST_ITEM_SELECTED,
                             self.on_selection)
self.main_sizer.Add(self.search_results_olv, 1, wx.ALL | wx.EXPAND, 5)
self.update_ui()

self.results_txt = wx.TextCtrl(
    self, style=wx.TE_MULTILINE | wx.TE_READONLY)
self.main_sizer.Add(self.results_txt, 1, wx.ALL | wx.EXPAND, 5)

show_result_btn = wx.Button(self, label='Open Containing Folder')
show_result_btn.Bind(wx.EVT_BUTTON, self.on_show_result)
self.main_sizer.Add(show_result_btn, 0, wx.ALL | wx.CENTER, 5)
```

This bit of code adds the `ObjectListView` widget from before but it also adds a `wx.TextCtrl` that will be used for showing the actual string matches from within the search results. You can think of it as a meta-search viewer. You also add a button to open the folder that the search result is in.

The method that this button is bound to is called `on_choose_folder()` and is exactly the same as the one in the file search utility's code. You can actually just copy that method from that application's code into this one.

The method you will use to actually populate this text control happens to be what you'll write next:

```
def on_selection(self, event):
    current_selection = self.search_results_olv.GetSelectedObject()
    self.results_txt.SetValue('\n'.join(current_selection.data))
```

The `on_selection` event handler fires when the user selects a search result in the `ObjectListView` widget. You grab that selection and then set the value of the text control to the `data` attribute. The data attribute is a list of strings, so you need to use the string's join() method to join all those lines together using a newline character: \n. You want each line to be on its own line to make the results easier to read.

You can copy the on_show_result() method from the file search utility to this one as there are no changes needed for that method.

The next bit of new code to write is the on_search() method:

```python
def on_search(self, event):
    search_term = self.search_ctrl.GetValue()
    self.search(search_term)
```

The on_search() method is quite a bit simpler this time in that you only need to get the search_term. You don't have any filters in this version of the application, which certainly reduces the code clutter. Once you have your term to search for, you call search().

Speaking of which, that is the next method to create:

```python
def search(self, search_term):
    """
    Search for the specified term in the directory and its
    sub-directories
    """
    folder = self.directory.GetValue()
    config = ConfigParser()
    config.read(self.config)
    try:
        grin = config.get("Settings", "grin")
    except NoSectionError:
        self.show_error('Settings or grin section not found')
        return

    if not os.path.exists(grin):
        self.show_error(f'Grin location does not exist {grin}')
        return
    if folder:
        self.search_results = []
        SearchThread(folder, search_term)
```

The search() code will get the folder path and create a config object. It will then attempt to open the config file. If the config file does not exist or it cannot read the "Settings" section, you will show an error message. If the "Settings" section exists, but the path to the grin executable does not, you will show a different error message. But if you make it past these two hurdles and the folder itself is set, then you'll start the `SearchThread`. That code is saved in another module, so you'll have to wait to learn about that.

For now, let's see what goes in the `show_error()` method:

```python
def show_error(self, message):
    with wx.MessageDialog(None, message=message,
                          caption='Error',
                          style= wx.ICON_ERROR) as dlg:
        dlg.ShowModal()
```

This method will create a `wx.MessageDialog` and show an error to the user with the `message` that was passed to it. The function is quite handy for showing errors. You can update it a bit if you'd like to show other types of messages as well though.

When a search completes, it will send a `pubsub` message out that will cause the following code to execute:

```python
def update_search_results(self, results):
    """
    Called by pubsub from thread
    """
    for key in results:
        if os.path.exists(key):
            stat = os.stat(key)
            modified_time = stat.st_mtime
            result = SearchResult(key, modified_time, results[key])
            self.search_results.append(result)

    if results:
        self.update_ui()
```

This method takes in a `dict` of search results. It then loops over the keys in the `dict` and verifies that the path exists. If it does, then you use `os.stat()` to get information about the file and create a `SearchResult` object, which you then `append()` to your `search_results`.

The `update_ui()` code is pretty much exactly the same as the previous code:

```python
def update_ui(self):
    self.search_results_olv.SetColumns([
        ColumnDefn("File Path", "left", 800, "path"),
        ColumnDefn("Modified Time", "left", 150, "modified")
    ])
    self.search_results_olv.SetObjects(self.search_results)
```

The only difference here is that the columns are a bit wider than they are in the file search utility. This is because a lot of the results that were found during testing tended to be rather long strings.

The code for the wx.Frame has also changed as you now have a menu to add:

```python
class Search(wx.Frame):

    def __init__(self):
        super().__init__(None, title='Text Search Utility',
                         size=(1200, 800))
        pub.subscribe(self.update_status, 'status')
        panel = MainPanel(self)
        self.create_menu()
        self.statusbar = self.CreateStatusBar(1)
        self.Show()

    def update_status(self, search_time):
        msg = f'Search finished in {search_time:5.4} seconds'
        self.SetStatusText(msg)
```

Here you create the Search frame and set the size a bit wider than you did for the other utility. You also create the panel, create a subscriber and create a menu. The update_status() method is the same as last time.

The truly new bit was the call to create_menu() which is what's also next:

```python
def create_menu(self):
    menu_bar = wx.MenuBar()

    # Create file menu
    file_menu = wx.Menu()

    preferences = file_menu.Append(
        wx.ID_ANY, "Preferences",
        "Open Preferences Dialog")
    self.Bind(wx.EVT_MENU, self.on_preferences,
              preferences)
```

```
exit_menu_item = file_menu.Append(
    wx.ID_ANY, "Exit",
    "Exit the application")
menu_bar.Append(file_menu, '&File')
self.Bind(wx.EVT_MENU, self.on_exit,
        exit_menu_item)

self.SetMenuBar(menu_bar)
```

In this code you create the MenuBar and add a file_menu. Within that menu, you add two menu items; one for preferences and one for exiting the application.

You can create the exit code first:

```
def on_exit(self, event):
    self.Close()
```

This code will execute if the user goes into the **File** menu and chooses "Exit". When they do that, your application will Close(). Since the frame is the top level window, when it closes, it will also destroy itself.

The final piece of code in this class is for creating the preferences dialog:

```
def on_preferences(self, event):
    with PreferencesDialog() as dlg:
        dlg.ShowModal()
```

Here you instantiate the PreferencesDialog and show it to the user. When the user closes the dialog, it will be automatically destroyed.

When you are done coding the rest of this application, it will look like this:

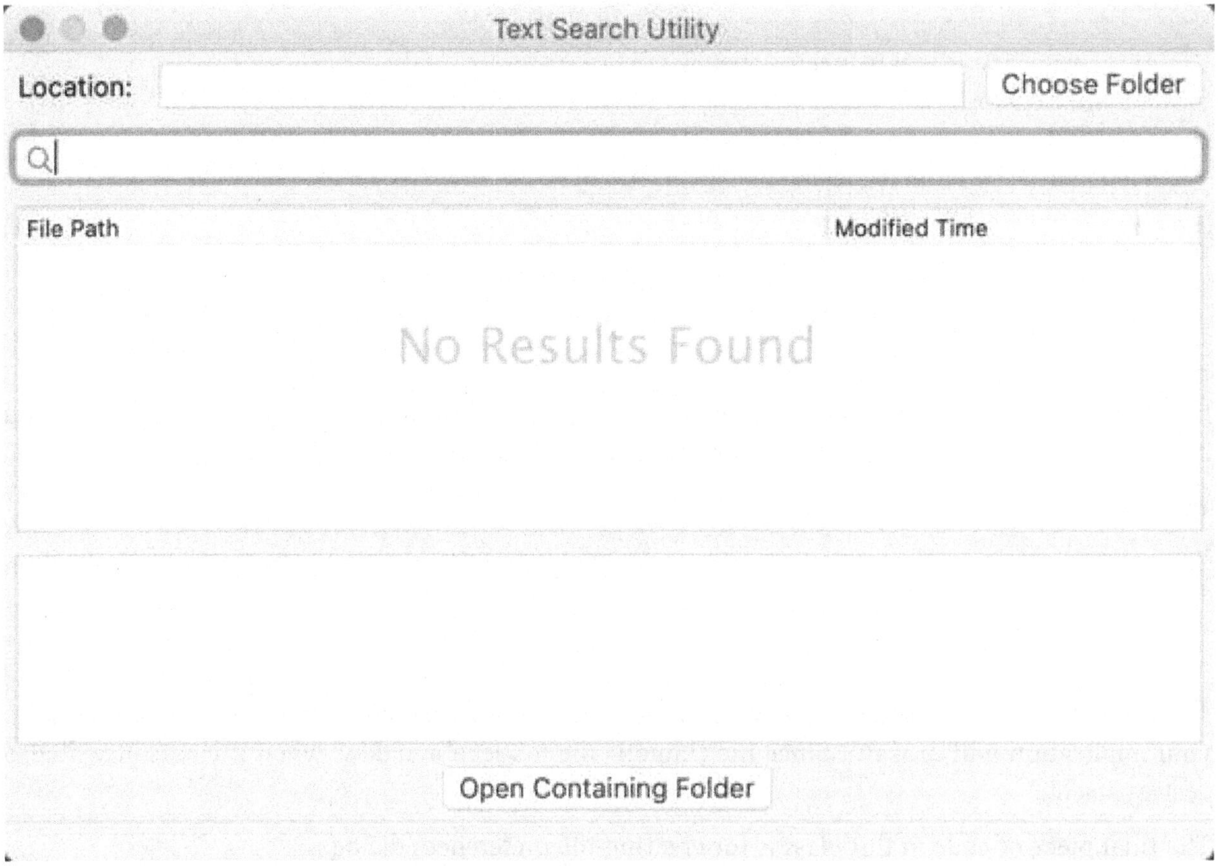

Fig. 11-4: Text Search Utility

The next step is to create the threading code!

The search_thread Module

The **search_thread** module contains your logic for searching for text within files using the grin3 executable. You only need one subclass of Thread in this module as you will always search subdirectories.

The first step is to create the imports:

```
# search_thread.py

import os
import subprocess
import time
import wx

from configparser import ConfigParser
from pubsub import pub
from threading import Thread
```

For the **search_thread** module, you will need access to the os, subprocess and time modules. The new one being the subprocess module because you will be launching an external application. The other new addition here is the ConfigParser, which you use to get the executable's path from the config file.

Let's continue and create the SearchThread itself:

```
class SearchThread(Thread):

    def __init__(self, folder, search_term):
        super().__init__()
        self.folder = folder
        self.search_term = search_term
        module_path = os.path.dirname(os.path.abspath( __file__ ))
        self.config = os.path.join(module_path, 'config.ini')
        self.start()
```

The __init__() method takes in the target folder and the search_term to look for. It also recreates the module_path to derive the location of the config file.

The last step is to start() the thread. When that method is called, it rather incongruously calls the run() method.

Let's override that next:

```python
def run(self):
    start = time.time()
    config = ConfigParser()
    config.read(self.config)
    grin = config.get("Settings", "grin")
    cmd = [grin, self.search_term, self.folder]
    output = subprocess.check_output(cmd, encoding='UTF-8')
    current_key = ''
    results = {}
    for line in output.split('\n'):
        if self.folder in line:
            # Remove the colon off the end of the line
            current_key = line[:-1]
            results[current_key] = []
        elif not current_key:
            # key not set, so skip it
            continue
        else:
            results[current_key].append(line)
    end = time.time()
    wx.CallAfter(pub.sendMessage,
                 'update',
                 results=results)
    wx.CallAfter(pub.sendMessage, 'status', search_time=end-start)
```

Here you add a `start` time and get the `config` which should be created at this point. Next you create a `list` of commands. The `grin` utility takes the search term and the directory to search as its main arguments. There are actually other arguments you could add to make the search more targeted, but that would require additional UI elements and your objective is to keep this application nice and simple.

The next step is to call `subprocess.check_output()` which takes the list of commands. You also set the `encoding` to UTF-8. This tells the `subprocess` module to return a string rather than byte-strings and it also verifies that the return value is zero.

The results that are returned now need to be parsed. You can loop over each line by splitting on the newline character. Each file path should be unique, so those will become the keys to your `results` dictionary. Note that you will need to remove the last character from the line as the key has a colon on the end. This makes the path invalid, so removing that is a good idea. Then for each line of data following the path, you append it to the value of that particular key in the dictionary.

Once done, you send out two messages via `pubsub` to update the UI and the status bar.

Now it's time to create the last module!

The preferences Module

The **preferences** module contains the code you will need for creating the `PreferencesDialog` which will allow you to configure where the `grin` executable is on your machine.

Let's start with the imports:

```python
# preferences.py

import os
import wx

from configparser import ConfigParser
```

Fortunately, the import section of the module is short. You only need the `os`, `wx` and `configparser` modules to make this work.

Now that you have that part figured out, you can create the dialog itself:

```python
class PreferencesDialog(wx.Dialog):

    def __init__(self):
        super().__init__(None, title='Preferences')
        module_path = os.path.dirname(os.path.abspath( __file__ ))
        self.config = os.path.join(module_path, 'config.ini')
        if not os.path.exists(self.config):
            self.create_config()

        config = ConfigParser()
        config.read(self.config)
        self.grin = config.get("Settings", "grin")

        self.main_sizer = wx.BoxSizer(wx.VERTICAL)
        self.create_ui()
        self.SetSizer(self.main_sizer)
```

Here you create the `__init__()` method and get the `module_path` so that you can find the `config`. Then you verify that the `config` exists. If it doesn't, then you create the config file, but don't set the executable location.

You do attempt to get its location via `config.get()`, but if it is blank in the file, then you will end up with an empty string.

The last three lines set up a sizer and call `create_ui()`.

You should write that last method next:

```python
def create_ui(self):
    row_sizer = wx.BoxSizer()
    lbl = wx.StaticText(self, label='Grin3 Location:')
    row_sizer.Add(lbl, 0, wx.ALL | wx.CENTER, 5)
    self.grin_location = wx.TextCtrl(self, value=self.grin)
    row_sizer.Add(self.grin_location, 1, wx.ALL | wx.EXPAND, 5)
    browse_button = wx.Button(self, label='Browse')
    browse_button.Bind(wx.EVT_BUTTON, self.on_browse)
    row_sizer.Add(browse_button, 0, wx.ALL, 5)
    self.main_sizer.Add(row_sizer, 0, wx.EXPAND)

    save_btn = wx.Button(self, label='Save')
    save_btn.Bind(wx.EVT_BUTTON, self.save)
    self.main_sizer.Add(save_btn, 0, wx.ALL | wx.CENTER, 5)
```

In this code, you create a row of widgets. A label, a text control that holds the executable's path and a button for browsing to that path. You add all of these to the sizer which is then nested inside of the main_sizer. Then you add a "Save" button at the bottom of the dialog.

Here is the code for creating a config from scratch:

```python
def create_config(self):
    config = ConfigParser()
    config.add_section("Settings")
    config.set("Settings", 'grin', '')

    with open(self.config, 'w') as config_file:
        config.write(config_file)
```

When the config does not exist, this code will get called. It instantiates a ConfigParser object and then adds the appropriate sections and settings to it. Then it writes it out to disk in the appropriate location.

The save() method is probably the next most important piece of code to write:

```
def save(self, event):
    grin_location = self.grin_location.GetValue()
    if not grin_location:
        self.show_error('Grin location not set!')
        return
    if not os.path.exists(grin_location):
        self.show_error(f'Grin location does not exist {grin_location}')
        return

    config = ConfigParser()
    config.read(self.config)
    config.set("Settings", "grin", grin_location)
    with open(self.config, 'w') as config_file:
        config.write(config_file)
    self.Close()
```

Here you get the location of the grin application from the text control and show an error if it is not set. You also show an error if the location does not exist. But if it is set and it does exist, then you open the config file back up and save that path to the config file for use by the main application. Once the save is finished, you Close() the dialog.

This last regular method is for showing errors:

```
def show_error(self, message):
    with wx.MessageDialog(None, message=message,
                          caption='Error',
                          style= wx.ICON_ERROR) as dlg:
        dlg.ShowModal()
```

This code is actually exactly the same as the show_error() method that you have in the **main** module. Whenever you see things like this in your code, you know that you should refactor it. This method should probably go into its own module that is then imported into the **main** and **preferences** modules. You can figure out how to do that on your own though.

Finally, you need to create the only event handler for this class:

```python
def on_browse(self, event):
    """

    Browse for the grin file

    """
    wildcard = "All files (*.*)|*.*"
    with wx.FileDialog(None, "Choose a file",
                       wildcard=wildcard,
                       style=wx.ID_OPEN) as dialog:
        if dialog.ShowModal() == wx.ID_OK:
            self.grin_location.SetValue(dialog.GetPath())
```

This event handler is called when the user presses the "Browse" button to go find the **grin** executable. When they find the file, they can pick it and the text control will be set to its location.

Now that you have the dialog all coded up, here is what it looks like:

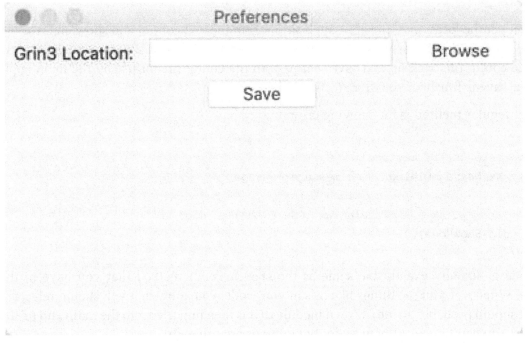

Fig. 11-5: Preferences Dialog

Wrapping Up

Creating search utilities is not particularly difficult, but it can be time consuming. Figuring out the edge cases and how to account for them is usually what takes the longest when creating software. In this chapter, you learned how to create two separate applications:

- A file search utility

- A text search utility

The first application used built-in Python libraries to search your file system. You used the os module here, but you could also have tried out glob. There is also fnmatch and if you wanted to get extra adventurous, there's re, Python's regex module.

For the text search utility, you leveraged a pre-made package called grin to search inside of text files. You went with the simplest approach which doesn't use all of grin's abilities, but it was effective nonetheless.

Here are a few enhancements that you could add to either of these programs:

- Add the ability to stop the search
- Prevent multiple searches from occurring at the same time
- Add other filters

For the text search tool you could also enhance it by adding support for more of grin's command line options. Check out grin's documentation for more information on that topic.

Chapter 12 - Creating an FTP Application

The File Transfer Protocol (FTP) used to be the primary way of uploading your files to your website. Nowadays you can create websites online without even using an FTP client. Instead, most of the time you can use your web browser for most of your website needs. However there are still many times where you do need to drop down to the FTP level. The Python language comes with a library builtin called `ftplib` that you can use for your basic FTP needs.

The `ftplib` supports normal FTP operations. You can also connect using Transport Layer Security (TLS). However if you want to use Secure FTP (SFTP), then you will need to download a separate package. The most popular one to use is called **paramiko**.

For the purposes of this chapter, you will focus on creating a simple FTP client that you can use to do the following:

- View files on a remote server using FTP
- Upload new files to the server
- Download files to the local machine
- Delete files on the remote server

You will also need to keep in mind that you may want to support adding SFTP in the future, so your mission will be to create an application that is modular and follows the **Separation of Concerns (SoC)** design principle.

Designing the FTP Client

There are lots of FTP client applications that you can use for inspiration. One of my favorites is called **Filezilla**. However that application's user interface is quite complex, so you should try to do something that's a bit easier to use.

For example, you know you will need the following information from the user:

- Host
- Port
- Username
- Password

Eventually, you can add **Protocol** to that list so that the user can choose between FTP and SFTP. Once you have that information, you should be able to connect to an FTP server.

Once you are connected, you will need a way to view what's on the remote machine. You can use a `wx.ListCtrl` or `ObjectListView` for that. You can make the control look more interesting by adding icons next to the items in the rows to mark them as files or folders.

Here is a mockup of what the UI could look like:

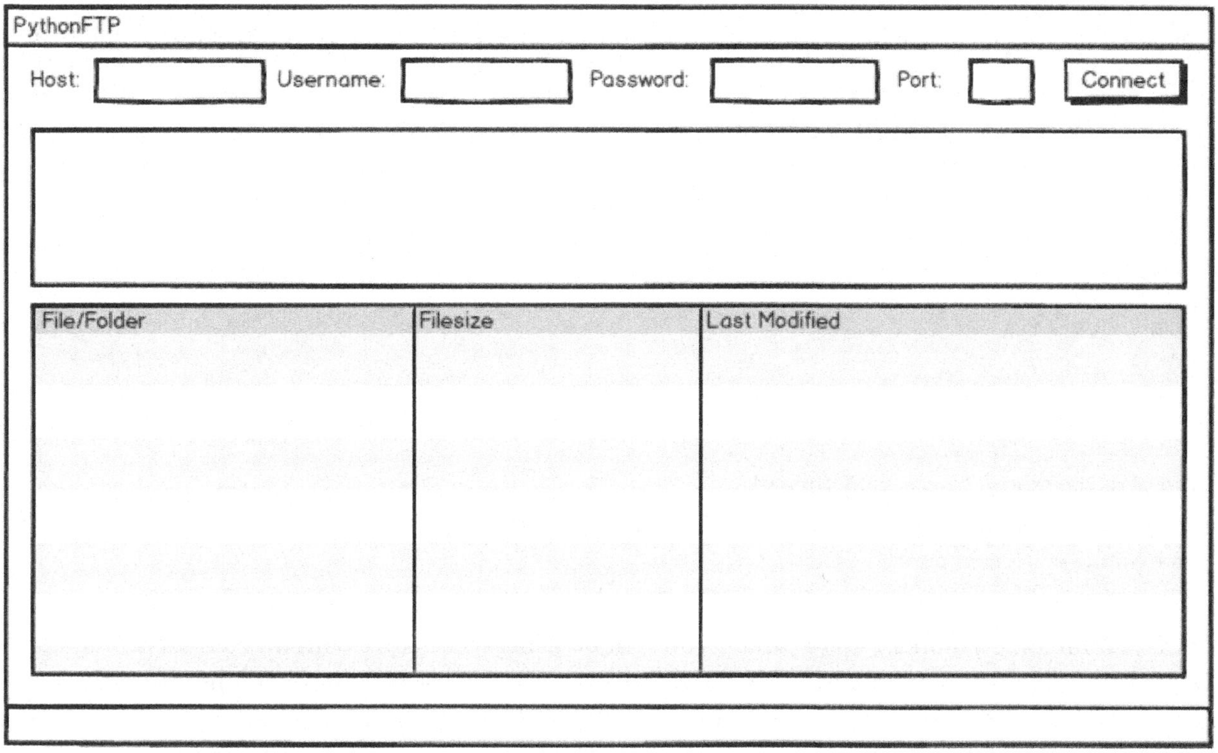

Fig. 12-1: Mockup FTP Application

You can aim for something like that for now.

Creating Your First Prototype

You will be creating the FTP Client Application in two iterations. The first iteration will be a prototype that allows you to connect to a server using FTP and view the contents of the folders there. You will be able to drill down into sub-directories as well as go back up the directory hierarchy.

The code will be split up into two files:

- main.py
- ftp_threads.py

Prototypes are small, runnable applications that do a very limited set of actions or tasks. They are useful for determining if your application's design is heading in the right or wrong direction. They are also useful as a demo for users or your boss and can help you get a project green lit.

Let's get started on your prototype now!

The main Module

The user interface code will go in your **main** module. Here you will set up all your widgets and interface logic.

You can get started by adding the following:

```python
# main.py

import ftplib
import sys
import time
import wx

from ftp_threads import FTPThread
from ObjectListView import ObjectListView, ColumnDefn
from pubsub import pub
```

Here you import Python's `ftplib` which you will be using to interact with an FTP server. You also import the `time` and `sys` modules from Python's standard library. The other imports include `wx`, `pubsub` and `ObjectListView` as well as the custom module, `ftp_threads`.

The first class for you to code is `FtpPanel`:

```python
class FtpPanel(wx.Panel):

    def __init__(self, parent):
        super().__init__(parent)

        self.ftp = None
        self.paths = []

        self.main_sizer = wx.BoxSizer(wx.VERTICAL)
        self.create_ui()
        self.SetSizer(self.main_sizer)
        pub.subscribe(self.update, 'update')
        pub.subscribe(self.update_status, 'update_status')
```

The __init__() method creates an ftp instance variable and sets it to None. This variable will eventually be an instance of ftplib.FTP(). The rest of the code here creates a sizer object and a couple of pubsub subscriptions to update various parts of your user interface.

The next step is to actually create the user interface:

```python
def create_ui(self):
    size = (150, -1)
    connect_sizer = wx.BoxSizer()
    # host, username, password, port, connect button
    host_lbl = wx.StaticText(self, label='Host:')
    connect_sizer.Add(host_lbl, 0, wx.ALL | wx.CENTER, 5)
    self.host = wx.TextCtrl(self, size=size)
    connect_sizer.Add(self.host, 0, wx.ALL, 5)
```

Here you set up a size tuple that represent 150 pixels wide by the default height or -1. This size will be applied to a couple of text controls in your application.

The first row of widgets that you will create will allow the user to set the following:

- Host
- Username
- Password
- Port number

The code above adds only the host widget.

The following code adds the widgets necessary to get the username and password from the user:

```python
user_lbl = wx.StaticText(self, label='Username:')
connect_sizer.Add(user_lbl, 0, wx.ALL | wx.CENTER, 5)
self.user = wx.TextCtrl(self, size=size)
connect_sizer.Add(self.user, 0, wx.ALL, 5)

password_lbl = wx.StaticText(self, label='Password:')
connect_sizer.Add(password_lbl, 0, wx.ALL | wx.CENTER, 5)
self.password = wx.TextCtrl(self, size=size, style=wx.TE_PASSWORD)
connect_sizer.Add(self.password, 0, wx.ALL, 5)
```

For the password widget, you set the wx.TE_PASSWORD style flag. This will make the text control hide the characters as the user types them.

The next two widgets to add are the port number and the connect button:

```
port_lbl = wx.StaticText(self, label='Port:')
connect_sizer.Add(port_lbl, 0, wx.ALL | wx.CENTER, 5)
self.port = wx.TextCtrl(self, value='21', size=(50, -1))
connect_sizer.Add(self.port, 0, wx.ALL, 5)

connect_btn = wx.Button(self, label='Connect')
connect_btn.Bind(wx.EVT_BUTTON, self.on_connect)
connect_sizer.Add(connect_btn, 0, wx.ALL, 5)
self.main_sizer.Add(connect_sizer)
```

Here you add the the port text control and the connect button in addition to a label. You default the
port to 21, although technically you could leave that blank as ftplib already defaults to port 21 if it
is blank.

The next-to-last widget to add is a multi-line text control:

```
self.status = wx.TextCtrl(self, style=wx.TE_MULTILINE)
self.main_sizer.Add(self.status, 1, wx.ALL | wx.EXPAND, 5)
```

This text control will be used to give the user up-to-state status information about what is happening.
For example, when you log in to the FTP server, the server's welcome message will appear here.
When you change folders, you can send that information here too.

The last widget to add is the ObjectListView for showing the folders and files on the server:

```
folder_ico = wx.ArtProvider.GetBitmap(
    wx.ART_FOLDER, wx.ART_TOOLBAR, (16, 16))
file_ico = wx.ArtProvider.GetBitmap(
    wx.ART_HELP_PAGE, wx.ART_TOOLBAR, (16, 16))

self.remote_server = ObjectListView(
    self, style=wx.LC_REPORT | wx.SUNKEN_BORDER)
self.remote_server.Bind(wx.EVT_LIST_ITEM_ACTIVATED,
                        self.on_change_directory)
self.remote_server.AddNamedImages('folder', smallImage=folder_ico)
self.remote_server.AddNamedImages('file', smallImage=file_ico)
self.remote_server.SetEmptyListMsg("Not Connected")
self.main_sizer.Add(self.remote_server, 2, wx.ALL | wx.EXPAND, 5)
self.update_ui()
```

This time around, you want to mark the rows in the widget with icons that show them to be either
a folder or a file. To keep things simple, you can use wx.ArtProvider for the images, but you could
also load icons yourself if you'd like a more custom look. Once you have the icons, you need to

add them to the widget, which is what the AddNamedImages() method is for. You add the images by giving them unique names and the icon object.

Now you are ready to create some logic:

```python
def on_connect(self, event):
    host = self.host.GetValue()
    username = self.user.GetValue()
    password = self.password.GetValue()
    port = int(self.port.GetValue())

    if host and username and password and port:
        self.ftp = ftplib.FTP()
        self.ftp.set_debuglevel(1)
        self.ftp.connect(host, port)
        self.ftp.login(username, password)
        self.update_status(self.ftp.getwelcome())
        thread = FTPThread(self.ftp)
```

The on_connect() method will connect your application to the specified FTP server using the username and password you give it. If these are not set, then the connect button will do nothing. One immediate improvement here would be to wrap this connection in a thread as it can take some time for the login process to complete. But this works fine for a prototype. You do call FTPThread at the end though, which is for getting a listing of the initial directory you end up in on the FTP server.

You need to create a helper method for getting the right image for the list items next:

```python
def image_getter(self, path):
    if path.folder:
        return "folder"
    else:
        return "file"
```

This method will get called by the ColumnDefn() class when you call update_ui(). The ObjectListView widget will pass that item's object through implicitly and you can then check its folder attribute to determine which image to return.

Now you may add the code for on_change_directory():

```python
def on_change_directory(self, event):
    current_selection = self.remote_server.GetSelectedObject()
    if current_selection.folder:
        thread = FTPThread(self.ftp, current_selection.filename)
```

The code above will fire if the user double-clicks on an item in the `ObjectListView` widget. It will then get the `current_selection` if there is a row selected and check to see if the item is a folder. If the item is a folder, then the widget will launch the `FTPThread` and pass in the `ftp` object and the folder name (`filename`).

You can write the `update()` method now:

```python
def update(self, paths):
    """
    Called by pubsub / thread
    """
    self.paths = paths
    self.update_ui()
```

When you are navigating the FTP server's file system, you need it to call back to your application and `update()` it. The method above gets called using `pubsub` from one of the threads that is doing something on the FTP server. If you make a change, such as uploading a file or changing to a different folder, then you want the contents of the `ObjectListView` to update accordingly.

You also need to update the status widget:

```python
def update_status(self, message):
    """
    Called by pubsub / thread
    """
    ts = time.strftime(time.strftime('%H:%M:%S',
                                     time.gmtime(time.time()
                                                 )
                                     )
                       )
    if '\n' in message:
        for line in message.split('\n'):
            line = f'{ts} {line}'
            self.status.WriteText(f'{line}\n')
    else:
        message = f'{ts} {message}'
        self.status.WriteText(f'{message}\n')
```

This method will write a message to the status text control. It is also called using pubsub from an external thread. This allows you to update the user with a notification that something has happened.

The final update method in this class is update_ui():

```python
def update_ui(self):
    self.remote_server.SetColumns([
        ColumnDefn("File/Folder", "left", 800, "filename",
                   imageGetter=self.image_getter),
        ColumnDefn("Filesize", "right", 80, "size"),
        ColumnDefn("Last Modified", "left", 150, "last_modified")
    ])
    self.remote_server.SetObjects(self.paths)
```

This method will update the ObjectListView widget using the list of paths. You update that list using the update() method, which also conveniently calls this method.

Now you can turn your attention to writing the frame code:

```python
class FtpFrame(wx.Frame):

    def __init__(self):
        super().__init__(None, title='PythonFTP', size=(1200, 600))
        panel = FtpPanel(self)
        self.create_toolbar()
        self.Show()
```

The FTPFrame class holds the code necessary to create the frame along with a toolbar and a statusbar. Currently, the application is called **PythonFTP**, but you can change that to whatever you want to. The size of the frame is also specified here. You may want to play around with that initial size depending on your computer's default resolution.

Let's go ahead and write the toolbar next:

```python
def create_toolbar(self):
    self.toolbar = self.CreateToolBar()

    add_ico = wx.ArtProvider.GetBitmap(
        wx.ART_GO_UP, wx.ART_TOOLBAR, (16, 16))
    add_file_tool = self.toolbar.AddTool(
        wx.ID_ANY, 'Upload File', add_ico,
        'Upload a file')
    self.Bind(wx.EVT_MENU, self.on_upload_file,
              add_file_tool)
```

```python
        add_ico = wx.ArtProvider.GetBitmap(
            wx.ART_GO_DOWN, wx.ART_TOOLBAR, (16, 16))
        add_file_tool = self.toolbar.AddTool(
            wx.ID_ANY, 'Download File', add_ico,
            'Download a file')
        self.Bind(wx.EVT_MENU, self.on_download_file,
                  add_file_tool)

        remove_ico = wx.ArtProvider.GetBitmap(
            wx.ART_MINUS, wx.ART_TOOLBAR, (16, 16))
        remove_tool = self.toolbar.AddTool(
            wx.ID_ANY, 'Remove File', remove_ico,
            'Remove file')
        self.Bind(wx.EVT_MENU, self.on_remove, remove_tool)

        self.toolbar.Realize()
```

The toolbar will have three buttons in it. One for uploading a file, one for downloading a file and one for removing a file. Once again, you use the wx.ArtProvider to get some generic icons for the toolbar buttons.

Since this is a prototype, you can stub out the methods that these buttons are bound to:

```python
def on_upload_file(self, event):
    pass


def on_download_file(self, event):
    pass


def on_remove(self, event):
    pass
```

These methods do not do anything, but they are required to exist for the application to run.

The last bit of code is for starting the wx.App:

```python
if __name__ == '__main__':
    app = wx.App(False)
    frame = FtpFrame()
    app.MainLoop()
```

When you run this application, you should end up seeing the following user interface:

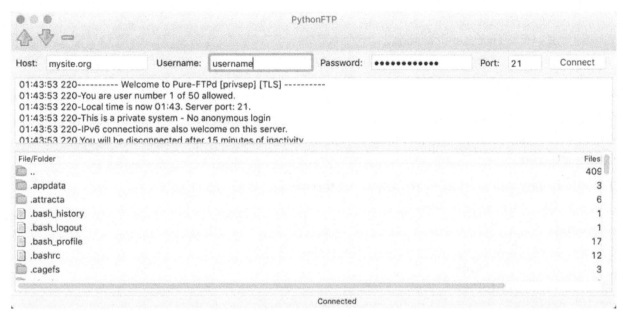

Fig. 12-2: **PythonFTP**

Of course, you will get an error if you don't have an **ftp_threads** module created. You can create an empty one just to run the UI, but the UI won't work very well unless you also add some code to this module. Let's do that next!

The ftp_threads Module

The **ftp_threads** module contains most of the code that you will use for getting directory listings on the FTP server. This is also where you could put the FTP connection code since that should probably be in a thread as well. Finally, you will be adding the class that the ObjectListView widget is using for its line items.

Here are the imports for this module:

```
# ftp_threads.py

import os
import wx

from pubsub import pub
from threading import Thread
```

These imports are rather mundane compared with the ones that were in the **main** module. You have Python's os module and the wx module, but you also have pubsub and the threading module. You can probably guess how you will use each of these.

To start off, you can create a helper function called send_status():

```python
def send_status(message):
    wx.CallAfter(pub.sendMessage,
                 'update_status',
                 message=message)
```

This function is for sending messages to the multi-line text control in the main application. It uses one of wxPython's thread-safe methods, wx.CallAfter, since you will be calling this function from within a thread.

The other thing you need to create before the thread class is a Path class:

```python
class Path:
    def __init__(self, ftype, size, filename, date):
        if 'd' in ftype:
            self.folder = True
        else:
            self.folder = False
        self.size = size
        self.filename = filename
        self.last_modified = f'{date}'
```

The Path class holds the metadata for the folders and files you load into the ObjectListView widget. The loading and parsing of this data is done in a thread and then the collection of Path objects is sent back to the main application using pubsub.

Speaking of which, you should write the thread class now:

```python
class FTPThread(Thread):

    def __init__(self, ftp, folder=None):
        super().__init__()
        self.ftp = ftp
        self.folder = folder
        self.start()
```

The FTPThread will take in the ftplib.FTP() object as its first argument and the folder it should change to, if any. These will both get set to instance attributes so they can be accessed elsewhere within the class.

To actually run your code, you will need to override the run() method:

```python
def run(self):
    if self.folder:
        self.ftp.cwd(self.folder)
        message = f'Changing directory: {self.folder}'
        send_status(message)
    self.get_dir_listing()
```

This code will first check to see if `folder` is set. If it is, then you will try to change to that directory. Regardless of whether you change folders, you will need to call `get_dir_listing()` to actually get the file and folder list from the FTP server.

You can implement that method next:

```python
def get_dir_listing(self):
    data = []
    contents = self.ftp.dir(data.append)
    self.parse_data(data)
```

This method will create an empty Python list called `data`. This list will hold all the data that is returned when you call `ftp.dir()`. Then you will need to call `parse_data()` to extract the relevant pieces of data that you care about.

You can create that method now:

```python
def parse_data(self, data):
    paths = []
    for item in data:
        parts = item.split()
        ftype = parts[0]
        size = parts[4]
        filename = parts[8]
        date = '{month} {day} {t}'.format(
            month=parts[5], day=parts[6], t=parts[7])
        if filename == '.':
            # Skip this one
            continue
        paths.append(Path(ftype, size, filename, date))

    wx.CallAfter(pub.sendMessage,
                 'update',
                 paths=paths)
```

Here you create a new list called `paths`. Then you loop over the `data` list and extract the file type, size, filename and date from the data. You also skip items that are a single period as those don't need to be represented in the user interface.

You may have noticed this already, but the `ftplib` code is kind of splintered between multiple files. When you add in trying to SFTP with `paramiko`, the code may get quite confusing when trying to figure out which method to call. This is one of the reasons why doing a prototype is useful. You will (hopefully) find issues quickly and be able to change the code before it's too late.

That is the topic of the next section!

Refactoring the Code

While this chapter won't get into actually implementing SFTP with `paramiko`, it is definitely a good idea to plan for its addition. One good method of preparation would be to put all the regular FTP code into its own module. When you add SFTP, it can go into its own module as well. Then in the main application, you can check a widget to see if the user wants to use FTP or SFTP and set the `self.ftp` variable to the appropriate module.

You will start by refactoring the **main** module.

Refactoring the main Module

The first step requires you to change the **main** module. You need to remove some imports and add some new ones.

Let's take a look:

```python
# main.py


import sys
import threading
import time
import wx


from ftp_client import FTP
from ObjectListView import ObjectListView, ColumnDefn
from pubsub import pub
```

You removed the `ftplib` module since that code needs to be in its own module. You basically replaced it with the `threading` module though. The other change is that you are importing from a new module called **ftp_client** instead of **ftp_threads**. The rest is the same as before.

You also need to copy the `send_status()` function into this module:

```
def send_status(message, topic='update_status'):
    wx.CallAfter(pub.sendMessage,
                 topic,
                 message=message)
```

The reason that this helper function is here now is that you will be using the threading module in this file. You will also be putting a copy of this function into **ftp_client**.

The FtpPanel class also needs to be modified. You won't need to touch any of the following methods:

- __init__()
- create_ui()
- image_getter()
- update()
- update_status()
- update_ui()

These methods stay the same as before.

Instead, the first method you need to change is on_connect():

```
def on_connect(self, event):
    host = self.host.GetValue()
    username = self.user.GetValue()
    password = self.password.GetValue()
    port = int(self.port.GetValue())
    self.frame.SetStatusText('Connecting...', 1)

    if host and username and password and port:
        self.ftp = FTP()
        try:
            self.ftp.disconnect()
        except:
            pass
        args = [self.ftp, host, port, username, password]
        self.thread = threading.Thread(
            target=self.connect_thread, args=args)
        self.thread.daemon = True
        self.thread.start()
```

Now when you connect to the FTP server, you first try to disconnect because connecting when you're already connected leads to goofy exceptions. You also put the actual connecting piece inside of a thread. This is done by creating a list of arguments and using the target argument of the Thread class to basically turn a regular function or method into a thread. Finally you daemonize the thread and start() it.

The method that you wrap in a thread is what you should write next:

```python
def connect_thread(self, ftp, host, port, username, password):
    """
    This method should only be run using a thread
    """
    ftp.connect(host, port, username, password)
```

This method is nice and short. You use the ftp object that you pass in and call its connect() method. You pass this method the other arguments that you passed in. Once connected, the thread ends and destroys itself implicitly. Note that this is **not** the connect() method from ftplib but one in your ftp_client code that you will be creating shortly.

Another method that should only be run in a thread is the change_dir_thread() method:

```python
def change_dir_thread(self, ftp, folder):
    """
    This method should only be run using a thread
    """
    ftp.change_directory(folder)
```

This method uses the change_directory() method from your ftp_client module. It will attempt to change directories, assuming that the one you passed in exists.

The change_directory() method is called by the following event handler:

```python
def on_change_directory(self, event):
    current_selection = self.remote_server.GetSelectedObject()
    if current_selection.folder:
        self.thread = threading.Thread(
            target=self.change_dir_thread,
            args=[self.ftp, current_selection.filename])
        self.thread.daemon = True
        self.thread.start()
```

This event handler fires when the user double-clicks on an item in the ObjectListView widget. When that occurs, it will get the current selection and run it in a thread in much the same way as the on_connect() event handler did.

That wraps up the changes to the FtpPanel class.

Now you are ready to change FtpFrame:

```python
class FtpFrame(wx.Frame):

    def __init__(self):
        super().__init__(None, title='PythonFTP', size=(1200, 600))
        self.panel = FtpPanel(self)
        self.create_toolbar()
        self.statusbar = self.CreateStatusBar(2)
        self.statusbar.SetStatusText('Disconnected', 1)
        pub.subscribe(self.update_statusbar, 'update_statusbar')
        self.Show()
```

The `create_toolbar()` method is the same in this version of the class as it was in the previous one. However, the other methods were just stubbed out before. Now is your chance to actually put some code into them.

Let's start with `on_upload_file()`, which will fire when you press the download button on the toolbar:

```python
def on_upload_file(self, event):
    if self.statusbar.GetStatusText(1) != 'Connected':
        return

    paths = None
    with wx.FileDialog(
        self, message="Choose a file",
        defaultDir='~',
        defaultFile="",
        wildcard="All files (*.*)|*.*",
        style=wx.FD_OPEN | wx.FD_MULTIPLE
        ) as dlg:
        if dlg.ShowModal() == wx.ID_OK:
            paths = dlg.GetPaths()
    if paths:
        self.thread = threading.Thread(
            target=self.panel.ftp.upload_files,
            args=[paths])
        self.thread.daemon = True
        self.thread.start()
```

This event handler will check the status bar to verify that you connected before doing anything. Then it will open up a `wx.FileDialog` to allow the user to choose a file or files to be uploaded. Once the user has made their choice or choices, you can call the ftp object's `upload_files()` method using a thread. That will do the necessary work for you and it will send an update back to the user interface when it finishes.

The `on_download_file()` method is similar:

```python
def on_download_file(self, event):
    if self.statusbar.GetStatusText(1) != 'Connected':
        return

    local_folder = None
    selections = self.panel.remote_server.GetSelectedObjects()
    if not selections:
        return

    with wx.DirDialog(
        self, "Choose a directory:",
        style=wx.DD_DEFAULT_STYLE,
        defaultPath='~') as dlg:
        if dlg.ShowModal() == wx.ID_OK:
            local_folder = dlg.GetPath()
    if local_folder and selections:
        # Filter out folder selections
        paths = [path.filename for path in selections
                 if not path.folder]
        self.thread = threading.Thread(
            target=self.panel.ftp.download_files,
            args=[paths, local_folder])
        self.thread.daemon = True
        self.thread.start()
```

In this event handler, you open up a `wx.DirDialog` which allows the user to choose what folder to save the file to, but does not allow the user to change the name of the file. Then you pass the path or paths along with the destination to the ftp object's `download_files()` method using the same thread trick that you saw in the last few examples.

The last event handler you need to add is `on_remove()`:

```python
def on_remove(self, event):
    selection = self.panel.remote_server.GetSelectedObject()
    if not selection:
        return

    # Ask user if they really want to delete the file
    with wx.MessageDialog(
        parent=None,
        message=f'Do you really want to delete {selection}?',
```

```
        caption='Confirmation',
        style=wx.OK | wx.CANCEL | wx.ICON_QUESTION) as dlg:
    if dlg.ShowModal() == wx.ID_OK:
        self.thread = threading.Thread(
            target=self.panel.ftp.delete_file,
            args=[selection.filename])
        self.thread.daemon = True
        self.thread.start()
```

This code will run when you press the Remove button on the toolbar. It will open up a wx.MessageDialog and ask the user to confirm the deletion of the selected file. If the user agrees, then it will start a thread that calls the delete_file() method from the ftp object.

The last method to create is update_statusbar(), which is used for updating the statusbar itself:

```
def update_statusbar(self, message):
    self.SetStatusText(message, 1)
```

This method is called via pubsub and updates the connection string therein. You will see it showing one of the following:

- Disconnected
- Connecting...
- Connected

This gives the user the ability to tell if your application is connected to the FTP server or not.

Now let's move on and create the FTP client code!

The ftp_client Module

The **ftp_client** module contains all the code for interacting with the FTP server. Note that if you create an SFTP implementation, you will want it to have the same methods as this one so that they can be used interchangeably.

Here are the imports for the module:

```
# ftp_client.py

import ftplib
import os
import wx

from model import Path
from pubsub import pub
```

These should be pretty familiar. The reason that you import wx here is to be able to use wx.CallAfter to send messages to the user interface. There is also a new module called model here that holds the code for the Path class. The primary reason for moving that class into its own module is so that you can import it into an SFTP module at some later point rather than having two copies of it.

This module also has a copy of the send_status() function, which you can just copy in here. It is not reproduced here since it is exactly the same as the one in the **main** module.

Let's get started by writing the __init__() method of the FTP class:

```
class FTP:

    def __init__(self, folder=None):
        self.folder = folder
```

The only item in the constructor is the folder instance attribute. This is for setting which folder you are in on the FTP server or None. You can assume that most, if not all, of the other methods in the class will be called from within a thread.

You can go ahead and create something a bit more useful, such as the connect() method:

```
def connect(self, host, port, username, password):
    try:
        self.ftp = ftplib.FTP()
        self.ftp.connect(host, port)
        self.ftp.login(username, password)
        send_status(self.ftp.getwelcome())
        send_status('Connected', topic='update_statusbar')
        self.get_dir_listing()
    except:
        send_status('Disconnected', topic='update_statusbar')
```

This method will connect to the FTP server using the provided credentials. It will also get the FTP server's "Welcome Message" and send that back to the status text control widget for display. You then update the statusbar and get the directory listing. Should something go awry when connecting, you update the statusbar with a "Disconnected" status.

The next method to create is the opposite of this one:

```
def disconnect(self):
    self.ftp.quit()
```

The disconnect() method is currently only called when the user attempts to connect. See the on_connect() event handler in the FtpPanel class. This will cause the FTP connection to end.

The next step is to create the method for changing directories on the FTP server:

```
def change_directory(self, folder):
    self.ftp.cwd(folder)
    self.get_dir_listing()
    current_directory = self.ftp.pwd()
    send_status(f'Changed directory to {current_directory}')
```

The change_directory() will attempt to change directories to the passed-in folder argument by using the cwd() method. If that works, then the code will get the directory listing again and also update the status in the main application.

You are probably wondering what is in the get_dir_listing() method, so let's do that next:

```
def get_dir_listing(self):
    data = []
    contents = self.ftp.dir(data.append)
    self.parse_data(data)
```

This method is actually the same as it was in the original code except that it has been moved into a new class. This method still calls parse_data() like it did before.

The parse_data() method is reproduced below for your convenience:

```
def parse_data(self, data):
    paths = []
    for item in data:
        parts = item.split()
        ftype = parts[0]
        size = parts[4]
        if len(parts) > 9:
            filename = ' '.join(parts[8:])
        else:
```

```
        filename = parts[8]
    date = '{month} {day} {t}'.format(
        month=parts[5], day=parts[6], t=parts[7])
    if filename == '.':
        # Skip this one
        continue
    paths.append(Path(ftype, size, filename, date))


wx.CallAfter(pub.sendMessage,
            'update',
            paths=paths)
```

This method will parse out the pieces of data that you care about and add them to the `paths` list before sending them over to the user interface.

The next new method to create is `delete_file()`:

```
def delete_file(self, filename):
    try:
        self.ftp.delete(filename)
        send_status(f'{filename} deleted successfully')
        self.get_dir_listing()
    except:
        send_status(f'Unable to delete {filename}')
```

This method uses the `delete()` method from `ftplib` to delete the specified filename. If the deletion works, you send an update back to the UI and update the directory listing accordingly. If it does not work, then you still send an update to the UI so that the user knows the deletion failed.

Now let's see how to download a file:

```
def download_files(self, paths, local_folder):
    for path in paths:
        try:
            full_path = os.path.join(local_folder, path)
            with open(full_path, 'wb') as local_file:
                self.ftp.retrbinary('RETR ' + path, local_file.write)
                message = f'Downloaded: {path}'
                send_status(message)
        except ftplib.error_perm:
            message = f'ERROR: Unable to download {path}'
            send_status(message)
```

The `download_files()` method is called by the Download toolbar button. It takes in a list of paths (i.e. filenames) and the folder to download the files to. Then it uses the `retrbinary()` method from `ftplib` to download the file. You also send out a status update back to the UI. The message you send will differ depending on whether or not the download is successful.

The final method to create is `upload_files()`:

```python
def upload_files(self, paths):
    txt_files = [".txt", ".htm", ".html"]
    for path in paths:
        _, ext = os.path.splitext(path)

        if ext in txt_files:
            with open(path) as fobj:
                self.ftp.storlines(
                    'STOR ' + os.path.basename(path), fobj)
        else:
            with open(path, 'rb') as fobj:
                self.ftp.storbinary(
                    'STOR ' + os.path.basename(path), fobj, 1024)
        send_status(f'Uploaded {path}')
    count = len(paths)
    send_status(f'{count} file(s) uploaded successfully')
    self.get_dir_listing()
```

This method will take in a list of filenames to upload. If the filename extension matches one in the `txt_files` list, it will be uploaded using the `storlines()` method. Otherwise it will use the `storbinary()` method. Once the file is uploaded, you send a message back to the UI. You also send a second message back when the entire list is done that includes a count of the items uploaded. Finally you update the directory listing.

Wrapping Up

Creating an FTP client application is fun. You learned how to connect to an FTP server using Python's built-in `ftplib` library. You were then able to view files and folders on the FTP server, add new files, delete files and download files. You also learned a new way to use Python's `threading` module with wxPython.

Here are some ideas for enhancing your FTP application:

- Add the ability to rename files / folders
- Create a directory on the FTP server

- Remove a directory on the FTP server
- Copy files / folders on the FTP server from one location to another
- Save connection details / credentials
- Add SFTP support with paramiko

There are lots of ways to improve the code and enhance the application. The ideas above don't take into consideration the user interface improvements you could make. For example, you could add a menubar with the same options as the ones in the toolbar. You could also add some UI to show the local file system in addition to the remote files. Play around with the code and add your own cool features. You will learn a lot in the process!

Chapter 13 - Creating an XML Editor

Markup languages are pretty common among software developers, especially if you develop web applications. A markup language is a computer language that describes data how that data should be arranged. There are many popular types of markup:

- HTML
- XML
- YAML

XML or **eXtensible Markup Language** is one of the most popular. Many businesses use it to store data and encode documents. One of the benefits of XML is that it is both human and machine readable. Python has built-in support for XML via its **xml** libraries. There are also 3rd party Python packages that you can download to work with XML.

In this chapter, you will be creating an XML Editor. This will allow you to open an XML document in a nice user interface and edit its contents. While the application won't work with every single XML document in existence, it will be a great way to learn how to make a nice UI and edit XML in Python.

The lxml Package

There is a popular XML toolkit called lxml that are bindings to some C libraries called libxml2 and libxslt. The reason that the lxml library is so popular is because of how fast and easy it is to use. I highly recommend using this library when you can. For this chapter, you will be using lxml for editing the XML data.

You could easily swap out the lxml package for Python's xml.etree.ElementTree library if you wanted to. I have done so in the past when I was unable to use lxml for certain projects.

To install lxml, you can use pip:

```
pip install lxml
```

If you run into any installation issues, it is recommended that you go to the lxml website and follow their installation directions here:

- https://lxml.de/installation.html

Now let's learn how to design your application!

Designing the Main App

There are many approaches that you could use for displaying and editing an XML document. One approach would be to look at the wxPython Demo package and just browse the widgets to attempt to find one that you think might work. A lot of developers think of XML nodes as trees, so perhaps you could use a Tree widget.

The wxPython GUI toolkit comes with a widget called `wx.TreeCtrl` that should work.

Next you will want some way to edit the values in the tree. There are also XML attribute sub-tags that you will need to be able to edit. One way to visualize these different data types is by putting them into two separate tabs, one for XML values and one for XML attributes.

If you go with this layout, you might come up with something like this:

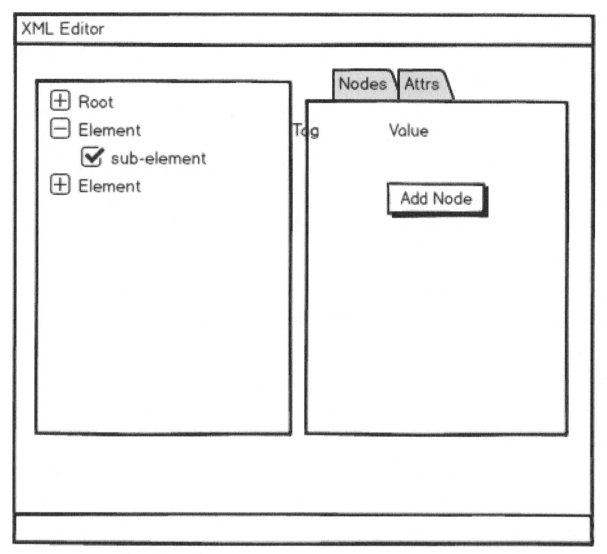

Fig. 13-1: Mockup XML Editor

Now that we have an idea of how to move forward, let's learn about one of your application's key components, the wx.TreeCtrl.

Introducing the wx.TreeCtrl

The wx.TreeCtrl widget is a bit more complicated than the basic widgets you have been using in the past. Most of the time, you will probably be subclassing it because you need to override one or more of its methods. This is something that you don't usually need to do with wx.Button, for example.

The first thing you will need is some XML to load into the widget.

Here's an example from Microsoft's MSDN website:

- https://msdn.microsoft.com/en-us/library/ms762271(v=vs.85).aspx

Here is the XML from the site:

```xml
<?xml version="1.0"?>
<catalog>
    <book id="bk101">
        <author>Gambardella, Matthew</author>
        <title>XML Developer's Guide</title>
        <genre>Computer</genre>
        <price>44.95</price>
        <publish_date>2000-10-01</publish_date>
        <description>An in-depth look at creating applications
        with XML.</description>
    </book>
</catalog>
```

This XML only shows one book in it. The full file has several book tags in it, but is too long to reproduce here.

Now let's move on and subclass wx.TreeCtrl and load an XML file into it:

```python
# xml_viewer.py

import wx

from lxml import etree, objectify


class XmlTree(wx.TreeCtrl):

    def __init__(self, parent):
        wx.TreeCtrl.__init__(self, parent)

        try:
            with open(parent.xml_path) as f:
                xml = f.read()
        except IOError:
            print('Bad file')
            return
        except Exception as e:
            print('Really bad error')
            print(e)
            return
```

Here you will need to import wx and a couple of modules from lxml: etree and objectify. The etree module is very similar to Python's own ElementTree implementation and can be swapped out for the other almost seamlessly. Here you subclass wx.TreeCtrl and attempt to open the XML file. The XML file's path is actually stored as an instance variable in the parent that was passed in to the wx.TreeCtrl.

If you have an exception, you can print out the issue. The exception handling here is a bit silly, but it's fun. You can make that more professional and useful at release time. The main thing is that if you do happen to pass in a bad file, it won't crash your application. One good enhancement you could add is to show a wx.MessageDialog here with the error message that occurred.

Let's add a few more lines of code to the __init__() to finish it up:

```
self.xml_root = objectify.fromstring(xml)

root = self.AddRoot(self.xml_root.tag)
self.SetItemData(root, ('key', 'value'))

for top_level_item in self.xml_root.getchildren():
    child = self.AppendItem(root, top_level_item.tag)
    self.SetItemHasChildren(child)
    if top_level_item.attrib:
        self.SetItemData(child, top_level_item.attrib)

self.Expand(root)
self.Bind(wx.EVT_TREE_ITEM_EXPANDING, self.onItemExpanding)
```

In this code, you use objectify to turn the contents of the XML into an object. Note that if the XML file is very large, you may want to load it up in chunks. But for now, you can just assume that the XML files are of a reasonable size. Next you need to set the root of the wx.TreeCtrl, so you grab the tag of the first element in the XML file, which should be the XML's root.

Then you set the root's data to a generic tuple. Next you iterate over the XML's children and append them to the root of the wx.TreeCtrl using AppendItem(). If the item has an attribute (i.e. attrib), then you set its data via SetItemData(). The function of SetItemData() is to save off information about that item in the tree. You can save any Python object here. In this case, you just save off the specific XML element's attribute field.

Finally you call Expand with the Tree's root as the sole parameter. This will expand the root for you and show all the immediate children underneath it. Then you bind the tree control to EVT_TREE_-ITEM_EXPANDING, which allows you to control what happens when someone expands items in the tree control.

Now let's write the event handler:

```
def onItemExpanding(self, event):
    item = event.GetItem()
    book_id = self.GetItemData(item)

    for top_level_item in self.xml_root.getchildren():
        if top_level_item.attrib == book_id:
            book = top_level_item
            self.SetItemData(item, top_level_item)
            self.add_book_elements(item, book)
            break
```

Here you extract the tree's item that you are expanding via GetItem(). Then you can get the book's id by pulling the item's data out. The next step is to iterate over the children of the root item and look for that specific id. When you find it, you reset the item data appropriately and you call add_book_elements() with the originally selected item object and the sub-item that matched the id.

This allows you to populate the sub-items in the tree on demand. You could pre-populate the entire tree, but that could be time-consuming if there is a lot of XML to load. So this is an example of optimization on the UI side.

Anyway, let's go ahead and write add_book_elements():

```
def add_book_elements(self, item, book):
    for element in book.getchildren():
        child = self.AppendItem(item, element.tag)
        if element.getchildren():
            self.SetItemHasChildren(child)

        if element.attrib:
            self.SetItemData(child, element.attrib)
```

This code is actually quite similar to the last piece. Here you will also loop over the sub-item's children. But this time you will append children to the sub-item. If the child has children itself, then you need to mark it as such with a call to SetItemHasChildren(). By doing so, you mark that sub-item's sub-item as expandable in the UI. If the sub-item's child has an attribute, then you set its data as you did before.

Now you need to create an instance of wx.Panel to put your wx.TreeCtrl into:

```
class TreePanel(wx.Panel):

    def __init__(self, parent, xml_path):
        wx.Panel.__init__(self, parent)
        self.xml_path = xml_path

        self.tree = XmlTree(self)

        sizer = wx.BoxSizer(wx.VERTICAL)
        sizer.Add(self.tree, 0, wx.EXPAND)
        self.SetSizer(sizer)
```

Here you create the panel as you normally would. You also set the xml_path attribute and instantiate the wx.TreeCtrl. Finally you add the tree widget to a sizer and expand it to fill up all the space.

Now to run the program, you will want to subclass wx.Frame:

```
class MainFrame(wx.Frame):

    def __init__(self, xml_path):
        wx.Frame.__init__(self, parent=None,
                          title='XML Viewer')
        panel = TreePanel(self, xml_path)
        self.Show()

if __name__ == '__main__':
    xml_path = 'sample.xml'
    app = wx.App(redirect=False)
    frame = MainFrame(xml_path)
    app.MainLoop()
```

This code should look familiar. You create the wx.Frame, add a panel and show it.

When I ran this code, it looked like this:

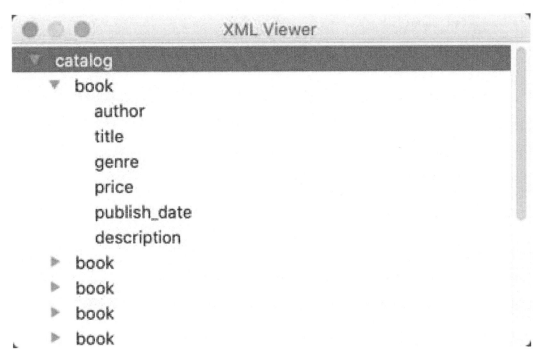

Fig. 13-2: XML Viewer

Admittedly, all this does is let you look at the top level tags in the XML document. You cannot see the tag's value, nor can you change them.

You will discover how to create the basic user interface next!

Creating the Basic User Interface

The first step in designing the interface is to figure out how to lay out the widgets. This first version of the code is pretty simplistic, but it will get you most of the way there visually. You will put most of the code into a single file called **xml_editor.py** that will be the code you will want to run to start your program. You will create the UI a class at a time.

Since this file will be several hundred lines of code, I will break it up into sections to make it easier to follow along.

Let's get started!

The imports (xml_editor.py)

The first piece of code in any new Python application is the imports and anything else you might need at the top of the script.

Let's take a look:

```
# xml_editor.py

import os
import wx
import wx.adv
import wx.lib.scrolledpanel as scrolled

from lxml import objectify
from pubsub import pub
from wx.lib.wordwrap import wordwrap

wildcard = "XML (*.xml)|*.xml|" \
"All files (*.*)|*.*"
```

Most of these imports should look pretty familiar to you. There are a couple of new ones though. The `wx.adv` sub-module contains some of wxPython's advanced widgets. You will learn how to use the `AboutDialogInfo` that comes from that sub-module soon. You also need to import `wx.lib.scrolledpanel`, which creates a version of the `wx.Panel` that will add a scrollbar automatically if enough widgets get added to it.

There is also the `lxml` import, which was discussed earlier in the chapter. The other import of interest is `wx.lib.wordwrap`, which you can use for wrapping long pieces of text automatically. You will be using that in conjunction with `AboutDialogInfo`.

Finally there is the variable, `wildcard`, which you will be using with a `wx.FileDialog` when you need to open an XML file.

The MainFrame Class (xml_editor.py)

The first class you should create is the `MainFrame` class since this is the class that will be the root of most of the rest of your application.

Let's start by taking a look at the `__init__`:

```
class MainFrame(wx.Frame):

    def __init__(self):
        size = (800, 600)
        super().__init__(
            None, title="XML Editor",
            size=size)
        self.panel = EditorPanel(self, size)
        self.create_menu()
        self.Show()
```

Here you instantiate the frame itself as well as create an instance of `EditorPanel`. You also set the size of the frame and pass that information along to the panel class. Then you create the menu and show the frame.

The menu creation method is next:

```python
def create_menu(self):
    menu_bar = wx.MenuBar()
    file_menu = wx.Menu()
    help_menu = wx.Menu()

    # add menu items to the file menu
    open_menu_item = file_menu.Append(
            wx.NewId(), 'Open', '')
    self.Bind(wx.EVT_MENU, self.on_open, open_menu_item)

    save_menu_item = file_menu.Append(
            wx.NewId(), 'Save', '')
    self.Bind(wx.EVT_MENU, self.on_save, save_menu_item)

    exit_menu_item = file_menu.Append(
            wx.NewId(), 'Quit', '')
    self.Bind(wx.EVT_MENU, self.on_exit, exit_menu_item)
    menu_bar.Append(file_menu, "&File")

    # add menu items to the help menu
    about_menu_item = help_menu.Append(
            wx.NewId(), 'About')
    self.Bind(wx.EVT_MENU, self.on_about_box, about_menu_item)
    menu_bar.Append(help_menu, '&Help')

    self.SetMenuBar(menu_bar)
```

Here we create a menu bar with two menus. The first menu is the typical **File** menu and the second is a **Help** menu. The **File** menu has three items in it: an open option, a save option and an exit option. The **Help** menu has one option that will open an about dialog. The next step is to hook up all the menu items.

Let's start by writing the `on_save` event handler:

```python
def on_save(self, event):
    """
    Event handler that saves the data to disk
    """
    pub.sendMessage('save_{}'.format(self.panel.page_id))
```

This method has only one line of code in it, besides the docstring. That line of code sends a message to the panel that tells it that it needs to save the XML file. Since this version of the code actually doesn't support editing the XML yet, this event handler essentially doesn't do anything. However this is nice to have for when you do get the save method finished.

The next event handler to create is on_about_box:

```python
def on_about_box(self, event):
    """
    Event handler that builds and shows an about box
    """
    info = wx.adv.AboutDialogInfo()
    info.Name = "About XML Editor"
    info.Version = "0.1 Beta"
    info.Copyright = "(C) 2019 Mike Driscoll"
    info.Description = wordwrap(
        "This is a Python-based XML editor ",
        350, wx.ClientDC(self.panel))
    info.WebSite = ("https://mousevspython.com",
                    "Mouse Vs Python")
    info.Developers = ["Mike Driscoll"]
    info.License = wordwrap("wxWindows Library Licence", 500,
                            wx.ClientDC(self.panel))
    # Show the wx.AboutBox
    wx.adv.AboutBox(info)
```

This is the bit of code where you learn how to use wx.adv.AboutDialogInfo. Basically, what you need to do is instantiate it. Then you can set a few of its attributes as you can see above. The Description attribute uses wordwrap and wx.ClientDC. The wx.ClientDC is used for drawing the text to the screen instead of using wx.StaticText. You can see a second instance of this sort of thing with the License attribute. Finally to show the information that you have created, you pass that instance to wx.adv.AboutBox.

Now let's write the code to open an XML file:

```python
def on_open(self, event):
    """
    Event handler that is called when you need to open an XML file
    """
    path = None
    default_dir=os.path.expanduser('~')
    with wx.FileDialog(
        self, message="Choose a file",
        defaultDir=default_dir,
        defaultFile="",
        wildcard=wildcard,
        style=wx.FD_OPEN | wx.FD_CHANGE_DIR
        ) as dlg:
        if dlg.ShowModal() == wx.ID_OK:
            path = dlg.GetPath()

    if path:
        self.panel.open_xml(path)
```

Here you create a wx.FileDialog using the wildcard you created earlier. This particular dialog is an open dialog. The type of dialog is set by the wx.FD_OPEN style flag. Once the user picks an XML file, you call the panel open_xml() to attempt to open the file.

To wrap up the event handlers, go ahead and write the on_exit() method:

```python
def on_exit(self, event):
    """
    Event handler that closes the application
    """
    self.Destroy()
```

This is another one-liner method. All it does is call Destroy(), which effectively ends the program.

The final bit to cover here is how to initialize the frame:

```python
if __name__ == '__main__':
    app = wx.App(False)
    frame = MainFrame()
    app.MainLoop()
```

As usual, you need to create an instance of wx.App and then an instance of the frame widget itself. Then start the MainLoop() and your application should be off and running!

The EditorPanel Class (xml_editor.py)

The EditorPanel class is where the main widgets are created and laid out. Fortunately, the code for this class is fairly brief because you will be splitting off the widgets that it contains into their own classes.

Let's take a look at the __init__() first:

```python
class EditorPanel(wx.Panel):

    def __init__(self, parent, size):
        super().__init__(parent)
        self.page_id = id(self)
        self.size = size
        pub.subscribe(self.save, 'save_{}'.format(self.page_id))
        pub.subscribe(self.add_node,
                      'add_node_{}'.format(self.page_id))

        self.xml_path = None
        self.open_xml()
```

This code is kind of interesting. Here you create a unique page_id. The reason is that eventually it would be nice to be able to have more than one XML document open at once. If you do that, then you will need a unique ID so that you know which XML edits go to which files. You also save off the initial size of the frame. The other bits here are setting up a couple of listeners in Pubsub, one for saves and one for adding nodes to the XML. The last piece is where you attempt to open the XML file.

Let's do that next:

```python
def open_xml(self, path='sample.xml'):
    try:
        with open(path) as f:
            self.xml = f.read()
    except IOError:
        print('Bad file')
        return
    except Exception as e:
        print('Really bad error')
        print(e)
        return
    self.create_editor()
```

Here is the code where you attempt to open the XML file and raise different sorts of errors if the file is bad. Once again, you could enhance this code by putting in some kind of dialog to tell the user that the file was bad. However, if the file opens successfully, then you call create_editor().

Go ahead and add that to your code now:

```python
def create_editor(self):
    """
    Create the XML editor widgets
    """
    page_sizer = wx.BoxSizer(wx.VERTICAL)

    splitter = wx.SplitterWindow(self)
    self.tree_panel = TreePanel(splitter, self.page_id, self.xml)

    xml_editor_notebook = wx.Notebook(splitter)
    xml_editor_panel = XmlEditorPanel(xml_editor_notebook,
                                      self.page_id)
    xml_editor_notebook.AddPage(xml_editor_panel, 'Nodes')

    attribute_panel = AttributeEditorPanel(
        xml_editor_notebook, self.page_id)
    xml_editor_notebook.AddPage(attribute_panel, 'Attributes')

    splitter.SplitVertically(self.tree_panel, xml_editor_notebook)
    splitter.SetMinimumPaneSize(self.size[0] / 2)
    page_sizer.Add(splitter, 1, wx.ALL|wx.EXPAND, 5)

    self.SetSizer(page_sizer)
    self.Layout()
```

The create_editor() method will create a wx.SplitterWindow that contains two widgets. The left-hand widget contains the TreePanel while the right-hand side contains a wx.Notebook. The notebook is a tabbed widget that you can add panels to. In this case, you add two panels:

- XmlEditorPanel - Which contains the widgets necessary to edit XML values and add nodes
- AttributeEditorPanel - Which contains the widgets you need to edit the XML node's attributes

You then use SplitVertically() to make the two different panels take their respective sides and you set the pane size to half the width of the frame's initial size.

Now let's stub out the last two methods of this class:

```python
def save(self):
    """ Save the XML file """
    print('Saving')

def add_node(self):
    """
    Add a sub-node to the selected item in the tree

    Called by pubsub
    """
    print('Add node')
```

The save() method will be used to save your XML file while the add_node() method would be used for adding a node to the XML.

Let's learn how to create the TreePanel next!

The TreePanel Class (xml_editor.py)

The TreePanel class is just a regular wx.Panel that creates an instance of the wx.TreeCtrl.

Let's take a look:

```python
class TreePanel(wx.Panel):

    def __init__(self, parent, page_id, xml):
        super().__init__(parent)

        self.page_id = page_id
        self.xml = xml

        self.tree = XmlTree(
            self, wx.ID_ANY, wx.DefaultPosition, wx.DefaultSize,
            wx.TR_HAS_BUTTONS)

        sizer = wx.BoxSizer(wx.VERTICAL)
        sizer.Add(self.tree, 1, wx.EXPAND)
        self.SetSizer(sizer)
```

Here you simply create an instance of XmlTree, which is a subclass of wx.TreeCtrl and add it to a sizer. The tree control is set to expand and fill the panel.

Now you are ready to learn about the other panel in the splitter window.

The XmlEditorPanel Class (xml_editor.py)

The `XmlEditorPanel` is the panel that sits on the right side of your application and contains the widgets necessary to edit XML values.

Let's find out what's in its __init__():

```python
class XmlEditorPanel(scrolled.ScrolledPanel):
    """
    The panel in the notebook that allows editing of XML
    element values
    """

    def __init__(self, parent, page_id):
        """Constructor"""
        scrolled.ScrolledPanel.__init__(
            self, parent, style=wx.SUNKEN_BORDER)
        self.main_sizer = wx.BoxSizer(wx.VERTICAL)
        self.widgets = []
        self.page_id = page_id
        pub.subscribe(self.update_ui,
                      'ui_updater_{}'.format(self.page_id))

        self.SetSizer(self.main_sizer)
```

This is your first encounter with the `ScrolledPanel` widget. You can add a sunken border to the widget via the aptly-named `style` flag. Since the widgets on this panel will be dynamically added and removed, you need to keep a list of them. You will also subscribe to an update message so that when the user changes their selection, this panel's contents will update.

Let's find out how the updating code works:

```python
def update_ui(self, xml_obj):
    """
    Update the panel's user interface based on the data
    """
    sizer = wx.BoxSizer(wx.HORIZONTAL)
    self.clear()

    tag_lbl = wx.StaticText(self, label='Tag', size=(25, 25))
    value_lbl = wx.StaticText(self, label='Value')
    sizer.Add(tag_lbl, 0, wx.ALL, 5)
    sizer.Add(0, 55, 0)
    sizer.Add(value_lbl, 0, wx.ALL, 5)
```

```
self.main_sizer.Add(sizer)

self.widgets.extend([tag_lbl, value_lbl])
```

These first few lines of update_ui() set up two labels that go at the top of the page. You add these labels to the widgets list. Also note that at the top of the method, you call clear(). The clear() method will remove all the current widgets on the page so that you can add new ones.

Let's go ahead and look at the rest of the code for this method:

```
if xml_obj is not None:
    lbl_size = (75, 25)
    for child in xml_obj.getchildren():
        if child.getchildren():
            continue
        sizer = wx.BoxSizer(wx.HORIZONTAL)
        tag_txt = wx.StaticText(
            self, label=child.tag, size=lbl_size)
        sizer.Add(tag_txt, 0, wx.ALL, 5)
        self.widgets.append(tag_txt)

        text = child.text if child.text else ''

        value_txt = wx.TextCtrl(self, value=text)
        sizer.Add(value_txt, 1, wx.ALL|wx.EXPAND, 5)
        self.widgets.append(value_txt)

        self.main_sizer.Add(sizer, 0, wx.EXPAND)

    if getattr(xml_obj, 'tag') and getattr(xml_obj, 'text'):
        if xml_obj.getchildren() == []:
            self.add_single_tag_elements(xml_obj, lbl_size)

    add_node_btn = wx.Button(self, label='Add Node')
    add_node_btn.Bind(wx.EVT_BUTTON, self.on_add_node)
    self.main_sizer.Add(add_node_btn, 0, wx.ALL|wx.CENTER, 5)
    self.widgets.append(add_node_btn)

    self.SetAutoLayout(1)
    self.SetupScrolling()
```

Here you do a check to make sure that xml_obj is set to something. If so, then you will loop over its children and add create widgets for them. For each widget, you also set the value to the corresponding XML value. The last check at the end is to see if there is an `xml_obj` with a `tag` and `text`, but doesn't have children. In that case, you will only want to add a single tag element.

You also want to add a new node button so that you can add new nodes to the XML. Finally, you will need to call `SetAutoLayout()` so that items lay out correctly in the panel and turn on scrolling via `SetupScrolling()`.

Now let's add a single tag:

```python
def add_single_tag_elements(self, xml_obj, lbl_size):
    """
    Adds the single tag elements to the panel
    This function is only called when there should be just one
    tag / value
    """
    sizer = wx.BoxSizer(wx.HORIZONTAL)
    tag_txt = wx.StaticText(self, label=xml_obj.tag, size=lbl_size)
    sizer.Add(tag_txt, 0, wx.ALL, 5)
    self.widgets.append(tag_txt)

    value_txt = wx.TextCtrl(self, value=xml_obj.text)
    sizer.Add(value_txt, 1, wx.ALL|wx.EXPAND, 5)
    self.widgets.append(value_txt)
    self.main_sizer.Add(sizer, 0, wx.EXPAND)
```

This method is needed primarily because I stumbled onto sort of an edge case where you will have a single tag element that you need to edit. This just adds the right widgets when that happens.

Let's write the `clear()` method:

```python
def clear(self):
    """
    Clears the widgets from the panel in preparation for an update
    """
    sizers = {}
    for widget in self.widgets:
        sizer = widget.GetContainingSizer()
        if sizer:
            sizer_id = id(sizer)
            if sizer_id not in sizers:
                sizers[sizer_id] = sizer
        widget.Destroy()

    for sizer in sizers:
```

```
            self.main_sizer.Remove(sizers[sizer])

    self.widgets = []
    self.Layout()
```

Here you will iterate over the widgets list that you made in the last two functions. For each widget, you get its sizer and add it to a sizer dictionary if it's not already in the dictionary. Then you destroy the widget. Next you loop over the sizer dictionary and remove the sizers from the top level sizer. Finally you reset the widgets list and call Layout() which will force the panel / sizer to refresh the layout of its contents.

The last method to look at is a stub version of on_add_node():

```
def on_add_node(self, event):
    pub.sendMessage(f'add_node_{self.page_id}')
```

Eventually you will write the listener for this publisher, but for now, this is good enough. It will broadcast the message and nothing will happen.

Now you are ready to learn about the XMLTree class.

The XmlTree Class (xml_editor.py)

The XmlTree class is what you will be using to represent the XML tags. You looked at how this worked in the first section. The following code has been enhanced a bit to make it more useful.

Let's take a look:

```
class XmlTree(wx.TreeCtrl):

    def __init__(self, parent, id, pos, size, style):
        super().__init__(parent, id, pos, size, style)
        self.page_id = parent.page_id
        self.expanded= {}

        self.xml_root = objectify.fromstring(parent.xml)

        root = self.AddRoot(self.xml_root.tag)
        self.SetItemData(root, ('key', 'value'))

        wx.CallAfter(pub.sendMessage,
                     'ui_updater_{}'.format(self.page_id),
                     xml_obj=self.xml_root)
```

```
        if self.xml_root.getchildren():
            for top_level_item in self.xml_root.getchildren():
                child = self.AppendItem(root, top_level_item.tag)
                if top_level_item.getchildren():
                    self.SetItemHasChildren(child)
                self.SetItemData(child, top_level_item)

        self.Expand(root)
        self.Bind(wx.EVT_TREE_ITEM_EXPANDING, self.onItemExpanding)
        self.Bind(wx.EVT_TREE_SEL_CHANGED, self.on_tree_selection)
```

First off, you have a new expanded dictionary that you will use to keep track of which tags have been expanded. Then you add the root to the tree control the same way as you did before. Here you use wx.CallAfter() to send a message to another class. The reason for using wx.CallAfter is that you want a slight delay so that the tree control and the right-side will be in sync when the application loads. Then you loop over the children in the XML nodes and update the tree control accordingly.

Finally you expand the root and bind a couple of events.

The first event handler to override is onItemExpanding():

```
def onItemExpanding(self, event):
    item = event.GetItem()
    xml_obj = self.GetItemData(item)

    if id(xml_obj) not in self.expanded and xml_obj is not None:
        for top_level_item in xml_obj.getchildren():
            child = self.AppendItem(item, top_level_item.tag)
            self.SetItemData(child, top_level_item)
            if top_level_item.getchildren():
                self.SetItemHasChildren(child)

    self.expanded[id(xml_obj)] = ''
```

This method is called when you expand a node in the tree control. When you do that, you will check if the node has been previously expanded and that the tree item's data returns an XML object. If one of those things doesn't happen, you cannot expand it or it was already expanded. The rest of the code is pretty much what you've seen before.

Now let's take a look at the final event handler:

```python
def on_tree_selection(self, event):
    """
    A handler that fires when an item in the tree is selected
    This will cause an update to be sent to the XmlEditorPanel
    to allow editing of the XML
    """
    item = event.GetItem()
    xml_obj = self.GetItemData(item)
    if xml_obj is not None and hasattr(xml_obj, 'getchildren'):
        pub.sendMessage('ui_updater_{}'.format(self.page_id),
                        xml_obj=xml_obj)
```

Whenever the user selects an item in the tree control, it will cause on_tree_selection() to fire. This method will extract the xml_obj and send a message out to update the right-hand side of your application so that you can edit the values and attributes of the selected XML node.

The AttributeEditorPanel Class (xml_editor.py)

The AttributeEditorPanel represents the second tab in the notebook control that appears on the right hand side of your application. It will allow the user to edit XML node attributes.

Let's find out how all this works:

```python
class AttributeEditorPanel(wx.Panel):

    def __init__(self, parent, page_id):
        super().__init__(parent)
        self.page_id = page_id
        self.widgets = []
        pub.subscribe(self.update_ui,
                      'ui_updater_{}'.format(self.page_id))
        self.main_sizer = wx.BoxSizer(wx.VERTICAL)
        self.SetSizer(self.main_sizer)
```

Here you once again create a widgets list and create a listener. The user interface for this panel will get updated when another class sends out the appropriate message type.

The update_ui() method is actually quite similar to the one in XmlEditorPanel.

Let's check it out anyway though:

```python
def update_ui(self, xml_obj):
    """

    Update the user interface to have elements for editing
    XML attributes

    Called via pubsub
    """
    self.clear()
    self.xml_obj = xml_obj

    sizer = wx.BoxSizer(wx.HORIZONTAL)
    attr_lbl = wx.StaticText(self, label='Attribute')
    value_lbl = wx.StaticText(self, label='Value')
    sizer.Add(attr_lbl, 0, wx.ALL, 5)
    sizer.Add(0, 55, 0)
    sizer.Add(value_lbl, 0, wx.ALL, 5)
    self.widgets.extend([attr_lbl, value_lbl])

    self.main_sizer.Add(sizer)

    for key in xml_obj.attrib:
        _ = wx.BoxSizer(wx.HORIZONTAL)
        attr_name = wx.TextCtrl(self, value=key)
        _.Add(attr_name, 1, wx.ALL|wx.EXPAND, 5)
        self.widgets.append(attr_name)

        val = str(xml_obj.attrib[key])
        attr_val = wx.TextCtrl(self, value=val)
        _.Add(attr_val, 1, wx.ALL|wx.EXPAND, 5)

        self.widgets.append(attr_val)
        self.main_sizer.Add(_, 0, wx.EXPAND)

    add_attr_btn = wx.Button(self, label='Add Attribute')
    add_attr_btn.Bind(wx.EVT_BUTTON, self.on_add_attr)
    self.main_sizer.Add(add_attr_btn, 0, wx.ALL|wx.CENTER, 5)
    self.widgets.append(add_attr_btn)

    self.Layout()
```

In this case, you once again call this class's `clear()` method as soon as possible. Once again, this will clear out the widgets and sizers as before. Then the rest of this code create the sizers and widgets necessary for the user to edit their XML's attributes.

The next method is the on_add_attr() event handler stub:

```python
def on_add_attr(self, event):
    pass
```

Since all you are trying to do with this code is make the user interface, this event handler doesn't need to do anything other than exist.

Now let's take a quick look at the clear() method:

```python
def clear(self):
    """
    Clears the panel of widgets
    """
    sizers = {}
    for widget in self.widgets:
        sizer = widget.GetContainingSizer()
        if sizer:
            sizer_id = id(sizer)
            if sizer_id not in sizers:
                sizers[sizer_id] = sizer
        widget.Destroy()

    for sizer in sizers:
        self.main_sizer.Remove(sizers[sizer])

    self.widgets = []
    self.Layout()
```

This code is actually exactly the same as the code in the XmlEditorPanel class. Whenever you see two pieces of code that are the same or nearly the same, that is a clue that you need to refactor it. This method should be moved into something else so that both of the classes can call it. You could create a super class that these two other classes inherit from, for example. Another simple solution would be to move common methods like this into their own module that the classes then use.

At this point, the code should run. On my machine, it looked like this:

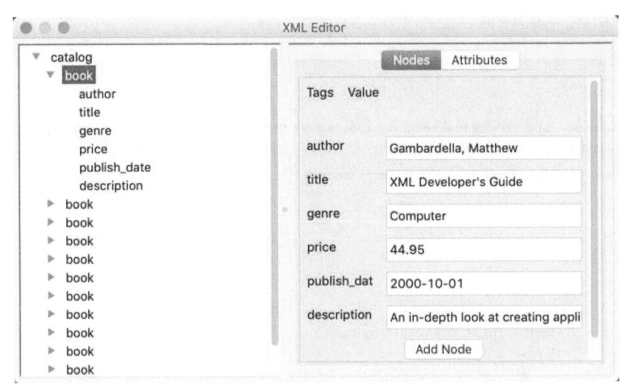

Fig. 13-3: XML Editor (non-working)

If you switch to the Attributes tab, it will look like this:

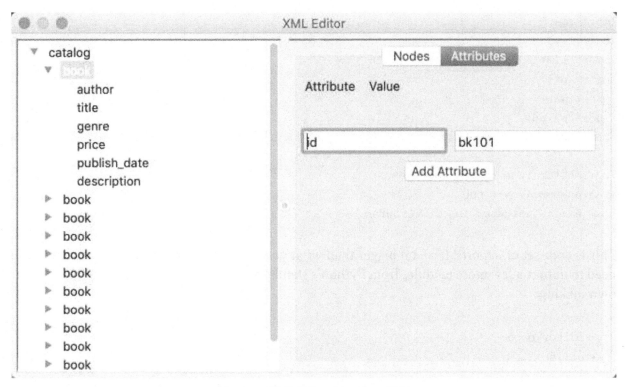

Fig. 13-4: XML Editor (Attribute Tab)

The last item you need to accomplish is making the code work!

Creating an XML Editor

Let's copy all this code you created into a new folder. In the Github repo, the folder you want to look at is **version_2_working_ui**. Now that you have a new copy of the code, you can take the time to split it up into multiple modules. This is also a good time to do any refactoring of the code that you want to do. The reason that most developers will split their code up is that it makes managing the code easier and it also allows much easier collaboration with other members of your team.

You will also be adding a new feature to your editor. That feature is the ability to have more than one XML file open at a time.

The main.py module

Most of the time, the main entry point for your code will be in a file named **main.py** by convention or it will be the name of the application. For example, if we called this application "Python XML Editor", the entry point name would probably be something like **xml_editor.py** or **wx_xml_editor.py**. The name doesn't matter all that much as long as you know what the name is.

```
import os
import sys
import time
import utils
import wx
import wx.adv
import wx.lib.agw.flatnotebook as fnb

from editor_page import NewPage
from pubsub import pub
from wx.lib.wordwrap import wordwrap
```

This is your set of imports. It's a bit bigger than what you had in the earlier sections. This time you need to import a few more modules from Python's standard library as well as some modules of your own making:

- editor_page
- utils

You will also be using wx.lib.agw.flatnotebook, which is a nice notebook that will allow you to load up multiple XML files at once.

Let's take a look at the MainFrame class code below:

```
class MainFrame(wx.Frame):

    def __init__(self):
        self.size = (800, 600)
        wx.Frame.__init__(self, parent=None, title='XML Editor',
                          size=(800, 600))

        self.full_tmp_path = ''
        self.full_saved_path = ''
        self.changed = False
        self.notebook = None
        self.opened_files = []
        self.last_opened_file = None
        self.current_page = None
```

This code is pretty self-explanatory. You have a lot of instance attributes that you are setting up, most of which are flags. You also keep a list of opened_files and which page is the current_page.

There are a few more lines to add to the __init__() though:

```python
self.current_directory = os.path.expanduser('~')
self.app_location = os.path.dirname(os.path.abspath( sys.argv[0] ))
self.recent_files_path = os.path.join(
    self.app_location, 'recent_files.txt')


pub.subscribe(self.save, 'save')

self.main_sizer = wx.BoxSizer(wx.VERTICAL)
self.panel = wx.Panel(self)
self.panel.SetSizer(self.main_sizer)


self.create_menu_and_toolbar()


self.Bind(wx.EVT_CLOSE, self.on_exit)


self.Show()
```

Here you set the current directory you will open XML files from. You always need to start somewhere after all. Then there's a pubsub subscription, some sizers and a call to create_menu_and_toolbar().

But before we get to that method, let's write create_new_editor() instead:

```python
def create_new_editor(self, xml_path):
    """
    Create the tree and xml editing widgets when the user loads
    an XML file
    """
    if not self.notebook:
        self.notebook = fnb.FlatNotebook(
            self.panel)
        self.main_sizer.Add(self.notebook, 1, wx.ALL|wx.EXPAND, 5)
        style = self.notebook.GetAGWWindowStyleFlag()
        style |= fnb.FNB_X_ON_TAB
        self.notebook.SetAGWWindowStyleFlag(style)
        self.notebook.Bind(
            fnb.EVT_FLATNOTEBOOK_PAGE_CLOSING, self.on_page_closing)

    if xml_path not in self.opened_files:
        self.current_page = NewPage(self.notebook, xml_path, self.size,
                                    self.opened_files)
        self.notebook.AddPage(self.current_page,
                              os.path.basename(xml_path),
                              select=True)
```

```
        self.last_opened_file = xml_path

        self.opened_files.append(self.last_opened_file)

    self.panel.Layout()
```

The main thrust of this code is that it will generate the notebook widget if it doesn't already exist. It also sets a few flags on the FlatNotebook that affect the notebook's display. For example, FNB_X_-ON_TAB adds an X to each tab to allow the user to close that tab by clicking the X. You also need to bind to EVT_FLATNOTEBOOK_PAGE_CLOSING so that you can destroy the page correctly.

The last conditional statement above is used for creating a page in the notebook. It verifies that you are not trying to open the same file twice and then creates the page with NewPage.

The next method to look at is create_menu_and_toolbar():

```
def create_menu_and_toolbar(self):
    """
    Creates the menu bar, menu items, toolbar and accelerator table
    for the main frame
    """
    menu_bar = wx.MenuBar()
    file_menu = wx.Menu()
    help_menu = wx.Menu()

    # add menu items to the file menu
    open_menu_item = file_menu.Append(
        wx.NewId(), 'Open', '')
    self.Bind(wx.EVT_MENU, self.on_open, open_menu_item)

    save_menu_item = file_menu.Append(
        wx.NewId(), 'Save', '')
    self.Bind(wx.EVT_MENU, self.on_save, save_menu_item)

    exit_menu_item = file_menu.Append(
        wx.NewId(), 'Quit', '')
    self.Bind(wx.EVT_MENU, self.on_exit, exit_menu_item)
    menu_bar.Append(file_menu, "&File")

    self.SetMenuBar(menu_bar)
```

To keep things short, I removed the toolbar portion from this section. You can refer to the final version of the code to see how that works. This method just creates a series of menus, as you have seen before.

Now let's learn how to open an XML file:

```python
def open_xml_file(self, xml_path):
    """
    Open the specified XML file and load it in the application
    """
    self.create_new_editor(xml_path)
```

The `open_xml_file()` method will get called when you open a new XML file. All that it does is call `create_new_editor()` with the path to the XML file.

The `save()` method is next:

```python
def save(self):
    """
    Update the frame with save status
    """
    if self.current_page is None:
        utils.warn_nothing_to_save()
        return

    pub.sendMessage('save_{}'.format(self.current_page.page_id))

    self.changed = False
```

The `save()` method will attempt to save the file. If you try to save a file without actually having any open, then `warn_nothing_to_save()` will be called and a warning message will be shown.

This next method is related to opening the XML file:

```python
def on_open(self, event):
    """
    Event handler that is called when you need to open an XML file
    """
    xml_path = utils.open_file(self)

    if xml_path:
        self.last_opened_file = xml_path
        self.open_xml_file(xml_path)
```

The `on_open()` method calls the `open_file()` function from the `utils` module. If a path is returned, you set a flag and then call `open_xml_file()`.

Let's see what's next:

```python
def on_page_closing(self, event):
    """

    Event handler that is called when a page in the notebook is closing
    """
    page = self.notebook.GetCurrentPage()
    page.Close()
    if not self.opened_files:
        wx.CallAfter(self.notebook.Destroy)
        self.notebook = None
```

The on_page_closing() method was mentioned earlier. Here you grab the current page and Close() it. Then you check to see if there are any open files left. If not, then you close the notebook itself.

Only two more event handlers to go:

```python
def on_save(self, event):
    """

    Event handler that saves the data to disk
    """
    self.save()
```

The on_save() event handler is nice and short. It's only duty is to call save() itself.

The last event handler closes the program:

```python
def on_exit(self, event):
    """

    Event handler that closes the application
    """
    self.Destroy()
```

The on_exit() event handler is also short and sweet. It tells wxPython to Destroy() the frame and end the program.

The utils.py module

The **utils.py** module contains reusable functions that other classes in your application can use. It's a module that is used for holding common utilities.

The first few lines of the module are as follows:

```
import os
import wx

wildcard = "XML (*.xml)|*.xml|" \
    "All files (*.*)|*.*"
```

Here you have the imports and a module-level variable called wildcard. You can probably guess what the variable is used for, but in case you haven't figured it out, it's for opening a file dialog.

Speaking of which, let's see how that works:

```
def open_file(self, default_dir=os.path.expanduser('~')):
    """
    A utility function for opening a file dialog to allow the user
    to open an XML file of their choice
    """
    path = None
    with wx.FileDialog(
        self, message="Choose a file",
        defaultDir=default_dir,
        defaultFile="",
        wildcard=wildcard,
        style=wx.FD_OPEN | wx.FD_CHANGE_DIR
        ) as dlg:
        if dlg.ShowModal() == wx.ID_OK:
            path = dlg.GetPath()

    if path:
        return path
```

The open_file() function will open a wx.FileDialog() so that the user can open an XML file. If they pick a file, then this function will return the full path to that file back to the caller. You can also pass in the default directory that the dialog should open to. In the event that you don't pass in a directory, it defaults to the user's home folder.

The save_file() function is pretty similar:

```python
def save_file(default_dir):
    """

    A utility function that allows the user to save their XML file
    to a specific location using a file dialog
    """

    path = None
    with wx.FileDialog(
        self, message="Save file as ...",
        defaultDir=default_dir,
        defaultFile="", wildcard=wildcard,
        style=wx.FD_SAVE
        ) as dlg:
        if dlg.ShowModal() == wx.ID_OK:
            path = dlg.GetPath()

    if path:
        return path
```

The primary difference between the function above and the open_file() function is that you need to use the wx.FD_SAVE instead of the wx.FD_OPEN style flag. The rest of the code is essentially the same. You could theoretically refactor these two functions into a single function that just accepts style flags if you so desired.

The last function in the **utils.py** module is this one:

```python
def warn_nothing_to_save():
    """

    Warns the user that there is nothing to save
    """
    msg = "No Files Open! Nothing to save."
    with wx.MessageDialog(
        parent=None,
        message=msg,
        caption='Warning',
        style=wx.OK|wx.ICON_EXCLAMATION
        ) as dlg:
        dlg.ShowModal()
```

The warn_nothing_to_save() function is only called when you select the **Save** menu item without having any XML files open. When that happens, you show a dialog to let the user know that there is nothing to save. The wx.ICON_EXCLAMATION style flag will show a warning symbol on the dialog. There are other flags you can use too. Check out the documentation for additional details.

You could also just not do anything or just disable the menu item until an XML file has been opened.

The editor_page.py module

The **editor_page.py** module contains the code for creating the editor portion of the code. This is where you put the splitter window and instantiate the tree control and the notebook classes. You will find that a lot of this code looks familiar, but it has been split out into multiple modules and improved.

Let's get started by looking at the imports:

```python
import lxml.etree as ET
import os
import sys
import time
import utils
import wx


from attribute_editor import AttributeEditorPanel
from xml_tree import XmlTreePanel
from xml_editor import XmlEditorPanel
from pubsub import pub
```

This module will use lxml.etree instead of objectify like you used in the previous version of the code. While I personally really like objectify, there are times where it gets confused with certain types of tags, so I have found etree a bit more flexible. The other benefit of using etree is that it's easy to swap it out for Python's own ElementTree if you need to.

The rest of the code imports some custom-made modules that you will learn about soon as well as the pubsub module.

Let's go ahead and find out what the NewPage class is all about:

```python
class NewPage(wx.Panel):
    """

    Create a new page for each opened XML document. This is the
    top-level widget for the majority of the application
    """


    def __init__(self, parent, xml_path, size, opened_files):
        wx.Panel.__init__(self, parent)
        self.page_id = id(self)
        self.xml_root = None
        self.size = size
        self.opened_files = opened_files
        self.current_file = xml_path
        self.title = os.path.basename(xml_path)
```

The NewPage class creates all the pieces of the editor. Its parent is the FlatNotebook that you created in **main.py**. These first few lines set up some flags and save off a unique id for each page. You also need to know what files are already open and set the title of the page.

Let's look at the next few lines in the __init__() method:

```
self.app_location = os.path.dirname(os.path.abspath( sys.argv[0] ))
self.tmp_location = os.path.join(self.app_location, 'drafts')
pub.subscribe(self.save, 'save_{}'.format(self.page_id))
self.parse_xml(xml_path)

current_time = time.strftime('%Y-%m-%d.%H.%M.%S', time.localtime())
self.full_tmp_path = os.path.join(
    self.tmp_location,
    current_time + '-' + os.path.basename(xml_path))
```

These instance variables / attributes define various folders that you care about, parse the passed in XML and save off the current time. You also need to subscribe to the save message. This allows you to tell the editor to save on demand from other classes.

You also set up a temporary directory location for saving the file(s) to. This allows you to do periodic saves in a temporary location so that you could theoretically recover your file if the program crashed.

Here is the rest of the __init__() method's code:

```
if not os.path.exists(self.tmp_location):
    try:
        os.makedirs(self.tmp_location)
    except IOError:
        raise IOError('Unable to create file at {}'.format(
            self.tmp_location))

if self.xml_root is not None:
    self.create_editor()
```

Here you create the temporary location if it does not exist. On the off chance that the folder creation fails, you raise an error. You could potentially have an alternate temporary location that you could fall back to instead of raising an error though.

Finally you create the editor itself if the XML's root exists.

Speaking of creating the editor, that's what you will learn about next:

```python
def create_editor(self):
    """
    Create the XML editor widgets
    """
    page_sizer = wx.BoxSizer(wx.VERTICAL)

    splitter = wx.SplitterWindow(self)
    tree_panel = XmlTreePanel(splitter, self.xml_root, self.page_id)

    xml_editor_notebook = wx.Notebook(splitter)
    xml_editor_panel = XmlEditorPanel(xml_editor_notebook, self.page_id)
    xml_editor_notebook.AddPage(xml_editor_panel, 'Nodes')

    attribute_panel = AttributeEditorPanel(
        xml_editor_notebook, self.page_id)
    xml_editor_notebook.AddPage(attribute_panel, 'Attributes')

    splitter.SplitVertically(tree_panel, xml_editor_notebook)
    splitter.SetMinimumPaneSize(self.size[0] / 2)
    page_sizer.Add(splitter, 1, wx.ALL|wx.EXPAND, 5)

    self.SetSizer(page_sizer)
    self.Layout()

    self.Bind(wx.EVT_CLOSE, self.on_close)
```

This code demonstrates how to create the `wx.SplitterWindow`. It also shows how to add a panel with a `wx.TreeCtrl` in it and a `wx.Notebook` to the splitter. Note that you are using a regular `wx.Notebook` here instead of a `FlatNotebook`. It doesn't actually matter which notebook type you use here, although `wx.Notebook` will look more native on the target platform. Anyway, the rest of this code is pretty similar to some code you saw earlier in this chapter.

Let's take a quick look at how `parse_xml()` has changed:

```python
def parse_xml(self, xml_path):
    """
    Parses the XML from the file that is passed in
    """
    self.current_directory = os.path.dirname(xml_path)
    try:
        self.xml_tree = ET.parse(xml_path)
    except IOError:
        print('Bad file')
```

```
        return
    except Exception as e:
        print('Really bad error')
        print(e)
        return


    self.xml_root = self.xml_tree.getroot()
```

This method gets called when you want to load in a new XML file. The big difference here is that you will be using lxml.etree instead of objectify. The rest of the code is pretty much the same.

Now let's learn about the save() method:

```
def save(self, location=None):
    """
    Save the XML to disk
    """
    if not location:
        path = utils.save_file(self.current_directory)
    else:
        path = location

    if path:
        if '.xml' not in path:
            path += '.xml'

        # Save the xml
        self.xml_tree.write(path)
        self.changed = False
```

The save() method will call utils.save_file() to save the XML file that the user is editing. It will pass along the current_directory which is nice because then the user doesn't have to navigate back to a previously-set folder. If the user saves the file without specifying the extension of the file, you will add .xml yourself before writing the file out.

The last step is to set the changed attribute to False. The point of this attribute is that it keeps track of when a change to the XML has occurred. If you have a periodic save enabled, then you can use this attribute to determine if there is something new to save.

The final method / event handler in this module is on_close():

```python
def on_close(self, event):
    """

    Event handler that is called when the panel is being closed
    """
    if self.current_file in self.opened_files:
        self.opened_files.remove(self.current_file)

    if os.path.exists(self.full_tmp_path):
        try:
            os.remove(self.full_tmp_path)
        except IOError:
            print('Unable to delete file: {}'.format(self.full_tmp_path))
```

When closing a page in the notebook, you will want to remove the file from the `opened_files` list. You will also want to remove the temporary file path. This would be a good place to add some code to prompt the user if there was a change detected that wasn't saved. Right now, your code will blithely close the file and you may lose data.

Now let's move on to the next module!

The attribute_editor.py module

The `attribute_editor.py` module holds the code used for editing XML attributes.

To get you started, it is always nice to see what you import:

```python
import wx

from attribute_dialog import AttributeDialog
from functools import partial
from pubsub import pub
```

This module is fairly short and sweet in that it doesn't require a lot of imports. You will see the `AttributeDialog` getting instantiated and learn how to use `functools.partial` to send along extra information to an event handler in this module.

But first, let's look at the `State` class:

```python
class State():
    """

    Class for keeping track of the state of the key portion
    of the attribute
    """

    def __init__(self, key, val_widget):
        self.current_key = key
        self.previous_key = None
        self.val_widget = val_widget
```

This class is meant to hold information related to the attribute. This is helpful for keeping track of which attribute maps to which value. You will see this used shortly.

But first, you will need to create a new wx.Panel:

```python
class AttributeEditorPanel(wx.Panel):
    """

    A class that holds all UI elements for editing
    XML attribute elements
    """

    def __init__(self, parent, page_id):
        wx.Panel.__init__(self, parent)
        self.page_id = page_id
        self.xml_obj = None
        self.widgets = []

        pub.subscribe(self.update_ui, 'ui_updater_{}'.format(self.page_id))

        self.main_sizer = wx.BoxSizer(wx.VERTICAL)
        self.SetSizer(self.main_sizer)
```

This panel holds the widgets you need to edit XML attributes. In this code, you keep track of the page_id, the xml_obj and the children widgets on the panel. You also subscribe to the ui_updater_ topic so that this panel updates when the tree control updates.

Let's go ahead and see how update_ui() works:

```python
def update_ui(self, xml_obj):
    """

    Update the user interface to have elements for editing
    XML attributes

    Called via pubsub
    """
    self.clear()
    self.xml_obj = xml_obj

    sizer = wx.BoxSizer(wx.HORIZONTAL)
    attr_lbl = wx.StaticText(self, label='Attribute')
    value_lbl = wx.StaticText(self, label='Value')
    sizer.Add(attr_lbl, 0, wx.ALL, 5)
    sizer.Add((133,0))
    sizer.Add(value_lbl, 0, wx.ALL, 5)
    self.widgets.extend([attr_lbl, value_lbl])

    self.main_sizer.Add(sizer)
```

The code above is just the first third of the code that goes into update_ui(). Here you clear() out all the old widgets and sizers and add new ones. In this case, you just add the two header labels and the main_sizer.

The next piece of code adds the rest of the widgets dynamically:

```python
for key in xml_obj.attrib:
    _ = wx.BoxSizer(wx.HORIZONTAL)
    attr_name = wx.TextCtrl(self, value=key)
    _.Add(attr_name, 1, wx.ALL|wx.EXPAND, 5)
    self.widgets.append(attr_name)

    val = str(xml_obj.attrib[key])
    attr_val = wx.TextCtrl(self, value=val)
    _.Add(attr_val, 1, wx.ALL|wx.EXPAND, 5)

    # keep track of the attribute text control's state
    attr_state = State(key, attr_val)

    attr_name.Bind(
        wx.EVT_TEXT, partial(
            self.on_key_change, state=attr_state))
    attr_val.Bind(
```

```
        wx.EVT_TEXT, partial(
            self.on_val_change,
            attr=attr_name
        ))

    self.widgets.append(attr_val)
    self.main_sizer.Add(_, 0, wx.EXPAND)
else:
    add_attr_btn = wx.Button(self, label='Add Attribute')
    add_attr_btn.Bind(wx.EVT_BUTTON, self.on_add_attr)
    self.main_sizer.Add(add_attr_btn, 0, wx.ALL|wx.CENTER, 5)
    self.widgets.append(add_attr_btn)


self.Layout()
```

Here you loop over the attributes field of the current XML node and add the appropriate number of widgets. You create a State instance that basically maps the current attribute to its value. Then you add that state to the wx.EVT_TEXT event binding using partial which allows you create an ad-hoc function on the fly. Now when the attribute name changes, it won't mess up its link to its value because of the state that you have saved.

The last bit of code will give the user the ability to add a new attribute to their XML file.

Let's find out how that works:

```
def on_add_attr(self, event):
    """
    Event handler to add an attribute
    """
    dlg = AttributeDialog(
        self.xml_obj,
        page_id=self.page_id,
        title = 'Add Attribute',
        label_one = 'Attribute',
        label_two = 'Value'
    )
    dlg.Destroy()
```

When the user presses the "Add Attribute" button, you need to instantiate the AttributeDialog with the right data. Once the user finishes entering the new attribute information or cancels the dialog, you Destroy() it. Note that you aren't using Python's with statement here. You could if you wanted to, but I thought it would be good to show the slightly older method of showing and destroying dialogs here as well.

The clear() method is next on your list:

```python
def clear(self):
    """
    Clears the panel of widgets
    """
    sizers = {}
    for widget in self.widgets:
        sizer = widget.GetContainingSizer()
        if sizer:
            sizer_id = id(sizer)
            if sizer_id not in sizers:
                sizers[sizer_id] = sizer
        widget.Destroy()

    for sizer in sizers:
        self.main_sizer.Remove(sizers[sizer])

    self.widgets = []
    self.Layout()
```

This code remains unchanged from the version you saw earlier. As before, you just loop over the widgets and sizers and Destroy() or Remove() them respectively.

Now let's learn what happens when the user edits an attribute's name:

```python
def on_key_change(self, event, state):
    """
    Event handler that is called on text change in the
    attribute key field
    """
    new_key = event.GetString()
    if new_key not in self.xml_obj.attrib:
        if state.current_key in self.xml_obj.attrib:
            self.xml_obj.attrib.pop(state.current_key)
        self.xml_obj.attrib[new_key] = state.val_widget.GetValue()
        state.previous_key = state.current_key
        state.current_key = new_key
```

The on_key_change() event handler is called when the user edits the attribute's name or key. When that happens, you have to pop the old value from the XML file and add the new one. While this code doesn't show it, you can save the previous key's value in case you might want to undo your change. That code isn't in this version, but it does add the capability to enhance this code more easily in the future.

The last event handler to look at is the one called when the user changes an attribute's value:

```
def on_val_change(self, event, attr):
    """
    Event handler that is called on text change in the
    attribute value field
    """
    new_val = event.GetString()
    self.xml_obj.attrib[attr.GetValue()] = new_val
```

Here you extract the text from the widget by using event.GetString(). Then you can update the XML's attribute dictionary using the attr.GetValue() call to update the right mapping. Note that this could be improved by using the dictionary's get() method instead. This would prevent a KeyError from being raised if there was some weird issue where the attribute didn't appear in the dictionary correctly.

Now you're ready to learn about the **xml_tree.py** module!

The xml_tree.py module

The **xml_tree.py** module is made up of two classes:

- XmlTree - The subclass of wx.TreeCtrl
- XmlTreePanel - The panel that is the parent for XmlTree

Let's start with the top of the file:

```
import lxml.etree as ET
import wx

from add_node_dialog import NodeDialog
from pubsub import pub
```

The module needs access to lxml and to the NodeDialog class in addition to wx and pubsub.

Let's see how the XmlTree class has changed:

```python
class XmlTree(wx.TreeCtrl):
    """

    The class that holds all the functionality for the tree control
    widget
    """


    def __init__(self, parent, wx_id, pos, size, style):
        wx.TreeCtrl.__init__(self, parent, wx_id, pos, size, style)
        self.expanded= {}
        self.xml_root = parent.xml_root
        self.page_id = parent.page_id
        pub.subscribe(self.update_tree,
                      'tree_update_{}'.format(self.page_id))
```

The first few lines of the __init__() contain references to the expanded dictionary, the page_id and the xml_root. The dictionary is still being used to help keep track of which nodes in the tree control have been expanded or not.

Now let's finish up the __init__():

```python
root = self.AddRoot(self.xml_root.tag)
self.expanded[id(self.xml_root)] = ''
self.SetItemData(root, self.xml_root)
wx.CallAfter(pub.sendMessage,
             'ui_updater_{}'.format(self.page_id),
             xml_obj=self.xml_root)


if self.xml_root.getchildren():
    for top_level_item in self.xml_root.getchildren():
        child = self.AppendItem(root, top_level_item.tag)
        if top_level_item.getchildren():
            self.SetItemHasChildren(child)
        self.SetItemData(child, top_level_item)

self.Expand(root)
self.Bind(wx.EVT_TREE_ITEM_EXPANDING, self.on_item_expanding)
self.Bind(wx.EVT_TREE_SEL_CHANGED, self.on_tree_selection)
```

Here you add the root to the wx.TreeCtrl and update the root with various children by looping over the XML root's children. You also expand the root and bind a couple of events to the widget.

Now let's find out what those event handlers do:

```
def on_item_expanding(self, event):
    """
    A handler that fires when a tree item is being expanded

    This will cause the sub-elements of the tree to be created
    and added to the tree
    """
    item = event.GetItem()
    xml_obj = self.GetItemData(item)

    if id(xml_obj) not in self.expanded and xml_obj is not None:
        for top_level_item in xml_obj.getchildren():
            child = self.AppendItem(item, top_level_item.tag)
            self.SetItemData(child, top_level_item)
            if top_level_item.getchildren():
                self.SetItemHasChildren(child)

    self.expanded[id(xml_obj)] = ''
```

The first event handler, on_item_expanding, is called when the user expands a node in the tree. You will loop over that node's children, if it has any, and create children underneath that node as necessary. If these sub-nodes have children as well, you can mark the node as expandable via SetItemHasChildren().

The other event handler is on_tree_selection():

```
def on_tree_selection(self, event):
    """
    A handler that fires when an item in the tree is selected

    This will cause an update to be sent to the XmlEditorPanel
    to allow editing of the XML
    """
    item = event.GetItem()
    xml_obj = self.GetItemData(item)
    pub.sendMessage('ui_updater_{}'.format(self.page_id),
                    xml_obj=xml_obj)
```

When the user selects a node in the tree, the on_tree_selection() is fired. It will extract the data it needs from the node and update the XML value and attribute portion of the editor, which appears on the right hand side of the application.

The update_tree() method comes into play when the tree itself needs updating:

```python
def update_tree(self, xml_obj):
    """
    Update the tree with the new data
    """
    selection = self.GetSelection()
    selected_tree_xml_obj = self.GetItemData(selection)

    if id(selected_tree_xml_obj) in self.expanded:
        child = self.AppendItem(selection, xml_obj.tag)
        if xml_obj.getchildren():
            self.SetItemHasChildren(child)
        self.SetItemData(child, xml_obj)

    if selected_tree_xml_obj.getchildren():
        self.SetItemHasChildren(selection)
```

This method is called via pubsub and updates the tree control itself. This will happen when you add a new node to the XML. The first step in the process is to get the currently-selected node and then append the newly created one. You will want to expand the currently-selected node to make the current and the new node visible to the user.

Now let's move on to the panel that holds the tree control:

```python
class XmlTreePanel(wx.Panel):
    """
    The panel class that contains the XML tree control
    """

    def __init__(self, parent, xml_obj, page_id):
        wx.Panel.__init__(self, parent)
        self.xml_root = xml_obj
        self.page_id = page_id

        pub.subscribe(self.add_node,
                      'add_node_{}'.format(self.page_id))
        pub.subscribe(self.remove_node,
                      'remove_node_{}'.format(self.page_id))

        self.tree = XmlTree(
            self, wx.ID_ANY, wx.DefaultPosition, wx.DefaultSize,
            wx.TR_HAS_BUTTONS)

        sizer = wx.BoxSizer(wx.VERTICAL)
```

```
        sizer.Add(self.tree, 1, wx.EXPAND)
        self.SetSizer(sizer)
```

The `XmlTreePanel` is the panel that will hold your tree control widget. It takes in the `xml_obj` and subscribes to a couple of messages with `pubsub`. It also sets up the `wx.TreeCtrl` and expands it to fit the panel.

Now you are ready to learn how to add a node:

```python
def add_node(self):
    """
    Add a sub-node to the selected item in the tree
    """
    node = self.tree.GetSelection()
    data = self.tree.GetItemData(node)
    dlg = NodeDialog(data,
                     page_id=self.page_id,
                     title = 'New Node',
                     label_one = 'Element Tag',
                     label_two = 'Element Value'
                     )
    dlg.Destroy()
```

The `add_node()` method is called via `pubsub`. When that happens, you will get the currently-selected tree node, extract the XML data from it and open the `NodeDialog` to add a node.

The `remove_node()` method is the last method to look at in this module:

```python
def remove_node(self):
    """
    Remove the selected node from the tree
    """
    node = self.tree.GetSelection()
    xml_node = self.tree.GetItemData(node)

    if node:
        msg = 'Are you sure you want to delete the {node} node'
        with wx.MessageDialog(
            parent=None,
            message=msg.format(node=xml_node.tag),
            caption='Warning',
            style=wx.YES_NO|wx.YES_DEFAULT|wx.ICON_EXCLAMATION
            ) as dlg:
            if dlg.ShowModal() == wx.ID_YES:
```

```
parent = xml_node.getparent()
parent.remove(xml_node)
self.tree.DeleteChildren(node)
self.tree.Delete(node)
```

Here you will once again grab the currently-selected node in the tree and extract the XML node from it. Assuming that there is a tree node selected, you will pop up a wx.MessageDialog asking the user if they really want to delete the node. If so, then you use lxml to remove() it. Then you have to delete all the children from the node in the tree control (DeleteChildren()) and then Delete() the tree node itself.

Now you are ready to move on to the XML editor class itself.

The xml_editor.py module

The **xml_editor.py** is where the user will go to edit XML values. The widgets for this part of your application reside in a wx.lib.scrolledpanel.

Let's take a look:

```python
import wx
import wx.lib.scrolledpanel as scrolled

from functools import partial
from pubsub import pub


class XmlEditorPanel(scrolled.ScrolledPanel):
    """
    The panel in the notebook that allows editing of XML element values
    """

    def __init__(self, parent, page_id):
        """Constructor"""
        scrolled.ScrolledPanel.__init__(
            self, parent, style=wx.SUNKEN_BORDER)
        self.main_sizer = wx.BoxSizer(wx.VERTICAL)
        self.page_id = page_id
        self.widgets = []
        self.label_spacer = None

        pub.subscribe(self.update_ui, 'ui_updater_{}'.format(self.page_id))

        self.SetSizer(self.main_sizer)
```

This code doesn't have any custom module imports. Instead these are all pretty run-of-the-mill. You subclass `ScrolledPanel` and add a `widgets` list and a spacer. You also subscribe to `ui_updater_` again.

The `update_ui()` method is mostly the same as it was in the previous iteration of this class. However, there was the addition of the following event handler:

```
value_txt.Bind(wx.EVT_TEXT, partial(self.on_text_change, xml_obj=child))
```

For each XML node's text control, you need to bind it to `wx.EVT_TEXT` to detect text changes. When those changes occur, you use `partial` to call `on_text_change()` with an XML object.

Moving on, the `add_single_tag_elements()` has been updated slightly:

```python
def add_single_tag_elements(self, xml_obj, lbl_size):
    """
    Adds the single tag elements to the panel

    This function is only called when there should be just one
    tag / value
    """
    sizer = wx.BoxSizer(wx.HORIZONTAL)
    tag_txt = wx.StaticText(self, label=xml_obj.tag, size=lbl_size)
    sizer.Add(tag_txt, 0, wx.ALL, 5)
    self.widgets.append(tag_txt)

    value_txt = wx.TextCtrl(self, value=xml_obj.text)
    value_txt.Bind(wx.EVT_TEXT, partial(
        self.on_text_change, xml_obj=xml_obj))
    sizer.Add(value_txt, 1, wx.ALL|wx.EXPAND, 5)
    self.widgets.append(value_txt)

    self.main_sizer.Add(sizer, 0, wx.EXPAND)
```

The main difference here is the sort of update as happened with `update_ui()` in that `add_single_-tag_elements()` now has a binding to `wx.EVT_TEXT` as well. In fact, these changes are nigh identical.

The `clear()` method is also the same as before, so you don't need to go over that again.

Instead, let's look at `on_text_change()`:

```python
def on_text_change(self, event, xml_obj):
    """
    An event handler that is called when the text changes in the text
    control. This will update the passed in xml object to something
    new
    """
    xml_obj.text = event.GetString()
```

Whenever the user changes the XML value, this method is called and you can just update the `xml_obj` directly since it is being kept handy in memory.

The `on_add_node()` method is also the same as last time, so you can safely ignore it this time around

The next section covers the actual dialog used to add an XML node.

The add_node_dialog.py module

The **add_node_dialog.py** module gives the user the ability to add a new node to their XML file.

Let's find out how:

```python
import lxml.etree as ET
import wx

from edit_dialog import EditDialog
from pubsub import pub
```

This code imports `lxml.etree` since you will need to edit the XML. You are also going to be subclassing from the `EditDialog`, which is a class you will be learning about shortly.

In the meantime, let's find out what the `NodeDialog` is:

```python
class NodeDialog(EditDialog):
    """
    A class for adding nodes to your XML objects
    """

    def on_save(self, event):
        """
        Event handler that is called when the Save button is
        pressed.

        Updates the XML object with the new node element and
        tells the UI to update to display the new element
```

```
    before destroying the dialog
    """
    element = ET.SubElement(
        self.xml_obj, self.value_one.GetValue())
    element.text = self.value_two.GetValue()
    pub.sendMessage('tree_update_{}'.format(self.page_id),
                    xml_obj=element)


    self.Close()
```

This class adds an on_save() method to its superclass and reuses the superclass's __init__()
and other methods. The on_save() method is an event handler that creates a SubElement. Once
completed, it uses pubsub to send a message to the tree control to update itself.

The last bit of following code is useful for testing:

```
if __name__ == '__main__':
    app = wx.App(False)
    dlg = NodeDialog('', title='Test',
                     label_one='Element',
                     label_two='Value')
    dlg.Destroy()
    app.MainLoop()
```

When you are creating dialogs, I find it helpful to instantiate the dialog in an if statement at the
bottom of the module. This is helpful in making sure it lays out correctly and it makes the module
more stand-alone. It's kind of a unittest in a way. The other nice thing about it is that it demonstrates
how another person on your team can work on the dialogs and make sure they work while the main
UI is still being worked on.

Here is what the dialog looks like:

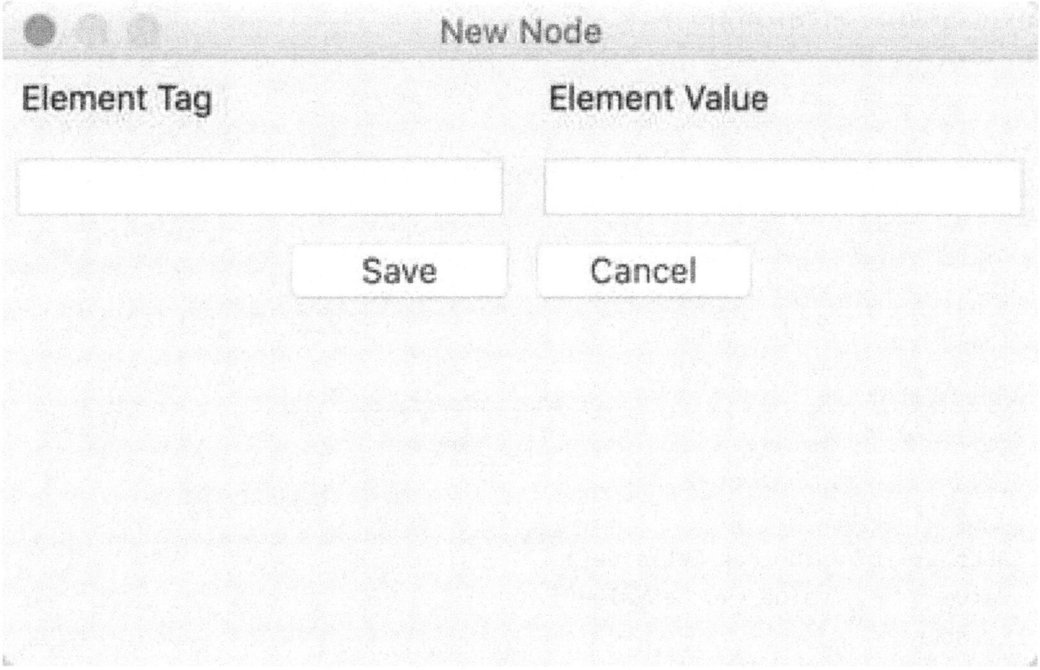

Fig. 13-5: XML Editor - Add Node

You may notice that there is a lot of whitespace following the buttons. If you do not like that, you can use the SetSizerAndFit() method or simply Fit() to make the dialog automatically resize to fit its contents.

Let's move on and find out about the other module that reuses the EditDialog.

The attribute_dialog.py module

The **attribute_dialog.py** module also subclasses EditDialog, but it does not need to use the lxml module directly.

Let's see how it works:

```python
import wx

from edit_dialog import EditDialog
from pubsub import pub
```

```python
class AttributeDialog(EditDialog):
    """
    Dialog class for adding attributes
    """

    def on_save(self, event):
        """
        Event handler that is called when the Save button is
        pressed.

        Updates the XML object with the new node element and
        tells the UI to update to display the new element
        before destroying the dialog
        """
        attr = self.value_one.GetValue()
        value = self.value_two.GetValue()
        if attr:
            self.xml_obj.attrib[attr] = value
            pub.sendMessage('ui_updater_{}'.format(self.page_id),
                            xml_obj=self.xml_obj)

        else:
            # TODO - Show a dialog telling the user that there is no attr to save
            raise NotImplemented

        self.Close()
```

Once again, you are adding an on_save() method. This time around, it gets the attribute and the attribute's value out of the dialog. Then it updates them accordingly using the provided xml_obj. Finally it sends out a message via pubsub that tells the rest of the application to update.

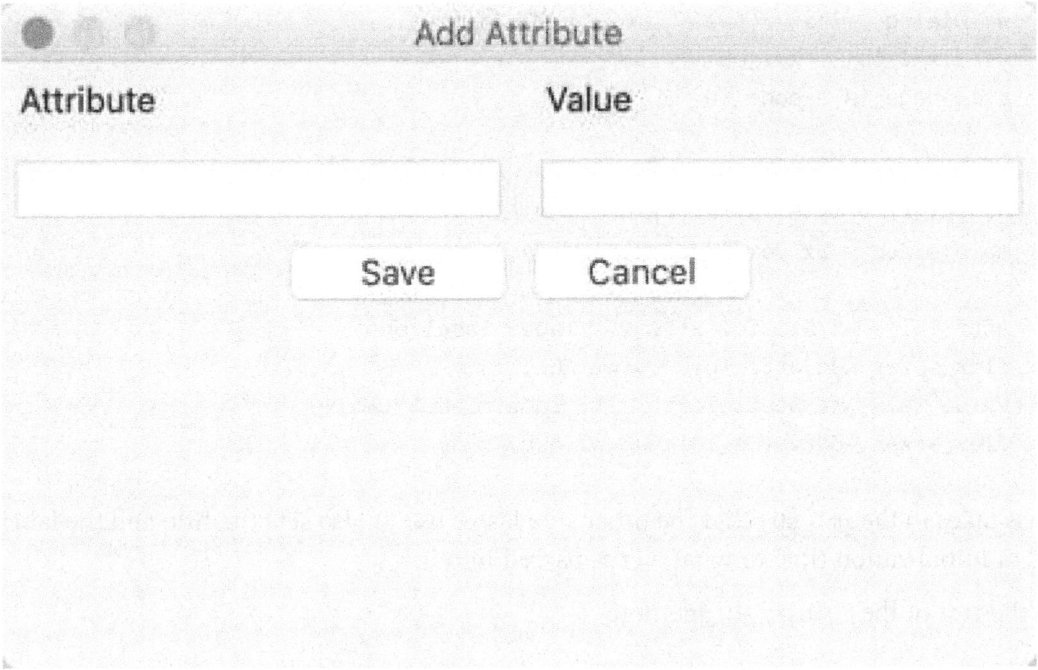

Fig. 13-6: XML Editor - Add Attribute

Now let's find out how the superclass works!

The edit_dialog.py module

The edit_dialog.py module contains the EditDialog superclass that the previous two classes used.
Let's see how it works:

```python
import wx


class EditDialog(wx.Dialog):
    """
    Super class to derive attribute and element edit
    dialogs from
    """

    def __init__(self, xml_obj, page_id, title, label_one, label_two):
        """
        @param xml_obj: The lxml XML object
        @param page_id: A unique id based on the current page being viewed
        @param title: The title of the dialog
        @param label_one: The label text for the first text control
        @param label_two: The label text for the second text control
        """
```

```
            wx.Dialog.__init__(self, None, title=title)
            self.xml_obj = xml_obj
            self.page_id = page_id

            flex_sizer = wx.FlexGridSizer(2, 2, gap=wx.Size(5, 5))
            btn_sizer = wx.BoxSizer(wx.HORIZONTAL)
            main_sizer = wx.BoxSizer(wx.VERTICAL)

            attr_lbl = wx.StaticText(self, label=label_one)
            flex_sizer.Add(attr_lbl, 0, wx.ALL, 5)
            value_lbl = wx.StaticText(self, label=label_two)
            flex_sizer.Add(value_lbl, 0, wx.ALL, 5)
```

This class takes in the `xml_obj` that the other subclasses use. It also sets the title and the labels of the widgets at initialization time to whatever is passed into it.

Here is the rest of the `__init__()` method:

```
self.value_one = wx.TextCtrl(self)
flex_sizer.Add(self.value_one, 1, wx.ALL|wx.EXPAND, 5)
self.value_two = wx.TextCtrl(self, style=wx.TE_PROCESS_ENTER)
self.value_two.Bind(wx.EVT_KEY_DOWN, self.on_enter)
flex_sizer.Add(self.value_two, 1, wx.ALL|wx.EXPAND, 5)
flex_sizer.AddGrowableCol(1, 1)
flex_sizer.AddGrowableCol(0, 1)

save_btn = wx.Button(self, label='Save')
save_btn.Bind(wx.EVT_BUTTON, self.on_save)
btn_sizer.Add(save_btn, 0, wx.ALL|wx.CENTER, 5)

cancel_btn = wx.Button(self, label='Cancel')
cancel_btn.Bind(wx.EVT_BUTTON, self.on_cancel)
btn_sizer.Add(cancel_btn, 0, wx.ALL|wx.CENTER, 5)

main_sizer.Add(flex_sizer, 0, wx.EXPAND)
main_sizer.Add(btn_sizer, 0, wx.CENTER)
self.SetSizer(main_sizer)

self.ShowModal()
```

Here you add the rest of the widgets necessary for editing. Since you are using a `wx.FlexGridSizer`, you set its columns to be growable. This allows the widgets to stretch to the full width of the dialog.

This dialog has two default event handlers:

```python
def on_enter(self, event):
    """

    Event handler that fires when a key is pressed in the
    attribute value text control
    """

    keycode = event.GetKeyCode()
    if keycode == wx.WXK_RETURN or keycode == wx.WXK_NUMPAD_ENTER:
        self.on_save(event=None)
    event.Skip()
```

The on_enter() event handler fires when the user presses the "Enter" or "Return" key while the second text control is in focus. When that happens, you call the on_save() method, which is not implemented here.

The other event handler in this dialog class is as follows:

```python
def on_cancel(self, event):
    """

    Event handler that is called when the Cancel button is
    pressed.

    Will destroy the dialog
    """

    self.Close()
```

The on_cancel() event handler will Close() the dialog.

You could improve this code a bit by using an AbstractBaseClass to enforce that the subclasses properly implement on_save().

Boomslang XML

The final version of the code for the XML Editor is called **Boomslang XML**. Boomslang is the name of a venomous tree snake and a fun name for the application. This is actually a project I did for fun a couple of years ago and has its own repository on Github in addition to having a copy of the code in this book's code repository. You can see it here:

- https://github.com/driscollis/boomslang

Boomslang has a bunch of additional features that are not covered in this chapter. For example, I added a timer that auto saves the file every so often and Boomslang also keeps track of recently opened files.

In addition, there is an XML preview widget:

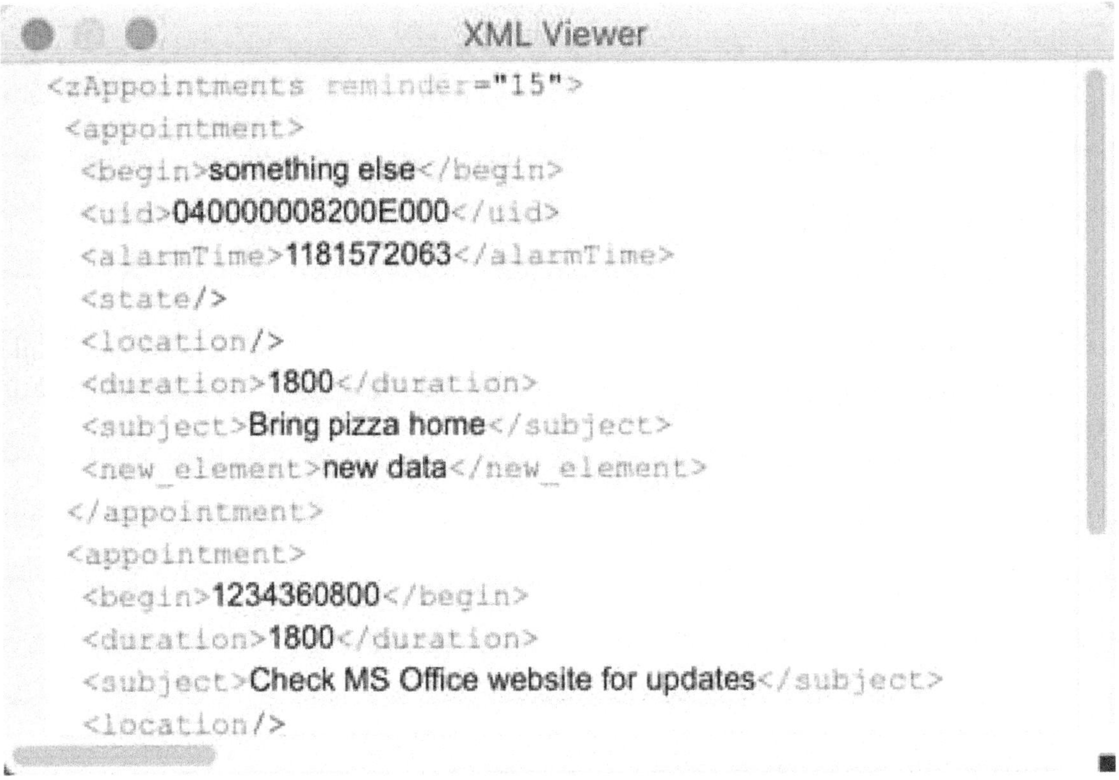

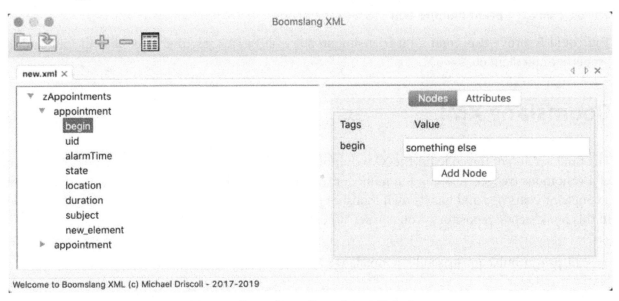

Fig. 13-7: Boomslang - XML Preview

The main application has a toolbar:

Fig. 13-8: Boomslang - Boomslang - Main App

And there is a context menu when right-clicking on the tree nodes among other things. Feel free to check out the code and learn how I did those features too.

Wrapping Up

You have learned a lot of new things in this chapter. You learned how to visualize XML with a Python GUI framework. You updated the XML viewer until it was able to edit XML documents. You also learned about more advanced layout techniques using `FlatNotebook` and `wx.SplitterWindow`.

There are many more enhancements that you can add to this program. Go to the book or the Boomslang code repository on Github and fork the code to give it a try.

Chapter 14 - Distributing Your Application

Now that you know how to write a GUI application with wxPython, how do you share it with the world? This is always the dilemma when you finish an amazing program. Fortunately, there are several ways you can share your code. If you want to share your code with other developers, then Github or a similar website is definitely a good way to go. I won't be covering using Git or Mercurial here. Instead what you will learn here is how to turn your application into an executable.

By turning your code into an executable, you can allow a user to just download the binary and run it without requiring them to download Python, your source code and your dependencies. All of those things will be bundled up into the executable instead.

There are many tools you can use to generate an executable:

- py2exe
- py2app
- PyInstaller
- cx_Freeze
- bbfreeze
- Nuitka

You will be using **PyInstaller** in this chapter. The main benefit to using PyInstaller is that it can generate executables for Windows, Mac and Linux. Note that it does **not** support cross-compiling. What that means is that you cannot run PyInstaller on Linux to create a Windows executable. Instead, PyInstaller will only create an executable for the OS that it is run on. In other words, if you run PyInstaller on Windows, it will create a Windows executable only.

Installing PyInstaller

Installing the PyInstaller package is nice and straightforward. All you need is `pip`.

Here is how you would install PyInstaller to your system Python:

```
pip install pyinstaller
```

You could also install PyInstaller to a virtual Python environment using Python's `venv` module or the `virtualenv` package.

Generating an Executable

The nice thing about PyInstaller is that it is very easy to use out of the box. All you need to do is run the `pyinstaller` command followed by the path to the main file of the application that you want to convert to an executable.

Here is a non-working example:

```
pyinstaller path/to/main/script.py
```

If the PyInstaller application is not found, you may have to specify a full path to it. By default, PyInstaller installs to Python's **Scripts** sub-folder, which is going to be in your system Python folder or in your virtual environment.

Let's take one of the applications that you created earlier in the book and turn it into an executable. For example, you could use **image_viewer_slideshow.py** from chapter 3.

If you wanted to turn it into an executable, you would run the following:

```
pyinstaller image_viewer_slideshow.py
```

Make sure that when you run this command, your current working directory is the one that contains the script you are converting to an executable. PyInstaller will be creating its output in whatever the current working directory is.

When you run this command, you should see something like this in your terminal:

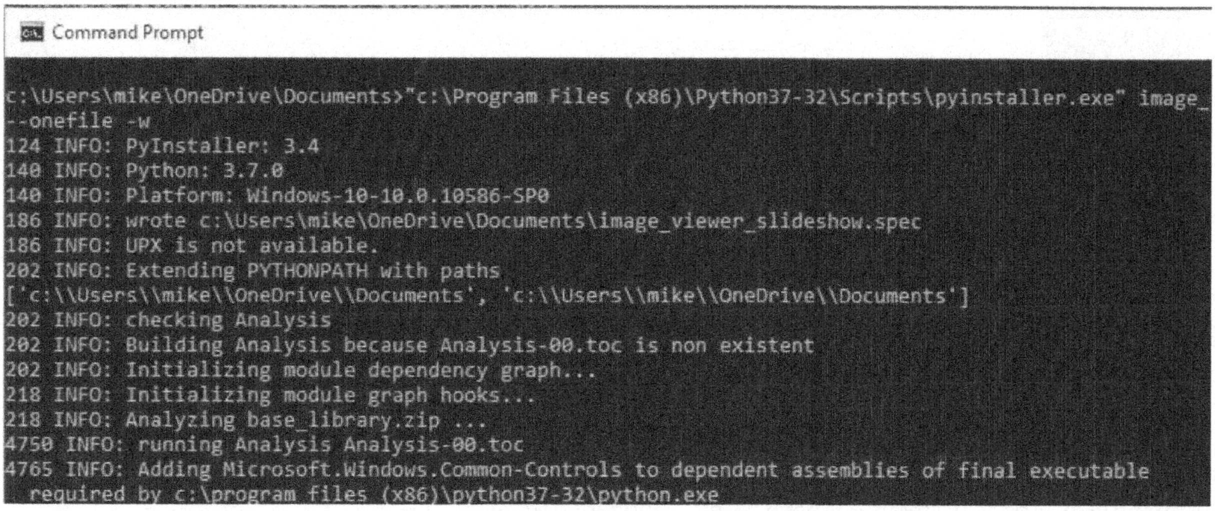

Fig. 14-1: **PyInstaller Output**

PyInstaller will create two folders in the same folder as the script that you are converting called **dist** and **build**. The **dist** folder is where you will find your executable if PyInstaller completes successfully. There will be many other files in the **dist** folder besides your executable. These are files that are required for your executable to run.

Now let's try running your newly created executable. When I ran my copy, I noticed that a terminal / console was appearing behind my application.

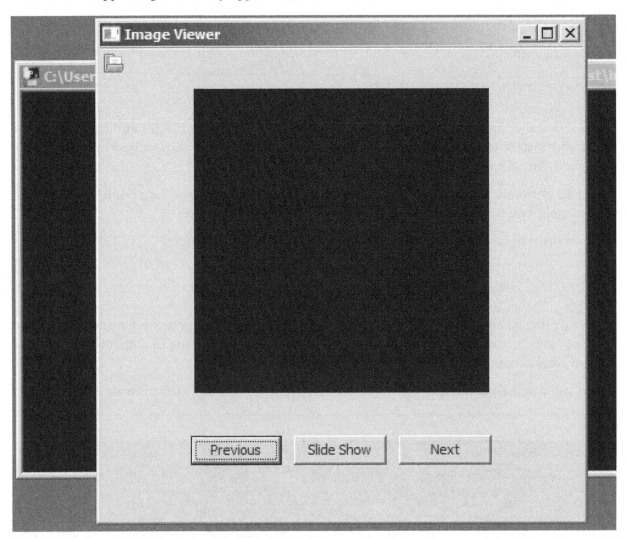

Fig. 14-2: Image Viewer with Console in Background

This is normal as the default behavior of PyInstaller is to build your application as if it were a command-line application, not a GUI.

You will need to add the --noconsole flag to remove the console:

```
pyinstaller image_viewer_slideshow.py --noconsole
```

Now when you run the result, you should no longer see a console window appearing behind your application.

It can be complicated to distribute lots of files, so PyInstaller has another command that you can use to bundle everything up into a single executable. That command is --onefile. As an aside, a lot of the commands that you use with PyInstaller have shorter aliases. For example, there is a shorter alias for --noconsole that you can also use called: -w. Note the single dash in -w.

So let's take that information and have PyInstaller create a single file executable with no console:

```
pyinstaller image_viewer_slideshow.py --onefile -w
```

You should now have just one file in the **dist** folder.

The spec file

PyInstaller has the concept of specification files. They are kind of like a **setup.py** script, which is something that you use with Python's distutils. These spec files tell PyInstaller how to build your executable. PyInstaller will generate one for you automatically with the same name as the file that you passed in to the script, but with a **.spec** extension. So if you passed in **image_viewer_-slideshow.py**, then you should see a **image_viewer_slideshow.spec** file after running PyInstaller. This spec file will be created in the same location as your application file.

Here is the contents of the spec file that was created from the last run of PyInstaller above:

```
# -*- mode: python -*-

block_cipher = None


a = Analysis(['image_viewer.py'],
             pathex=['C:\\Users\\mdriscoll\\Documents\\test'],
             binaries=[],
             datas=[],
             hiddenimports=[],
             hookspath=[],
             runtime_hooks=[],
             excludes=[],
             win_no_prefer_redirects=False,
             win_private_assemblies=False,
             cipher=block_cipher,
             noarchive=False)
pyz = PYZ(a.pure, a.zipped_data,
             cipher=block_cipher)
exe = EXE(pyz,
          a.scripts,
```

```
a.binaries,
a.zipfiles,
a.datas,
[],
name='image_viewer',
debug=False,
bootloader_ignore_signals=False,
strip=False,
upx=True,
runtime_tmpdir=None,
console=False )
```

While PyInstaller worked fine with the image viewer example, you may find that it won't work out of the box if you had other dependencies, such as NumPy or Pandas. If you run into issues with PyInstaller, it has very verbose logs that you can use to help you figure out the issue. One good location is the build/cli/warn-cli.txt file. You may also want to rebuild without the -w command so that you can see what is being printed to stdout in the console window.

There are also options for changing the log level during building that may help you uncover issues.

If none of those work, try Google or go to PyInstaller's support page and get help there:

- https://www.pyinstaller.org/support.html

Creating Executables for Mac

While the same commands should work on Mac OSX as it does on Windows, I found that I needed to run the following command to generate a working executable:

```
pyinstaller image_viewer_slideshow.py --windowed
```

The output that PyInstaller generates will be slightly different and the result is an application file.

Another popular option for generating applications on Mac is a Python package called **py2app**.

Creating Executables for Linux

For Linux, it is usually recommended that you build the executable with an old version of glibc because the newer glibc versions are not backwards compatible. By building with an old version of Linux, you can usually target a wider variety of Linux versions. But your mileage may vary.

After the files are generated, you can just tar them up into a gzipped tarball (.tar.gz). You could even using the archiving application you created in this book to do that for you, if you wanted.

An alternative would be to learn how to create a .deb or related file that most Linux versions can install.

Learning More About PyInstaller

This chapter is not meant to be an in-depth guide to PyInstaller. It will likely change much faster than wxPython, so it is recommended that you read the documentation for PyInstaller instead. It will always be the most up-to-date location to get the information you need on the project.

Here is a link:

- https://pyinstaller.readthedocs.io/en/stable/

What About Installers?

Windows users know that most of the time you have an installer application that you can run to install your application on your computer and put some shortcuts here and there. There are several useful free programs that you can use to create a Windows Installer as well as some paid ones

Here are the two freeware applications I see mentioned the most:

- NSIS - https://nsis.sourceforge.io/Main_Page
- Inno Setup - http://www.jrsoftware.org/isinfo.php

I have used Inno Setup to create a Windows installer on several occasions. It is easy to use and requires only a little reading of its documentation to get it working. I haven't used NSIS before, but I suspect it is quite easy to use as well.

Let's use Inno Setup as an example and see how to generate an installer with it.

Creating an Installer with Inno Setup

Inno Setup is a nice freeware application that you can use to create professional-looking installer programs. It works on most versions of Windows. I personally have used it for quite a few years. While Inno Setup is not open source, it is still a really nice program. You will need to download and install it from here:

- Inno Setup - http://www.jrsoftware.org/isinfo.php

Once installed, you can use this tool to create an installer for the executable you created earlier in this chapter.

To get started, just run Inno Setup and you should see the following:

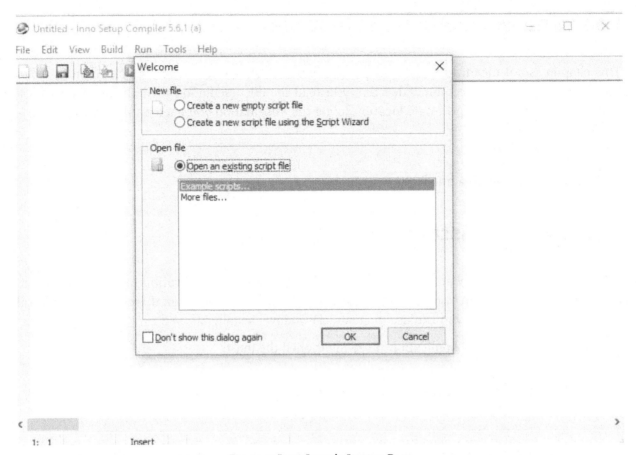

Fig. 14-3: Inno Setup's Startup Page

While Inno Setup defaults to opening an existing file, what you want to do is choose the second option from the top: "Create a new script file using the Script Wizard". Then press **OK**.

You should now see the first page of the Inno Setup Script Wizard. Just hit **Next** here since there's nothing else you can really do.

Now you should see something like this:

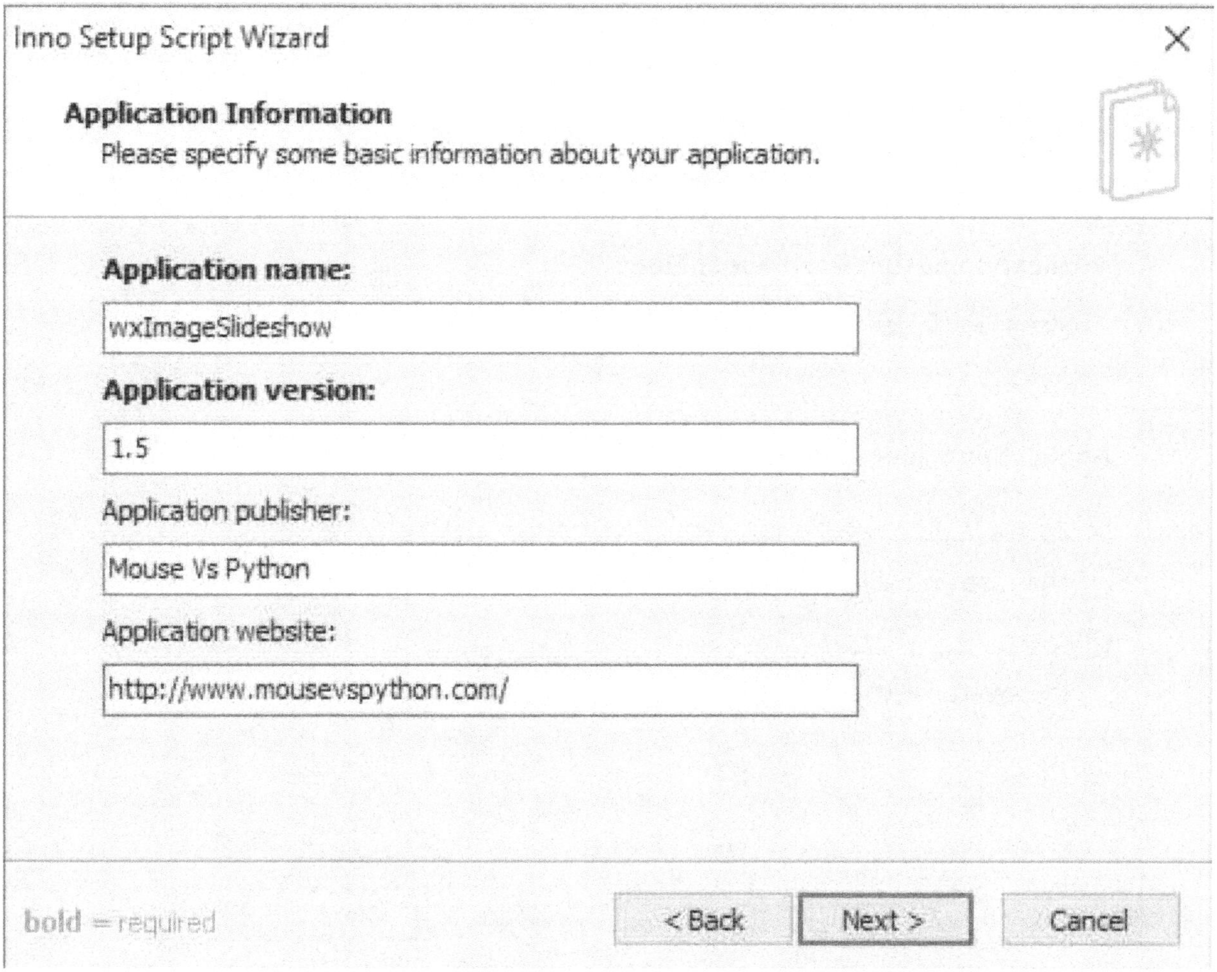

Fig. 14-4: Inno Setup Script Wizard Application Information Page

This is where you enter your application's name, its version information, the publisher's name and the application's website. I pre-filled it with some examples, but you can enter whatever you want to here.

Go ahead and press **Next** and you should see page 3:

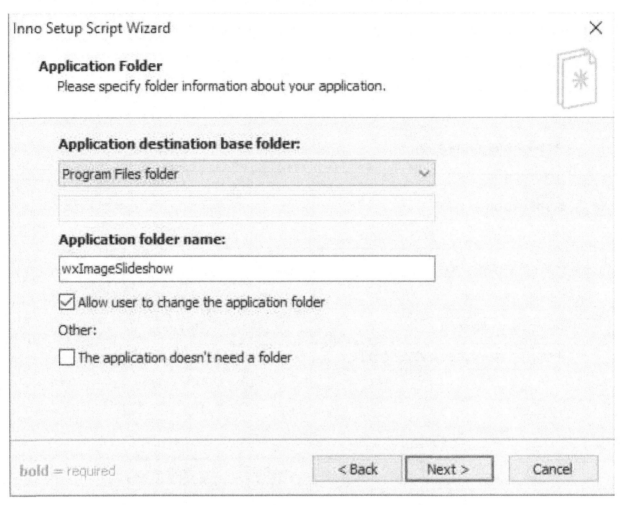

Fig. 14-5: Inno Setup Script Wizard Application Folder Page

This page of the wizard is where you can set the application's install directory. On Windows, most applications install to **Program Files**, which is also the default here. This is also where you set the folder name for your application. This is the name of the folder that will appear in Program Files. Alternatively, you can check the box at the bottom that indicates that your application doesn't need a folder at all.

Let's go to the next page:

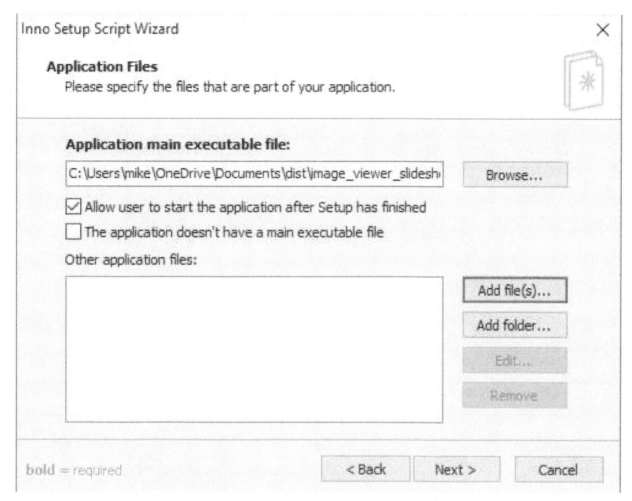

Fig. 14-6: Inno Setup Script Wizard Application Files Page

Here is where you will choose the main executable file. In this case, you want to choose the executable you created with PyInstaller. If you didn't create the executable using the `--onefile` flag, then you can add the other files using the **Add file(s)...** button. If your application requires any other special files, like a SQLite database file or images, this is also where you would want to add them.

By default, this page will allow the user to run your application when the installer finishes. A lot of installers do this, so it's actually expected by most users.

Let's continue:

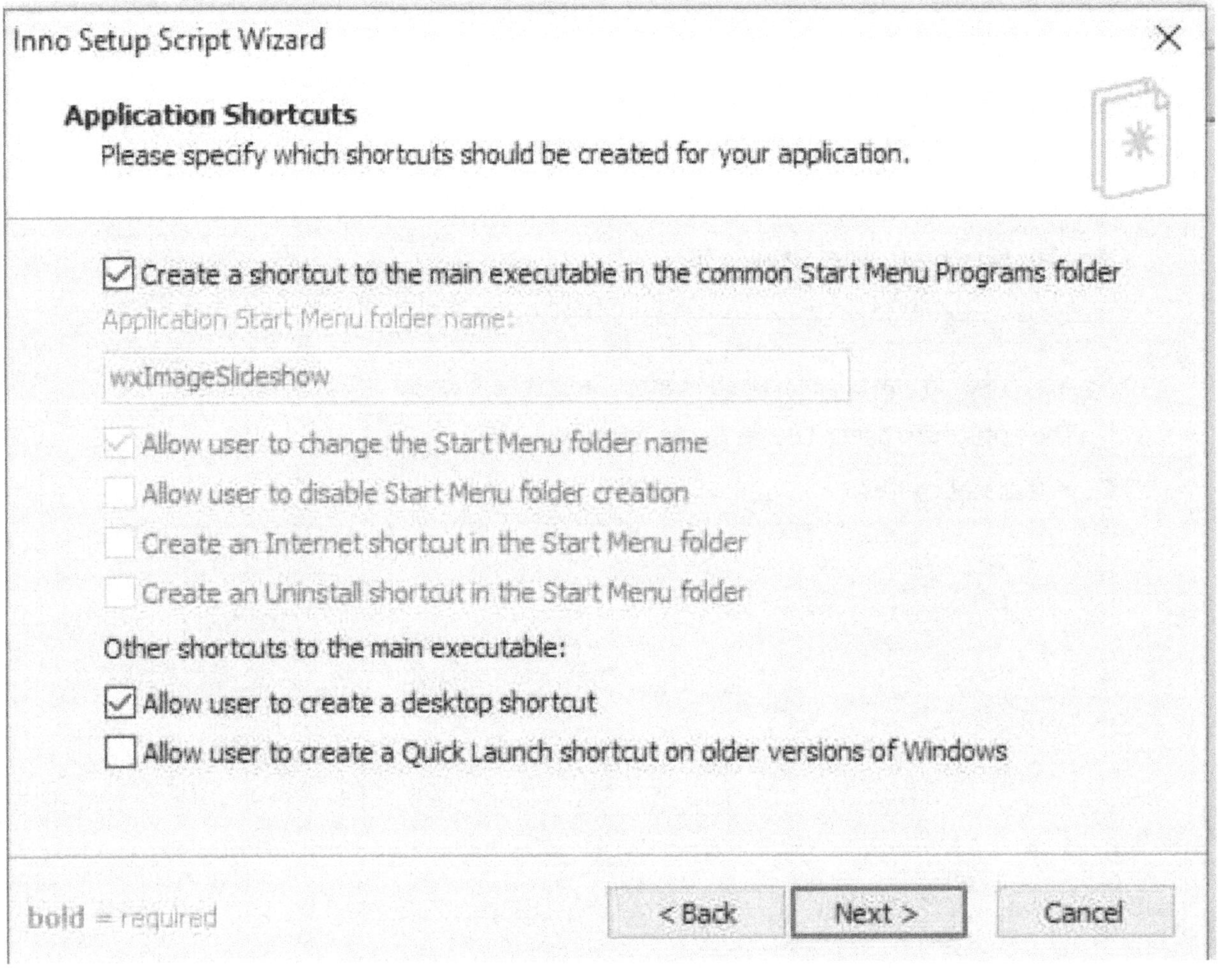

Fig. 14-7: Inno Setup Script Wizard Application Shortcuts Page

This is the **Application Shortcuts** page and it allows you to manage what shortcuts are created for your application and where they should go. The options are pretty self-explanatory. I usually just use the defaults, but you are welcome to change them however you see fit.

Let's find out what's on the documentation page:

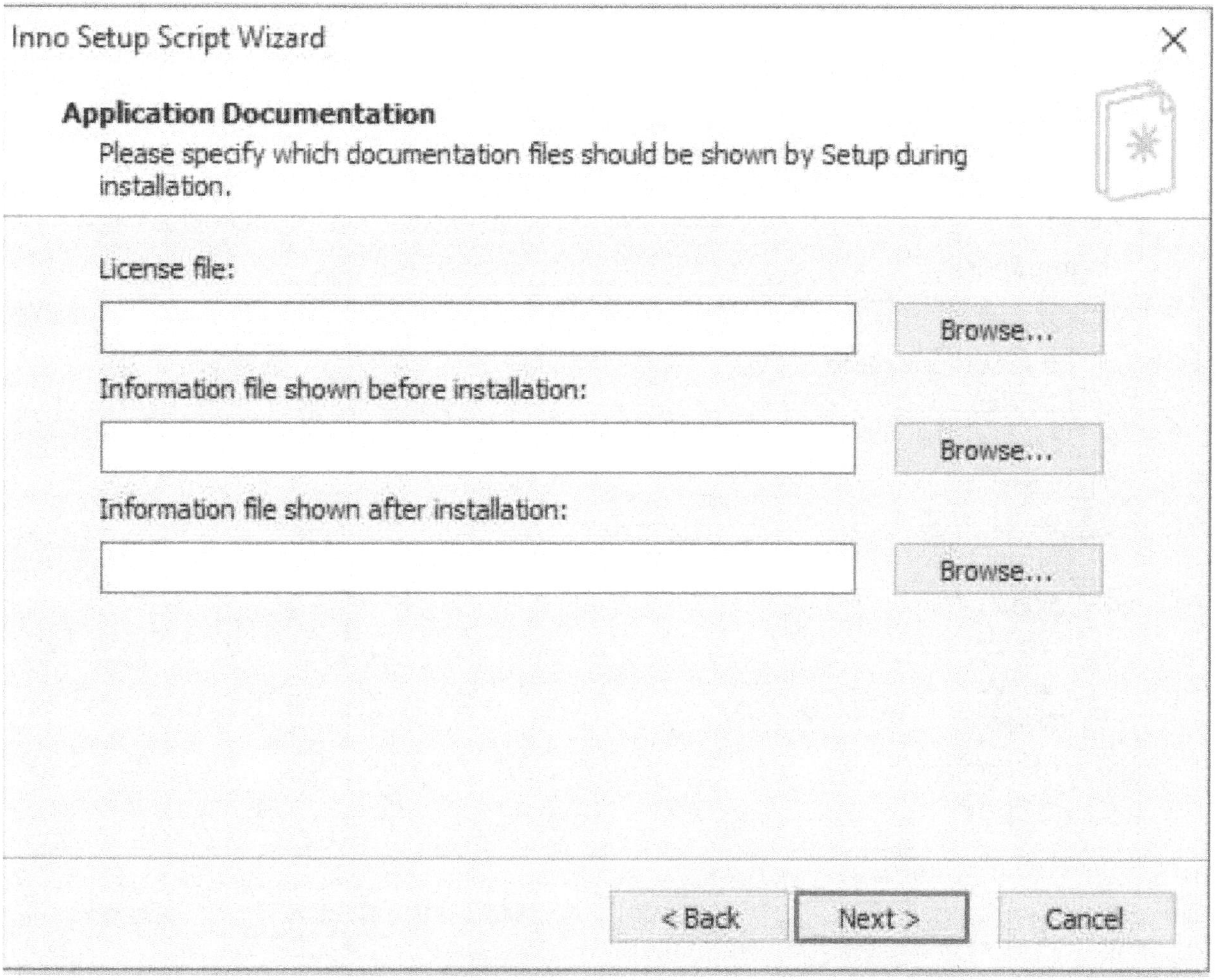

Fig. 14-8: Inno Setup Script Wizard Application Documentation Page

The **Documentation Page** of the wizard is where you can add your application's license file. For example, if you were putting out an open source application, you can add the GPL or MIT or whatever license file you need there. If this were a commercial application, this is where you would add your **End-User License Agreement (EULA)** file.

Let's see what's next:

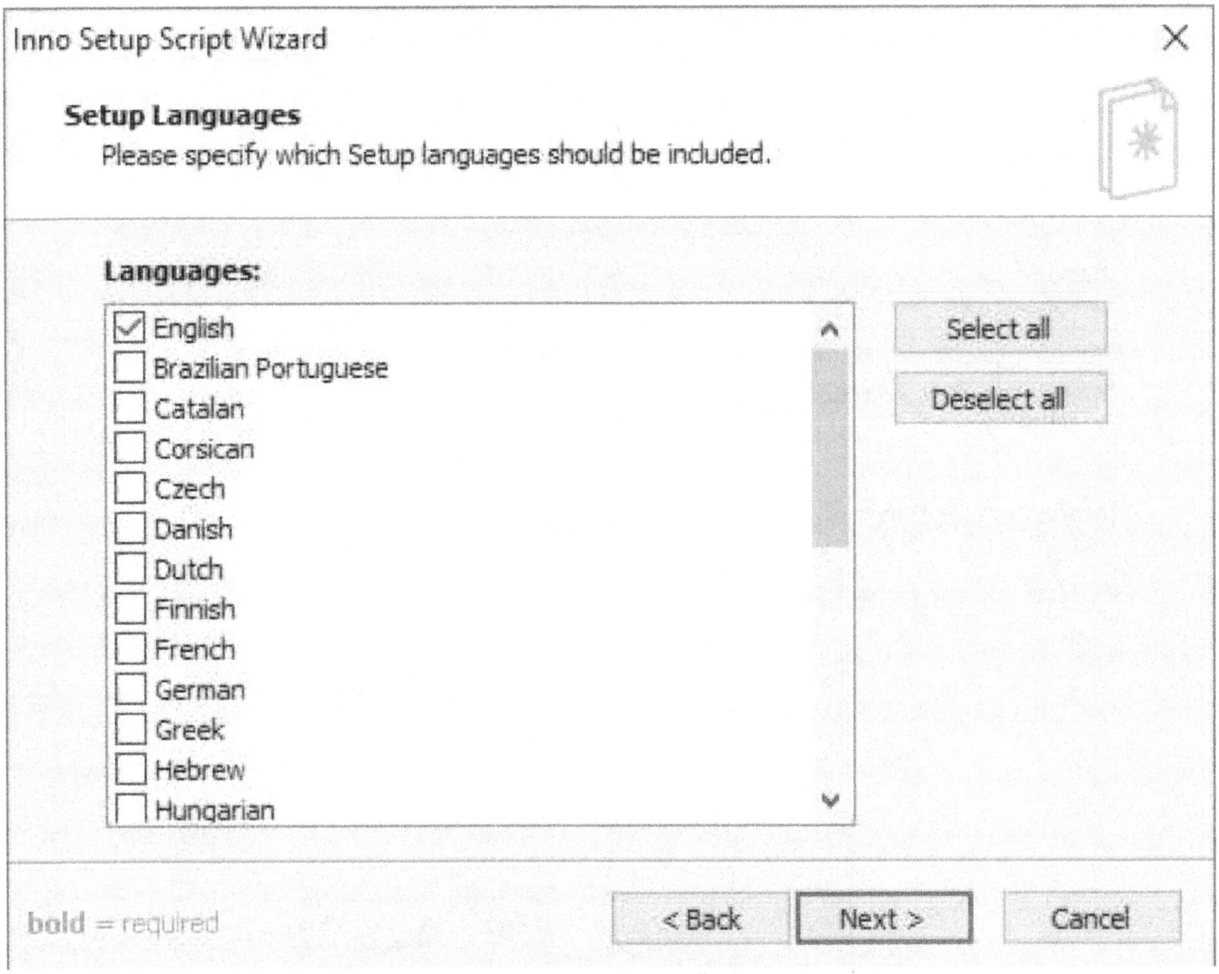

Fig. 14-9: Inno Setup Script Wizard Setup Languages Page

Here you can set up which setup languages should be included. Inno Setup supports quite a few languages, with English as the default choice.

Now let's find out what compiler settings are:

Fig. 14-10: Inno Setup Script Wizard Compiler Settings Page

The **Compiler Settings** page lets you name the output setup file, which defaults to simply **setup**. You can set the output folder here, add a custom setup file icon and even add password protection to the setup file. I usually just leave the defaults alone, but this is an opportunity to add some branding to the setup if you have a nice icon file handy.

The next page is for the preprocessor:

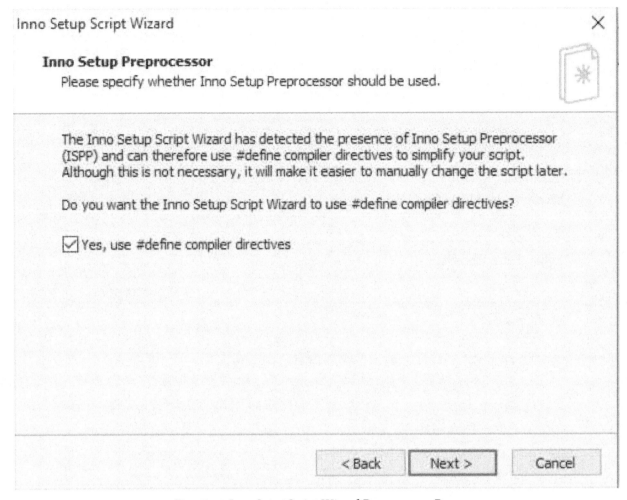

Fig. 14-10: Inno Setup Script Wizard Preprocessor Page

The preprocessor is primarily for catching typos in the Inno Setup script file. It basically adds some helpful options at compile time to your Inno Setup script.

Check out the following URL for full details:

- http://www.jrsoftware.org/ispphelp/

Click **Next** and you should see the last page of the wizard:

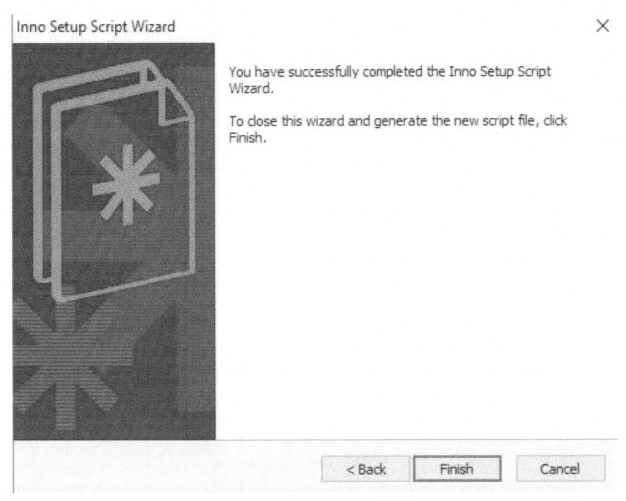

Fig. 14-10: Inno Setup Script Wizard End Page

Click **Finish** and Inno Setup will generate an Inno Setup Script (.iss) file. When it is finished, it will ask you if you would like to compile the file.

Go ahead and accept that dialog and you should see the following:

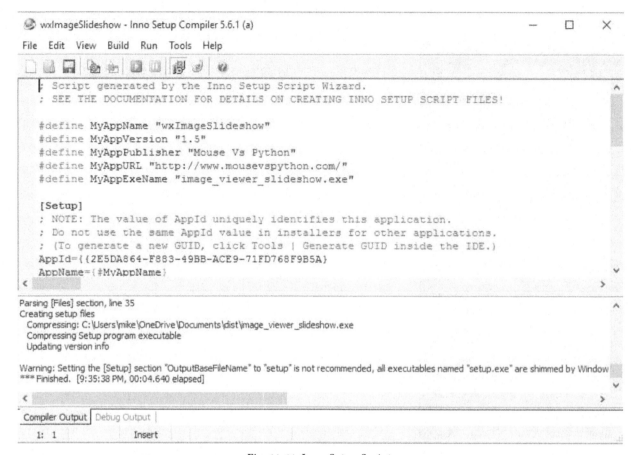

Fig. 14-11: Inno Setup Script

This is the Inno Setup Script editor with your newly generated script pre-loaded into it. The top half is the script that was generated and the bottom half shows the compiler's output. In this screenshot, it shows that the setup file was generated successfully but it also displays a warning that you might want to rename the setup file.

At this point, you should have a working installer executable that will install your program and any files it depends on to the right locations. It will also create shortcuts in the Windows Start menu and whichever other locations you specified in the wizard.

The script file itself can be edited. It is just a text file and the syntax is well documented on Inno Setup's website.

Code Signing

Windows and Mac OSX prefer that applications are signed by a corporation or the developer. Otherwise the person installing your application will see a warning that they are using an unsigned piece of code or software. The reason this matters is that it protects your application from being modified by someone else. You can think of code signing as a kind of embedded MD5 hash in your application. A signed application can be traced back to whomever signed it, which makes it more trustworthy.

If you want to sign code on Mac OSX, you can use XCode:

- https://developer.apple.com/support/code-signing/

Windows has several options for signing their code. Here is a URL for getting your application certified for Windows:

- https://docs.microsoft.com/en-us/windows/desktop/win_cert/windows-certification-portal

You can also purchase a certificate from various companies that specialize in code signing, such as **digicert**:

- https://www.digicert.com/code-signing/

There is also the concept of self-signed certificates, but that is not for production or for end users. You would only self-sign for internal testing, proof-of-concept, etc. You can look up how to do that on your own.

Wrapping Up

You have now learned how to generate executables using PyInstaller on Windows, Mac and Linux. The command to generate the executable is the same across all platforms. While you cannot create a Windows executable by running PyInstaller on Linux, it is still quite useful for creating an executable for the operating system it's running on.

You also learned how to use Inno Setup to create an installer for Windows. You can now use these skills to create executables for your own applications or for some of the other applications that you created in this book!

Appendix A - The wxPython Demo

Whenever I start a new project with wxPython and I need to use a widget I'm not very familiar with, I know I can probably find an example in the **wxPython Demo**. This demo contains examples of nearly all the widgets that are available for wxPython. It let's you run example code, change the code live and view how the widgets work. You can modify the code in the demo application itself. You can also take the code out of the demo and use it in your own code with just a few minor tweaks here and there in most cases.

If you'd like to get started using the demo, you can get it here:

- https://wxpython.org/pages/downloads/

Look under the **Extra files** section of the website. Or you can go directly to this URL:

- https://extras.wxpython.org/wxPython4/extras/

Click the latest version of wxPython and choose the tarball that has **demo** in its name. For example, the 4.0.3 version has a file named **wxPython-demo-4.0.3.tar.gz** in it at that URL. Once you have that downloaded and untarred, run the **demo.py** file that you will find in the **demo** folder. You should see the following when it loads up:

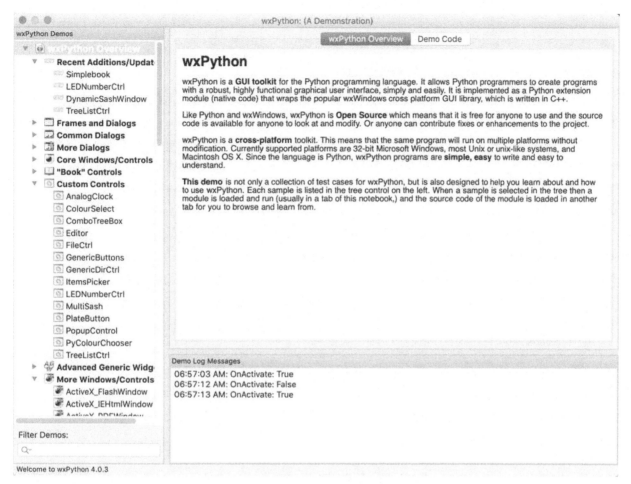

Fig. A-1: wxPython Demo

Let's try out the demo!

Learning to Use the Demo

There are several parts of the demo that you should know about. The first part is the tree control that you will find on the left-hand side of the demo. It is circled below:

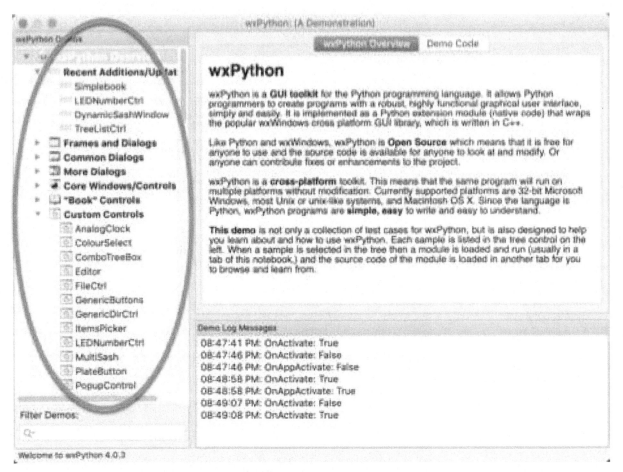

Fig. A-2: wxPython demos in a tree control

This is a list of demos. You may expand each of the categories to see more demos underneath. There is also a filter search tool at the bottom left, circled below:

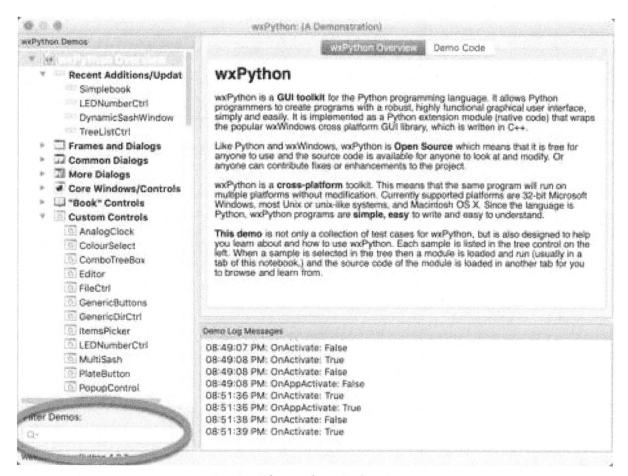

Fig. A-3: Filtering the wxPython Demos

Let's try entering the word "button" into the search control. When you do, you will see the tree widget update to look like this:

Fig. A-4: Example of the demo filtered

The search tool is very helpful for finding the right widgets that you want to use. You can also open up the demo's source code and learn how to write your own search button / filter function.

Let's move on to the next section of the demo. That is the top right-hand portion. Go ahead and click on BitmapButton in the filtered result that you had from earlier. Your screen should now look like this:

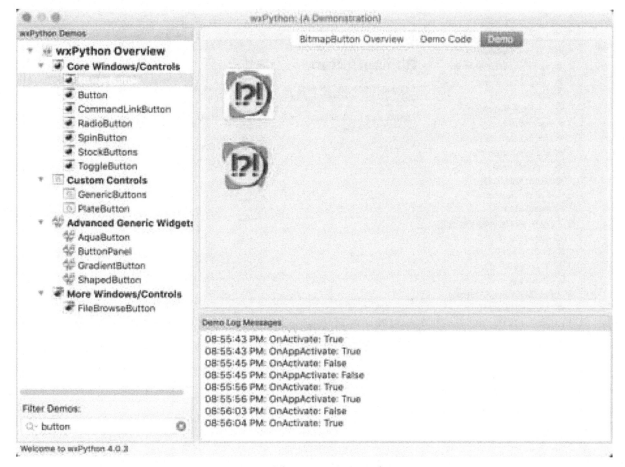

Fig. A-5: The BitmapButton demo

There are three pieces to each demo. The first is the **Overview** tab shown below. This section tells you a little about the currently selected widget.

Fig. A-6: The BitmapButton demo overview

The next tab is the **Demo Code** tab which looks like this:

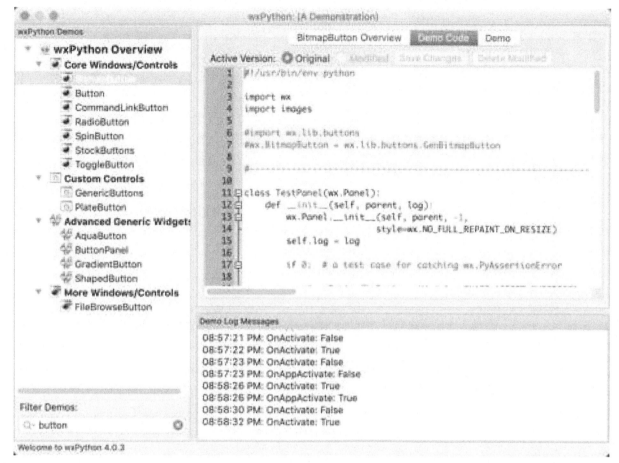

Fig. A-7: **The BitmapButton demo code**

This tab shows you the code for the demo. You can read the code and even modify it here. In fact, you will learn about modifying the demo later on in this chapter. But before we do that, you should check out the **Demo** tab:

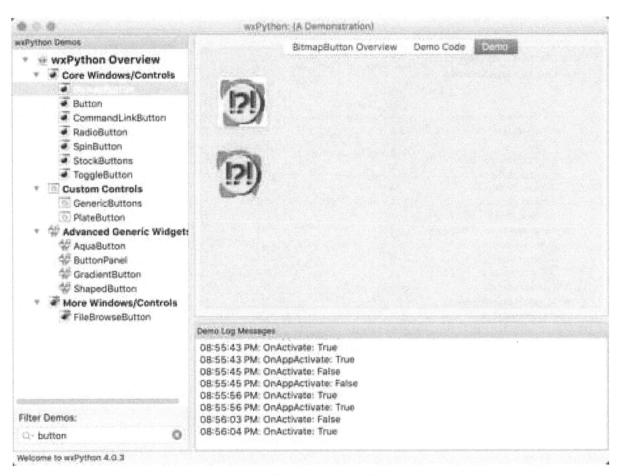

Fig. A-8: The BitmapButton demo

Here you can interact with the widget to see how it behaves. The widgets in the demo usually have events hooked up to them. If you click on one of the buttons above, you should see some output in the **Demo Log Messages** box at the bottom of the menu. This indicates that something happened and is useful for figuring out how the widget works when you go back to look at the demo's code.

Now let's learn how to edit a demo.

Modifying Demo Code

Modifying a working example of code is a great way to learn. Let's try going to the Button demo and learn how to modify the event handler so that it actually tells you which button you are pressing instead of the button's id. Open up the Button's **Demo Code** tab and scroll down to the OnClick method. Your screen should look something like this:

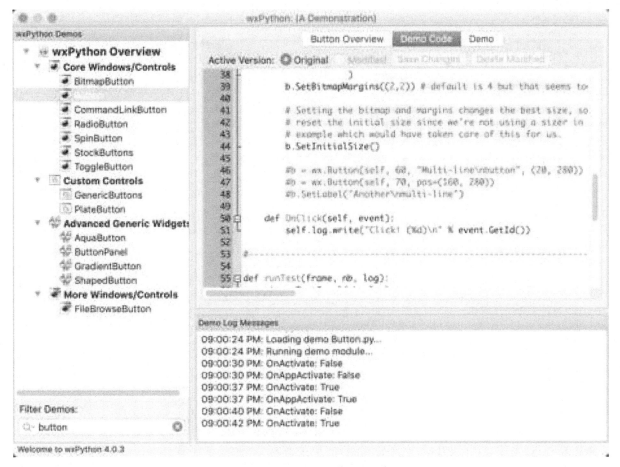

Fig. A-9: wx.Button demo code

The method that we want to change has the following code:

```python
def OnClick(self, event):
    self.log.write("Click! (%d)\n" % event.GetId())
```

Let's change this code to look like this:

```python
def OnClick(self, event):
    button = event.GetEventObject()
    label = button.GetLabel()
    msg = f'You pressed the button labeled "{label}"\n'
    self.log.write(msg)
```

Here you extract the actual button that was pressed using GetEventObject(). Then you grab the button's label and create a string that you then write to the log. The log in this case is actually the text control widget at the bottom of the demo. Now click on the **Save Changes** button:

Fig. A-10: Saving your changes

Assuming that you did everything correctly, when you press a button it should state which button label you pressed in the log. Go ahead and give it a try.

Once you are done playing around with that example, feel free to try modifying the code some more or choose a different demo to modify.

Note that is you mess up or just want to revert your changes, all you need to do is click the **Delete Modified** button:

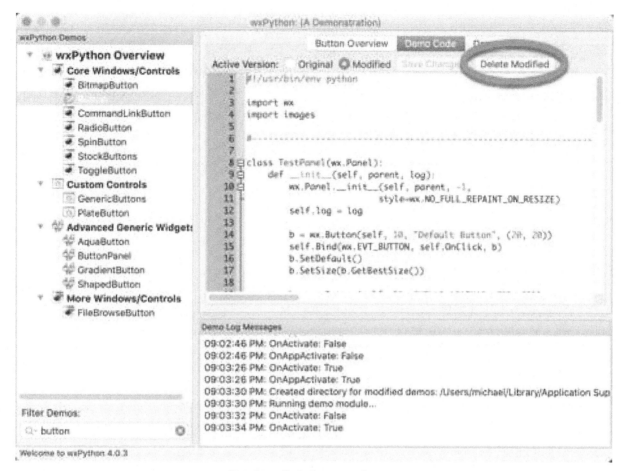

Fig. A-11: Deleting your changes

The code should now be exactly as it was before you modified it.

Extracting Demo Code

One of the best things about the wxPython demo is that you can see how a widget looks and how it works. You can also take the code from the demo and use it in your own application. However there is a little caveat to that. You may have noticed that the demos refer to something called self.log a lot. This is a reference to a text control that the demo logs messages to. Since your application probably won't have that, you do have to be careful not to copy lines like that from the demo into your own code. If you do, your code will not work correctly.

Let's try to extract a complicated control, such as the DataViewListCtrl (AKA DVC_ListCtrl). You can find it quickly by typing "dvc" or "list" into the search filter in the demo.

Once selected, your demo should look like this:

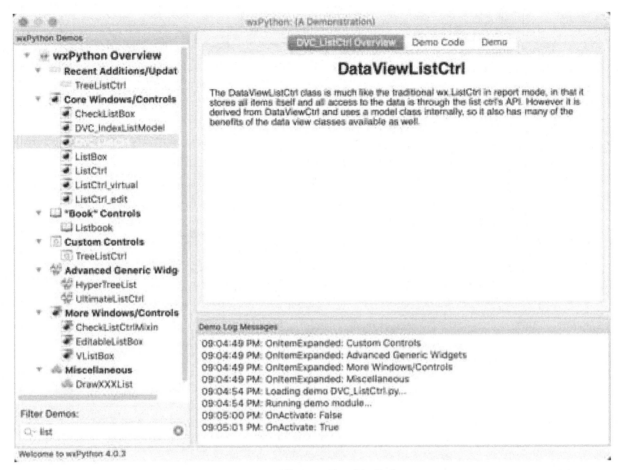

Fig. A-12: The DataViewListCtrl

To get started, you will need to create a simple skeleton application first.

Here's a good start:

```python
# initial_skeleton.py

import wx

class MyPanel(wx.Panel):

    def __init__(self, parent):
        super().__init__(parent)

class MyFrame(wx.Frame):

    def __init__(self):
        super().__init__(None,
                    title='DVC ListCtrl Demo Extraction')
```

```
        panel = MyPanel(self)
        self.Show()

if __name__ == '__main__':
    app = wx.App(False)
    frame = MyFrame()
    app.MainLoop()
```

This will create a wx.Frame with a single child widget, a wx.Panel. Now we need to add some of the code from the demo. Go and open the **Demo Code** tab for the DVC_ListCtrl demo. Let's try copying over the import and the code related to the DataViewListCtrl widget.

Your code should now look like this:

```python
# dvc_demo.py

import wx
import wx.dataview as dv


class MyPanel(wx.Panel):

    def __init__(self, parent):
        super().__init__(parent)
        self.dvlc = dvlc = dv.DataViewListCtrl(self)

        # Give it some columns.
        # The ID col we'll customize a bit:
        dvlc.AppendTextColumn('id', width=40)
        dvlc.AppendTextColumn('artist', width=170)
        dvlc.AppendTextColumn('title', width=260)
        dvlc.AppendTextColumn('genre', width=80)

        # Load the data. Each item (row) is added as a sequence of values
        # whose order matches the columns
        for itemvalues in musicdata:
            dvlc.AppendItem(itemvalues)

        # Set the layout so the listctrl fills the panel
        self.Sizer = wx.BoxSizer()
        self.Sizer.Add(dvlc, 1, wx.EXPAND)


class MyFrame(wx.Frame):
```

```
    def __init__(self):
        super().__init__(None,
                         title='DVC ListCtrl Demo Extraction')
        panel = MyPanel(self)
        self.Show()


if __name__ == '__main__':
    app = wx.App(False)
    frame = MyFrame()
    app.MainLoop()
```

This looks pretty good. You should try running it. When I ran it I got the following exception:

```
builtins.NameError: name 'musicdata' is not defined
```

Whoops! This is another thing about demos that you need to watch out for. Some of the demos use demo data, like the musicdata mentioned here. If you go back to the demo, you will notice that it is importing some module called ListCtrl. Try adding that import to your code and re-running your application.

When I ran it with that new import, I got this:

```
builtins.ModuleNotFoundError: No module named 'ListCtrl'
```

You know that wxPython has a ListCtrl, but it's not actually called ListCtrl. The real name of the widget is wx.ListCtrl. So that means that this import must be something that is included in the demo! If you browse the demo folder you will find that there is a ListCtrl.py file which is what this demo is importing. In fact, you can load that demo within the wxPython demo by clicking on ListCtrl in the tree widget. There you will find the musicdata dictionary that you need to complete your application.

Go ahead and copy that dictionary over and add it to the top of your script before you create your classes. It should look something like this:

```python
# dvc_demo_2.py

import wx
import wx.dataview as dv

musicdata = {
1 : ("Bad English", "The Price Of Love", "Rock"),
2 : ("DNA featuring Suzanne Vega", "Tom's Diner", "Rock"),
3 : ("George Michael", "Praying For Time", "Rock"),
}

musicdata = sorted(musicdata.items())
musicdata = [[str(k)] + list(v) for k,v in musicdata]

class MyPanel(wx.Panel):

    def __init__(self, parent):
        super().__init__(parent)
        self.dvlc = dvlc = dv.DataViewListCtrl(self)

        # Give it some columns.
        # The ID col we'll customize a bit:
        dvlc.AppendTextColumn('id', width=40)
        dvlc.AppendTextColumn('artist', width=170)
        dvlc.AppendTextColumn('title', width=260)
        dvlc.AppendTextColumn('genre', width=80)

        # Load the data. Each item (row) is added as a sequence of values
        # whose order matches the columns
        for itemvalues in musicdata:
            dvlc.AppendItem(itemvalues)

        # Set the layout so the listctrl fills the panel
        self.Sizer = wx.BoxSizer()
        self.Sizer.Add(dvlc, 1, wx.EXPAND)

class MyFrame(wx.Frame):

    def __init__(self):
        super().__init__(None,
                         title='DVC ListCtrl Demo Extraction')
        panel = MyPanel(self)
        self.Show()
```

```
if __name__ == '__main__':
    app = wx.App(False)
    frame = MyFrame()
    app.MainLoop()
```

Note that for brevity I cut the dictionary down in size, but you can copy the full dictionary in. The other change is to add in the sorting and the list comprehension from the DVC_ListCtrl demo. This formats the data so it can be consumed by the DataViewListCtrl widget. When you run this code, you should see the following:

id		artist	title
	1	Bad English	The Price Of Love
	2	DNA featuring Suzanne Vega	Tom's Diner
	3	George Michael	Praying For Time
	4	Gloria Estefan	Here We Are
	5	Linda Ronstadt	Don't Know Much
	6	Michael Bolton	How Am I Supposed To Live Witl
	7	Paul Young	Oh Girl
	8	Paula Abdul	Opposites Attract
	9	Richard Marx	Should've Known Better
	10	Rod Stewart	Forever Young
	11	Roxette	Dangerous

DVC ListCtrl Demo Extraction

Fig. A-13: The DataViewListCtrl extraction

There are lots of demos that you can try extracting code examples from. For example, if you had tried to extract code from the ListCtrl demo, you would have had to taken out the references to self.log that are scattered throughout it. That demo also makes use of a demo-only module called images.py. While you can copy those modules out for use in your own code, it is usually best to remove those references entirely or create your own custom code instead.

Wrapping Up

The wxPython demo is extremely rich and very useful for learning how wxPython's widgets work. You can find nearly all the widgets here so it's also a great way to see how they look to see if they will be a good fit for your project. Between the demo and the wxPython documentation, I think you will find enough example code to be able to use any widget in the toolkit.

Appendix B - The Widget Inspection Tool

The wxPython GUI toolkit comes with other nice tools besides the wxPython Demo Application. It also comes with a handy utility called the **Widget Inspection Tool**. The Widget Inspection Tool can be used for visualizing the layouts of your applications. Probably its biggest use is for debugging your user interface.

Let's learn how to use it now!

Using the Widget Inspection Tool

You can add the Widget Inspection Tool to your application by adding the following lines to your code:

```python
import wx.lib.inspection
wx.lib.inspection.InspectionTool().Show()
```

I usually recommend adding these lines in after creating the main window (i.e. wx.Frame) and before you call your App instance's MainLoop() method. Let's take the **sizer_with_two_widgets.py** script from chapter 1 and add the Widget Inspection Tool to it.

Here's the updated code:

```python
# sizer_with_two_widgets.py

import wx


class MyPanel(wx.Panel):

    def __init__(self, parent):
        super().__init__(parent)

        button = wx.Button(self, label='Press Me')
        button2 = wx.Button(self, label='Second button')

        main_sizer = wx.BoxSizer(wx.HORIZONTAL)
```

```
        main_sizer.Add(button, proportion=1,
                       flag=wx.ALL | wx.CENTER | wx.EXPAND,
                       border=5)
        main_sizer.Add(button2, 0, wx.ALL, 5)
        self.SetSizer(main_sizer)


class MyFrame(wx.Frame):

    def __init__(self):
        super().__init__(None, title='Hello World')
        panel = MyPanel(self)
        self.Show()


if __name__ == '__main__':
    app = wx.App(redirect=False)
    frame = MyFrame()
    import wx.lib.inspection
    wx.lib.inspection.InspectionTool().Show()
    app.MainLoop()
```

The two new lines are in the `if` statement at the end of the code example above. Here we just add an import to `wx.lib.inspection` and then instantiate the `InspectionTool` and `Show()` it.

When I ran this code, the inspection tool looked like this:

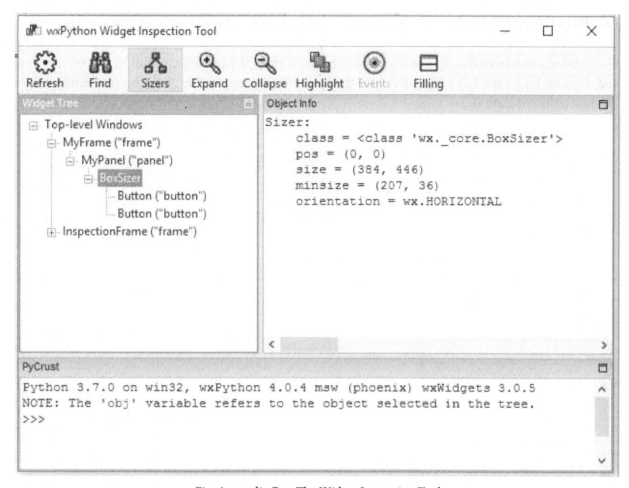

Fig. Appendix B-1: The Widget Inspection Tool

There are several buttons along the top of the Inspector.

Let's learn what they do:

- Refresh - Updates the Widget Tree to match whatever widgets are currently on-screen
- Find - Press this button and then click a button in your application to inspect it
- Sizers - Toggles the display of sizers in the Widget Tree
- Expand - Expands all the nodes in the Widget Tree
- Collapse - Collapse all the nodes in the Widget Tree
- Highlight - Highlight in the live window whatever is currently selected in the Widget Tree. The top-level widgets will be flickers while other widgets will have borders drawn on them for a few seconds
- Filling - Toggles the display of the **PyFilling** portion of the **PyCrust** Python interpreter at the bottom of the Inspector Tool

Note that on Xubuntu 18.04, the Highlight and Filling buttons did not work, so keep that in mind when using the tool.

Let's demonstrate how some of these features work.

Highlighting

If you would like to Highlight a widget, just choose it from the tree in the Widget Inspection Tool and then hit highlight. Let's try expanding the tree and clicking on one of the button entries. Then hit the Highlight button.

You should see something like this:

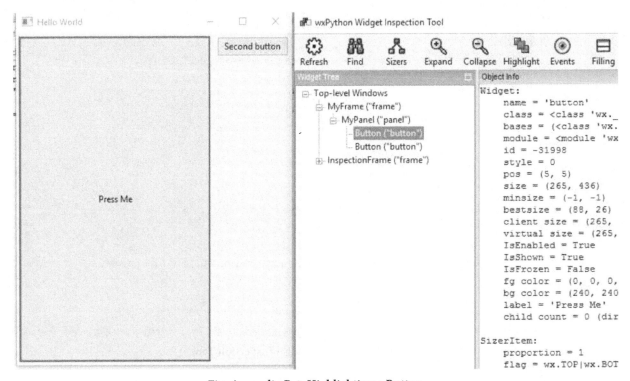

Fig. Appendix B-2: Highlighting a Button

Now click the **Sizers** button and select a sizer from the tree. Then click the Highlight button again.

You should now see this:

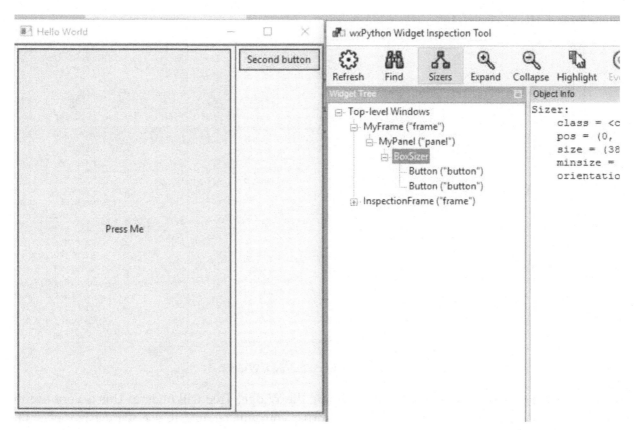

Fig. Appendix B-3: Highlighting a Sizer

Let's learn how to find a specific widget next!

Finding Widgets

Sometimes you need to know where a widget is on your screen. This may be because you are having weird layout issues or you have taken on a pre-existing project and you don't understand how the user interface is laid out.

To find a specific widget, you can click the **Find** button in the Widget Inspection Tool.

You should see something like this:

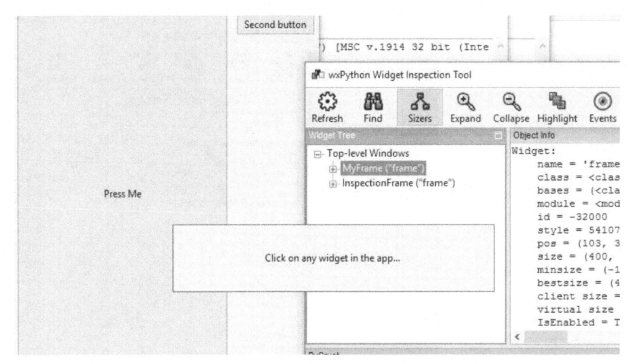

Fig. Appendix B-4: Finding a Widget

Now just click on a widget in your application and the Widget Tree will update. This is very useful for figuring out widget hierarchies. In other words, you will be able to see widget parent-child relationships and you will be able to see which sizers hold which widgets.

By using the Find and Highlight buttons you can debug pretty much any layout in wxPython.

Events

The Events button will open the Event Watcher. This is a separate dialog that is basically an event sniffer. This is useful for figuring out which widget is emitting which event or events.

Here is what the dialog looks like:

#	Event	Source	
6	EVT_SET_CURSOR	ToolBar "toolbar" (-31965)	^
7	EVT_SET_CURSOR	ToolBar "toolbar" (-31965)	
8	EVT_SET_CURSOR	ToolBar "toolbar" (-31965)	
9	EVT_SET_CURSOR	ToolBar "toolbar" (-31965)	
10	EVT_SET_CURSOR	ToolBar "toolbar" (-31965)	
11	EVT_MOTION	ToolBar "toolbar" (-31965)	
12	EVT_SET_CURSOR	ToolBar "toolbar" (-31965)	
13	EVT_MOTION	ToolBar "toolbar" (-31965)	
14	EVT_SET_CURSOR	ToolBar "toolbar" (-31965)	
15	EVT_MOTION	ToolBar "toolbar" (-31965)	
16	EVT_SET_CURSOR	ToolBar "toolbar" (-31965)	
17	EVT_MOTION	ToolBar "toolbar" (-31965)	
18	EVT_SET_CURSOR	ToolBar "toolbar" (-31965)	
19	EVT_TOOL_ENTER	ToolBar "toolbar" (-31965)	
20	EVT_MOTION	ToolBar "toolbar" (-31965)	
21	EVT_SET_CURSOR	ToolBar "toolbar" (-31965)	
22	EVT_MOTION	ToolBar "toolbar" (-31965)	
23	EVT_SET_CURSOR	ToolBar "toolbar" (-31965)	
24	EVT_MOTION	ToolBar "toolbar" (-31965)	
25	EVT_SET_CURSOR	ToolBar "toolbar" (-31965)	
26	EVT_LEAVE_WINDOW	ToolBar "toolbar" (-31965)	
27	EVT_TOOL_ENTER	ToolBar "toolbar" (-31965)	v

EventWatcher for ToolBar "toolbar" (-31965)

Clear	Add Module	Watch	>>>

Fig. Appendix B-5: Watching Events

By default, the Event Watcher will look for all events. If you want to limit the events it watches for, you can click the bottom right button that is marked with a >>>.

This will cause the Event Watcher to expand like so:

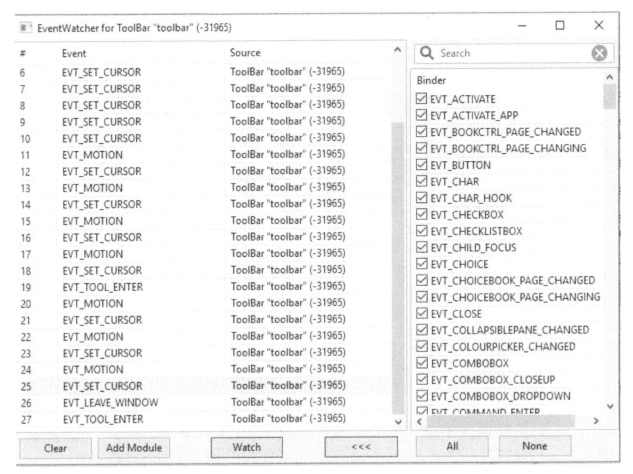

Fig. Appendix B-6: Choosing Which Events to Watch

Now you can configure which events to watch for.

There is also a **Watch** button at the bottom of the screen to toggle whether or not to record events.

Wrapping Up

You have learned the basics of using the Widget Inspection Tool in this appendix. It is extremely helpful when figuring out complex user interfaces. I have also used it when figuring out strange layout bugs where sizer's don't seem to be behaving in the way I expect. With a little practice, you will be able to using the Widget Inspection Tool productively in no time!

https://wxpython.org/Phoenix/docs/html/wx.lib.mixins.inspection.html